STOCK INDEX OPTIONS

STOCK INDEX OPTIONS

Powerful New Tools for Investing,
Hedging, and Speculating

Donald T. Mesler

Probus Publishing Company
118 North Clinton
Chicago, Illinois 60606

© Donald T. Mesler, 1985

ALL RIGHTS RESERVED. No part of this publication may be reproduced, stored in a retrieval system, or transmitted, in any form or by any means, electronic, mechanical, photocopying, recording, or otherwise, without the prior written permission of the publisher and the copyright holder.

This publication is designed to provide accurate and authoritative information in regard to the subject matter covered. It is sold with the understanding that the publisher is not engaged in rendering legal, accounting, or other professional service. If legal advice or other expert assistance is required, the services of a competent professional person should be sought.

FROM A DECLARATION OF PRINCIPLES JOINTLY ADOPTED BY A COMMITTEE OF THE AMERICAN BAR ASSOCIATION AND A COMMITTEE OF PUBLISHERS.

Library of Congress Cataloging in Publication Data

Mesler, Donald T.
  Stock index options.

  Bibliography: p.
  Includes index.
  1. Stock index futures. I. Title.
  HG6043.M47   1985   332.64'52   84–11472

ISBN 0-917253-02-7

Library of Congress Catalog Card No. 84:11472

Printed in the United States of America

1 2 3 4 5 6 7 8 9 0

To My Mother and Father

Foreword

Stocks will be less risky to own for those who master the strategies and tactics of using stock index options and index futures. In fact, use of these investment tools will open up totally new investment opportunities. This book provides the first intelligent and exclusively focused exposition of the ins and outs of stock index options.

The advent of index options and futures constitutes a revolution in the way things are done in the equity markets. These new capital market instruments allow the investor to assert himself in the stock market in ways that are both different and more efficient than what has been possible in the past.

This revolution will reflect itself permanently in the way money is deployed in the market. When used correctly, index options and futures will affect the performance of the small investor as well as that of the managers of multi-billion dollar portfolios. Use of the new capital market instruments is applicable to the most conservative, unleveraged long-term investment strategies as well as more aggressive, short-term leveraged approaches.

The implementation of risk-control measures, so well known and practiced in such diverse areas as insurance, race car driving, nuclear facilities, and NASA, has not been a routine part of investment management. To control risk not only must one be able to recognize that events are deviating significantly from acceptable outcomes, but also have the means to rapidly and cost effectively respond to those events to prevent things from getting worse than an acceptable margin of deviation.

Broadly speaking, there are two kinds of risk: stock-specific and broad-market risks. It has always been possible to manage stock-specific risk through rapid-response buying and selling. Broad-market risks, however, require managing two problems: degree of diversification and market timing. Diversification, for the purpose of avoiding stock-specific risks, however, involves costs. More stocks have to be researched and monitored and there are greater transactions costs. Moreover, the broader the extent of diversification the less is the return to stock picking skills.

Implementing market timing and asset allocation decisions presents yet other challenges for the investor. He must now monitor broad market fundamentals and technical variables and must be prepared to initiate buying and selling programs, involving trading in unison a portfolio of stocks against the other assets he is liquidating or accumulating, as his stock position is changed.

Since many investors, including those who are broadly diversified, tend to regard their portfolio with the same pride a craftsman has toward his work, it becomes difficult to expeditiously part with a hand-picked, hand-crafted portfolio.

Index options and futures are the solution to the problem. They allow the investor to alter his broad market exposure and risks without disturbing his portfolio. While the right hand is cultivating the garden, the left hand can be warding off predators. The ability to hedge against market risks means the investor can increase his staying power with his existing portfolio.

Efficiency in managing portfolio risks is another major advantage of stock index options and index futures. The index instruments can be traded quickly because the markets are highly liquid. Also, transaction costs are low. Both commissions and bid/ask spreads are a fraction of the costs associated with moving a similar dollar amount of stocks.

Finally, these new capital market instruments offer investors a unique strategic advantage. They give the equity trader the ability to trade based on perceived, broad-market opportunities in-between specific stock ideas. Sometimes it takes quite a bit of time to figure out which stocks are right to buy and sell, even though he may be convinced that the market is about to make a move. There is a tendency, therefore, for some investors to rush their decisions. This is no longer necessary. Time and perspective can be gained by trading the index options or futures first.

This book provides all the information an investor needs to learn about and start using stock index options effectively.

August 14, 1984

Gregory M. Kipnis
Vice President, Manager
Stock Index Department
Donaldson, Lufkin & Jenrette
New York, N.Y.

PREFACE

Nearly everyone, from taxicab drivers to corporate executives, has an opinion about the direction of the stock market. In the past, ways to capitalize on one's outlook were generally unsatisfactory, being indirect, complex, or very risky. Index options have completely altered this situation. Placing a market bet is now a snap. More importantly, portfolio managers now have a convenient, speedy way to hedge their holdings.

Because of these attributes, index options have been embraced throughout the investment community. They are the most successful new financial product in a decade.

This book explores index options in sufficient depth that investors can confidently direct transactions, and brokers and advisers can recommend positions responsibly. The book provides the background and tools necessary to develop the skills required for this level of competence.

Serious investors, brokers, analysts, money managers, and financial planners included, can use this book to gain insight into these powerful new tools. The focus of the book is on providing a working knowledge which can be applied immediately in the marketplace. The reader will learn:

What new strategies index options provide
Which underlying index should be selected
Which option should be purchased or sold
What are the contract terms
How many options are appropriate
What price should be paid for the option

This is the first major work devoted exclusively to index options. Until now, the only source of information was exchange or brokerage house literature which, by necessity, was abbreviated and superficial.

PREFACE

Index options, however, are complex instruments and a more penetrating analysis is required.

For example, in both composition and construction, the various underlying indexes are vastly different. It follows that the options also have unique characteristics. Options are available for thirteen different indexes and they are traded on four different exchanges. They are not interchangeable and care must be taken when selecting an option to assure that it will accomplish the intended purpose. This book is a compilation of information about all the options and all the underlying indexes. It provides comparisons between the different products, allowing the reader to make the optimum selection for a proposed strategy.

To properly incorporate these options into an investment program the reader needs a thorough understanding of indexes and averages. Therefore the book begins with a detailed discussion of the construction and components of these market measures. This is followed by a description of the index options, including all the special features, plus a comparison with equity options. With this background, the reader is prepared to explore applications. Twelve different investment approaches are presented with several examples worked in detail.

Once the strategy is selected and the appropriate underlying index determined, a specific option must be chosen. The book presents several alternatives for approaching this problem, ranging from computer data bases to investment advisory services. The final chapter covers a variety of facets unique to index options such as cash settlement, timing risk, and liquidity.

For readers with a limited background in listed options, a special supplement follows the main text. It is an overview of options in general, including a discussion of trading characteristics and basic strategies as well as definitions and terminology.

The book concludes with appendixes describing the indexes and the option contracts, sources of additional information, and a glossary. A thorough bibliography on indexes and options is provided for those wishing to pursue these subjects in further detail.

Donald T. Mesler
Chicago, Illinois

CONTENTS

INTRODUCTION	xv
THE OEX PHENOMENON	xvii

1 OVERVIEW — 1
MARKET BETS	1
EQUITY MARKETS VERSUS COMMODITY MARKETS	2
CONTROVERSIAL INSTRUMENT	2
DEFINITION OF INDEX OPTIONS	2
STOCK OPTIONS AND INDEX OPTIONS COMPARED	4
PREVIEW OF APPLICATIONS	5
LOOKING AHEAD	6

2 AVERAGES AND INDEXES — 7
INTRODUCTION	7
AVERAGES VERSUS INDEXES	7
Index Concentration	8
Index Complexity	8
INDEX OBJECTIVES	9
STOCK AVERAGES	10
DOW JONES INDUSTRIAL AVERAGE	14
Attributes and Shortcomings	15
Strengths	15
Weaknesses	16
STOCK INDEXES	16
Weighted Indexes	17
NEW YORK STOCK EXCHANGE COMPOSITE INDEX	19
Attributes and Shortcomings	20

CONTENTS

BROAD-BASED VERSUS NARROW-BASED INDEXES	21
Broad-Based Indexes	21
Narrow-Based Indexes	22
IMPORTANT INDEXES WITHOUT LISTED OPTIONS	23

3 COMPARING BROAD-BASED INDEXES — 27
- INTRODUCTION — 27
- GRAPHIC JUXTAPOSITION — 27
- CYCLICAL PERCENTAGE CHANGES — 38
- CORRELATION COEFFICIENT — 40
- USING THE COMPARISON MEASURES — 44

4 INDEX OPTION BASICS — 47
- INTRODUCTION — 47
- DEFINITION — 47
- HISTORY — 47
- CURRENT OFFERINGS — 49
- BASIC CHARACTERISTICS OF INDEX OPTIONS — 53
  - Contract Value — 53
  - Exercise Prices — 53
  - Premiums — 53
  - Expiration Cycles — 53
  - Cash Settlement — 54
  - Margin Requirements — 54
- COMPARING INDEX OPTIONS AND STOCK OPTIONS — 55
- THE OEX PHENOMENON — 56

5 APPLICATIONS — 59
- INTRODUCTION — 59
- BASIC STRATEGIES — 59
- INTRODUCTION TO RISK AND RETURN — 59
- RETURN CONCEPTS — 60
- RISK CONCEPTS — 61
  - Risk Decomposition — 61
  - Systematic Risk — 61
  - Unsystematic Risk — 62
  - Risk Unbundling — 62

CONTENTS

SPECULATIVE/TRADING STRATEGIES	64
HEDGING STRATEGIES	68
EXAMPLE TRANSACTIONS	71
Speculative Call Purchase	72
Protective Puts	73
"Covered" Call Writing	75
Straddle Sales	75
Straddle Purchases	77

6 OPTION EVALUATION — 79
SELECTING THE BEST OPTION	79
OPTION MODELS	79
FAIR VALUE	80
SCOPE OF UNDERTAKING	81
Alternative Information Sources	81
Computer Software	82
Computer Data Bases	82
Advisory Services	82
VALUE LINE OPTION EVALUATION	83

7 SPECIAL CONSIDERATIONS — 87
INTRODUCTION	87
LIQUIDITY	87
SENTIMENT AND ARBITRAGE	89
PORTFOLIO TRACKING	90
TIMING RISK	90
COMMISSIONS	91
COVERED WRITING	91
A Note about Covered Writing	92
ESCROW LETTERS	93
THE SPECTER OF MANIPULATION	94

SUPPLEMENT—OPTION FUNDAMENTALS	97
INTRODUCTION	97
OPTION DEFINITION	97

CONTENTS

CALL OPTIONS	97
Call Buyers	98
Call Writers	98
Option Diagram for Calls	100
DETERMINANTS OF PREMIUM LEVELS	101
Relationship of Stock Price to Exercise Price	102
Time until Expiration	102
Stock Volatility	102
Prevailing Interest Rate	102
Stock Dividend	102
TIME VALUE	103
PUT OPTIONS	104
Put Buyers	104
Put Writers	106
Option Diagram for Puts	107
STOCK OPTION TRADING	107
OPTION HEDGING	110
Covered Writing	111
Protective Puts	111
Straddles	114

APPENDIXES

APPENDIX A: OPTIONABLE INDEXES	121
APPENDIX B: NONOPTIONABLE INDEXES	151
APPENDIX C: INDEX OPTIONS (CONTRACT SPECIFICATIONS)	159
APPENDIX D: VALUE LINE EVALUATIONS	173
APPENDIX E: COMMON STOCKS HAVING LISTED OPTIONS	181
APPENDIX F: COMPUTER DATA BASES	187
APPENDIX G: ADVISORY SERVICES COVERING INDEX OPTIONS	189
APPENDIX H: EXCHANGE ADDRESSES	191
APPENDIX I: OPTION SYMBOL GUIDE	193
APPENDIX J: BIBLIOGRAPHY	197
APPENDIX K: GLOSSARY	201
INDEX	211

INTRODUCTION

Recently there has been an explosive growth in the number of new investment vehicles trading publicly. A partial list would include such items as commodity options, adjustable rate preferred stock, zero coupon bonds, warrants on debt instruments, adjustable rate convertible notes, volume indexed bonds, commodity indexed bonds, stock index futures, and stock index futures options. The latest, which of course is the reason for this book, is the stock index option.

These investment tools are proliferating faster than it is humanly possible to keep track. It is not only the public which is bewildered; investment professionals as well must constantly pursue educational programs to remain abreast of new developments. It would be rare indeed to find an individual who could run down the preceding list and describe each vehicle giving terms, specifications, purchase and sale guidelines, suitability, and currently attractive investment candidates. Nevertheless, these new tools are extremely valuable. Investors have an obligation to themselves to become knowledgeable about them as soon as possible. Of course index options fall into this classification. They offer new ways to capitalize on a market opinion and make possible a number of new investment strategies.

Reasons for the explosion in new products are multifold. Among them are the adoption of new technologies by the brokerage industry, increased volatility in the financial markets, and a new aggressiveness from a marketing standpoint within the industry itself.

Technological improvements came in two major areas, data processing and communications. The computer, of course, had a major impact in both areas. The paper work and manual labor which automation eliminated made high trading volume in an increasing number of financial instruments possible. Instantaneous dissemination of information makes trading in the rapidly changing markets feasible.

Increased volatility is not unique to any particular financial market

INTRODUCTION

but rather characterizes them all. No single culprit seems to be responsible either. Volatility increased in the currency markets when fixed exchange rates were abandoned and floating rates were instituted. Volatility increased in the debt markets when the country embraced inflationary policies and interest rates ratcheted to new highs. Volatility increased in the equity markets as institutions garnered an ever increasing share of trading volume and demonstrated that they too followed the herd instinct and often acted in concert. Finally, volatility increased in the commodity markets as investors thronged to tangibles in response to the ever decreasing value of currency.

The ingenuity and marketing expertise of the financial community should not be overlooked. In the face of doubters and disbelievers they molded exchange traded options into an unqualified success. In the face of regulatory morass they launched commodity options. In the face of criticism from those who claimed that financial markets were being transformed into gambling casinos they successfully introduced stock index futures, options on stock index futures, and finally options on stock indexes.

The financial explosion has not been without its problems. Brokerage firms accepted some of the new products rather coldly because neither staff nor facilities were properly prepared at the onset of trading. Had the educational process been initiated earlier, some of the products might have met with even greater success.

It would be incorrect to believe that everything attempted was successful. For example, options on the Value Line stock index futures were discontinued because of lack of interest. Index options were not universally accepted either. Three fatalities have already been recorded and no doubt others will fail to catch the public's interest. The environment also will be a major factor. For example, if interest rates stabilize the need for interest rate sensitive futures may disappear. Nevertheless, this influx of new financial instruments has been a godsend. To the brokerage industry it is a source of new revenue. To the exchanges it represents new growth. To investors it means new tools for investment, speculation, and risk control.

It is universally true that the new instruments are very complex—more so than initially meets the eye. Frequently they are modeled after existing instruments or are an outgrowth of existing trading so on the surface the differences may seem negligible. When examined in detail, however, the subtleties become topics for major investigation. A good understanding of the new nomenclature, contract terms, evaluation techniques, and investment strategies is not readily gained from a quick perusal of brief exchange or brokerage firm publications.

INTRODUCTION

So it is with stock index options. Many will be purchased and sold by individuals ignorant of the true nature of the beast they are dealing with. Hopefully this book will provide the information necessary to make skillful traders in this attractive new instrument.

THE OEX PHENOMENON

OEX is the ticker symbol for the S&P 100, the first index for which listed options were offered. It has become the most popular and most actively traded of all the indexes. Moreover, it is the most successful option product of the decade. Most investors are probably unaware of the magnitude of the success of OEX options. A few numbers should establish proper perspective.

On March 11, 1983, the first day of trading, total OEX volume was 4,575 contracts. Slightly over one year later—May 11, 1984—on a record volume day, 355,870 contracts changed hands. To an investor unacquainted with these instruments the activity suggests that there might just be something going on here worth looking into.

The CBOE (Chicago Board Options Exchange) is the largest options exchange in the country as measured by trading volume in index options and equity options. OEX volume averages in excess of 40 percent of total CBOE volume and has been higher than 50 percent. Trading in the single index option qualifies the OEX pit as the country's second largest exchange.

No written description can do justice to an explanation of trading on the exchange floor. The OEX pit has an area of 5,000 square feet. Depending on the market and the time of day, between 200 and 400 market makers and floor brokers battle with words and hand signals to trade these contracts. The visual and aural impression is that of organized pandemonium. The CBOE is one of Chicago's most interesting attractions. An invitation to visit the exchange should be accepted unhesitatingly.

1
OVERVIEW

MARKET BETS

Until recently it was difficult to translate a market opinion directly into a wager on the market. Further, a highly leveraged bet with low transaction costs was impossible. Possible substitutions for a market position were not totally satisfactory. They included concentrated portfolios (perhaps containing only one stock), diversified portfolios, mutual funds, closed-end funds (purchased on margin), and options on individual stocks. Unfortunately those alternatives have a major shortcoming: the performance of a collection of stocks and the market itself frequently do not coincide. In addition, these strategies do not provide other desirable characteristics such as high leverage and low execution costs. Also, planning the purchase and sale of these assets and monitoring open positions can be a time consuming process.

Now, however, several new products have been introduced which permit strategists to take a position directly in the market. The products include stock index futures, options on stock index futures, and stock index options. These instruments have many similar characteristics and applications. For all practical purposes what can be accomplished with one vehicle can be accomplished with the other. To keep the scope of this book bounded and to retain a sharp focus, index options will be addressed exclusively. Justification for this seemingly parochial approach will be addressed in subsequent sections.

The ability to take a position in the market directly has great importance not just to speculators. A primary benefit accrues also to equity owners. Now, as the market outlook changes, there is a simple means for offsetting risk through hedging transactions.

2

STOCK INDEX OPTIONS

EQUITY MARKETS VERSUS COMMODITY MARKETS

As stated earlier, this book will only touch briefly on indexes as they relate to vehicles in the futures markets. There is further justification for limiting this discussion. Index options can be executed through a stockbroker in a regular margin account. Equity investors and stock option users should be comfortable with this process.

On the other hand, orders for index futures and options on index futures must be placed with a commodities broker and executed in a commodities account. Successful incorporation of these instruments into an investment program requires an in-depth understanding of the futures markets and all the ramifications which trading in futures entails.

CONTROVERSIAL INSTRUMENT

Index options did not come of age without considerable debate. Proponents argued that the instruments offered a plethora of new techniques to hedge positions and they stressed the conservative nature of their attributes. Detractors, on the other hand, likened them only to a new and easily executed form of gambling.

It may be comforting to know that investment theory generally endorses this expansion in the financial markets. A multiplicity of investment alternatives lubricates the wheels of capitalism and optimizes resource allocation.

DEFINITION OF INDEX OPTIONS

Index options are puts and calls on the value of a composite of stocks; that is, an average or an index. In most respects they are identical to listed stock options. The index number can be viewed as the price of one share of an underlying stock and each contract as an option covering 100 shares of the index. The value of each options contract represents $100 times the current value of the underlying index.

When exercised, settlement does not occur by delivery of the securities comprising the index. The option holder who exercises receives cash equal to the difference between the closing dollar value of the index on the exercise date and the aggregate exercise price of the option. In effect, the exercising holder receives the amount by which the option is in-the-money.

OVERVIEW

Currently options are being traded on 13 different indexes. These are listed in Table 1-1. The indexes can be classified into two major types: broad-based and narrow-based. Broad-based indexes are those which are composed of a large number of stocks with the objective of reflecting movements in the overall market. An example of a broad-based index for which index options are available is the NYSE Composite Index. Narrow-based indexes, also called sub-indexes or industry indexes, are composed of a small number of stocks with the objective of reflecting a particular segment of the market. An example of a narrow-based index, one created exclusively for options trading, is the Amex Oil & Gas Index.

TABLE 1-1
OPTIONABLE INDEXES

Amex Computer Technology Index
Amex Major Market Index
Amex Market Value Index
Amex Oil & Gas Index
Amex Transportation Index
New York Stock Exchange Composite Index
New York Stock Exchange Telephone Index
Pacific Stock Exchange Technology Index
Philadelphia Stock Exchange Gaming/Hotel Index
Philadelphia Stock Exchange Gold/Silver Index
S&P 100 Index
S&P 500 Index
S&P Transportation Index

To clarify the parallels between equity options and index options the following comparison between a call purchase in both types of options is presented. More complex examples will be analyzed in Chapter 5.

Assume an investor is interested in call options for International Business Machines. At the time of this writing in mid-May 1984, IBM was trading at $111\frac{1}{8}$. The October 120 call option was quoted at $4\frac{1}{4}$. An order to purchase one contract for 100 shares would be stated as follows:

Buy 1 IBM Oct 120 (JD) @ $4\frac{1}{4}$ = $425

Similar instructions for the purchase of calls on optionable indexes are shown in Table 1-2. The listing begins with the index name, symbol, and level as of mid-May 1984. This is followed by a statement directing

STOCK INDEX OPTIONS

TABLE 1-2
SAMPLE INDEX OPTION PURCHASE TRANSACTIONS

Amex Computer Technology Index			XCI	85.41
Buy 1	XCI	Aug 85 (HQ) @ 5½ =		$550.00
Amex Major Market Index			XMI	108.61
Buy 1	XMI	Jul 110 (GB) @ 2¼ =		$225.00
Amex Market Value Index			XAM	198.35
Buy 1	XAM	Aug 220 (HT) @ 5½ =		$550.00
Amex Oil & Gas Index			XOI	116.79
Buy 1	XOI	Jun 120 (FD) @ ¾ =		$ 75.00
Amex Transportation Index			XTI	114.84
Buy 1	XTI	Jun 115 (HC) @ 5¼ =		$525.00
NYSE Composite Index			NYA	87.25
Buy 1	NYA	Dec 85 (LQ) @ 6⅜ =		$637.50
NYSE Telephone Index			NTI	97.24
Buy 1	NTI	Jan 100 (AT) @ 2½ =		$250.00
Pacific Stock Exchange Technology Index			PSE	99.56
Buy 1	PSE	Sep 100 (IT) @ 6 =		$600.00
Philadelphia Stock Exchange Gaming/Hotel Index			XGH	77.12
Buy 1	XGH	Dec 80 (LP) @ 5¼ =		$525.00
Philadelphia Stock Exchange Gold/Silver Index			XAU	112.70
Buy 1	XAU	Dec 110 (LB) @ 13 =		$1,300.00
S&P 100 Index			OEX	150.40
Buy 1	OEX	Aug 160 (HL) @ 1⅜ =		$137.50
S&P 500 Index			SPX	151.78
Buy 1	SPX	Jun 160 (FL) @ ½ =		$50.00
S&P Transportation Index			OTN	126.20
Buy 1	OTN	Aug 130 (HF) @ 4½ =		$450.00

Note: For each example above, line 1 states the index, the index symbol, and the index level. Line 2 states the order, the option expiration month, the exercise price, the option symbol, the option price (premium) and the total transaction value.

purchase of one contract. This sequence is repeated for each of the 13 optionable indexes.

STOCK OPTIONS AND INDEX OPTIONS COMPARED

A familiarity with listed stock options makes an understanding of index options relatively simple. For all practical purposes buying and selling index options is like buying and selling listed stock options. The excep-

STOCK INDEX OPTIONS

tions, to be discussed in detail in later chapters, are few and easy to understand.

The real challenge in using index options is selection of the appropriate underlying index. Thirteen optionable indexes having vastly different characteristics are already available to investors. Needless to say, they do not all perform similarly. For speculators it is critical to select the index which participates in a perceived market move. For hedgers it is crucial to select the index which mirrors movement in the portfolio being protected.

PREVIEW OF APPLICATIONS

Index options can be used in most of the strategies in effect for stock options. In addition, some new strategies and some variations on old strategies are unique to index options. Before going into detail about these investment approaches it is necessary to investigate the underlying indexes and the option contracts in more detail. The rationale for the strategies and the methods for implementation will then have greater meaning. At this point, however, there is no harm in surveying a few of the potential applications. A sample should include the following:

1. Speculate on the overall market.
2. Speculate on segments of the market.
3. Hedge an equity portfolio in anticipation of a market decline.
4. Separate market risk from stock and industry group risk.
5. Establish a market position prior to receipt of funds.

The most exciting prospect for index options is in conjunction with select groups of securities or with one-of-a-kind special situations uncovered on an infrequent basis by alert observers of the markets. A sample might include the following:

1. Hedge commodity indexed warrants and convertibles with narrow-based index options.
2. Hedge publicly-traded (closed-end) funds trading at a premium or discount to net asset value with broad-based index options.
3. Hedge portfolios of convertible securities with broad-based index options.
4. Hedge index funds or diversified mutual funds with broad-based index options.
5. Hedge specialized mutual funds with narrow-based index options.

STOCK INDEX OPTIONS

The creative investor should have no trouble concocting other innovative investments. In the current environment the securities industry is regularly devising new investment vehicles and new approaches for trading them. The resourceful investor should have a veritable field day. Potential is limited only by the imagination of the analyst.

LOOKING AHEAD

If the future unfolds as it is currently programmed, today's opportunities will seem sparse by comparison. In mid 1983 the SEC imposed a moratorium limiting each of the exchanges to options on two industry indexes. This moratorium expired February 1, 1984 and as of this writing a host of new indexes had been announced or were under consideration. Whereas only 13 indexes are currently trading, several times that number could be available in the future.

The NYSE, for example, filed with the SEC an additional 14 sub-indexes. The CBOE filed for trading 17 Standard & Poor's industry indexes. Is more really better? Are there benefits from additional index options which cannot be provided by existing options? Those questions will be left unanswered as far as the general public is concerned; however, for the resourceful individual this variety of industry index options provides a broad new spectrum of investment opportunity. The proliferation of narrow-based index options insures greater probability that they can be coupled with other highly individualistic and perhaps mispriced securities to create interesting risk controlled investments.

There will be deletions from the list as well. Public consumption of this product is not easy to predict and initial optimism is already being tempered. Three sub-index options (the S&P Computer and Business Equipment Index, the S&P Integrated International Oil Index, and the S&P Telephone Index) have already failed and the prognosis for some of the others is poor. The stock market itself may determine the ultimate popularity of the new index options. If the stock market is active and individual stocks exhibit high volatility, interest is likely to be directed to index options. In a less dynamic environment index puts and calls may not thrive and grow.

2

AVERAGES AND INDEXES

INTRODUCTION

The degree to which incorporation of index options in an investment strategy is successful depends largely upon the behavior of the underlying index. An understanding of this behavior can be greatly enhanced by examining the objective, components, construction, and price history of the various indexes. In addition, performance comparisons between indexes are also revealing.

Only after studying these characteristics can the best index be selected for the intended purpose. As stated previously, speculators want to select an index providing the most bang for the buck. Hedgers, on the other hand, need to ascertain which index will most likely duplicate movements in a vulnerable portfolio.

AVERAGES VERSUS INDEXES

Averages and indexes are closely related, in fact, an index is a special form of average. An average is simply the mean value of a group of stock prices. In its simplest form, an index is nothing more than an average expressed in terms of a base value (usually 100) at some earlier period. Indexes are by far the more prevalent of the two reporting schemes.

Although the terms average and index should not be used interchangeably, there is no rigid code forcing developers of these indicators to adhere to the proper nomenclature. For example, the Value Line Composite Average—as it is formally known—is really an index. Contrariwise, the Amex Major Market Index is in reality an average.

STOCK INDEX OPTIONS

Throughout the remainder of this book the term index will be used when discussing indexes specifically or indexes and averages in general. The term average will be used only when discussing a specific indicator calculated as a true average.

Index Concentration

In designing an indicator preference is usually given to the index form. In fact, of the thirteen optionable indexes only three are true *averages;* namely, the Amex Major Market Index, the Amex Transportation Index, and the Pacific Stock Exchange Technology Index. This is not an indictment on the usefulness of averages, however. Because the Major Market Index (an average) mimics the Dow it should find widespread application and its importance cannot be overstated. A speculator anticipating a blue-chip rally might find the Amex Major Market Index options to be the ideal vehicle to capitalize on this outlook. An investor holding high quality issues might find the Amex Major Market Index to be the ideal vehicle for hedging that portfolio.

Index Complexity

Although widely used and quoted, indexes are complex indicators often poorly understood and improperly used. This is not surprising because the theory of indexes is complex and there is controversy even in academic circles as to which is the best method of construction and how distortions can develop.

The experienced and erudite as well as amateurs can be ensnared by index complexities. For example, in 1966 the American Stock Exchange (Amex) introduced a new index, the American Stock Exchange Price Level Index. The objective of this index was to reflect changes in all stocks traded on the Amex. Design of the index had been contracted to Arthur D. Little, Inc., the prestigious think tank, working in conjunction with exchange officials. In the next few years, however, the index began to drift from its intended objective and it became the object of intense criticism in the financial press. The calculation scheme was finally abandoned and a new approach developed which has been more satisfactory.

On a somewhat lighter note officials at the Vancouver Stock Exchange were embarassed to say the least when a flaw in their index surfaced. An investigation was triggered after the index gradually dropped from 1000 to 520 during a period when the component stocks were stable or perhaps even higher.

9

AVERAGES AND INDEXES

The index was established in January 1982 at a level of 1000 and the method of calculation gave all stocks equal weight. Whenever the price of any of the approximately 1400 stocks in the index changed the index was recomputed, an event which occurred about 2,800 times on an average day.

The index was calculated to five decimal places. However, it was recorded with only three digits, and the computer dropped the last two digits without rounding. For example, 540.32567 became 540.325 rather than the correctly rounded number 540.326. The error, made thousands of times daily, was cumulative and caused ever increasing distortion.

When this was reported in late 1983, the exchange was preparing to recalculate the index from its inception. It had also engaged a consultant to reevaluate the design of the index and its usefulness.

INDEX OBJECTIVES

Indexes and averages are designed to measure the overall level of stock prices usually by measuring performance of a representative sample of individual stocks. This noble objective, while simple enough in concept, is difficult to implement. The final conclusions from any foray into index study are that no index is perfect in every respect, no index is suitable for all applications, and no index will replicate its relative behavior with other indexes on every occasion. On the other hand, depending upon what the analyst is trying to achieve, one index may clearly be superior to another.

Several designs for indexes have been developed and there is diversity in the number and type of stocks included. Therefore, care must be taken when making broad general statements about these indicators. One type of index measures change in the total market value of a large number of common stocks. Therefore this is an economic indicator useful in assessing the overall level of prosperity. They are also suited for measurement of the performance of large portfolios. A second type of index attempts to measure change in stock prices. These indicators are most useful as benchmarks for comparing performance of individual stocks.

Numerous factors complicate the otherwise simple concepts of averages and indexes. For example, dividends can be reinvested to give an indication of the total return on the stocks involved. In many indexes weighting schemes are introduced to give large companies greater representation in the index than small companies.

STOCK INDEX OPTIONS

Maintaining the indexes is not always straightforward either. Special adjustments are required in calculating these indicators to avoid discontinuities caused by substitutions in the component stocks. Similarly, allowance must be made for stock splits, stock dividends, recapitalizations, and mergers.

In the next few sections the construction of averages and indexes is explained thoroughly. Following the section on averages, the Dow Jones Industrial Average is analyzed in detail as an illustrative example. Following the section on indexes the New York Stock Exchange Composite Index is analyzed in detail. Later sections include a brief description of every index for which options are available. Finally the chapter concludes with a discussion of a few important indexes not having listed options.

STOCK AVERAGES

The stock average is an elementary concept. The prices of a representative group of stocks are added together and this sum is divided by the total number of issues in the sample. The quotient thus formed is a simple arithmetic mean and, if the Dow Jones Industrial Average is any indication, it can be an important and respected market measure.

If stock splits or stock dividends never occurred averages would probably be more popular and the need for more complex indexes would be less pressing; however, stock splits create discontinuities in a price average and unless adjustment is made, distortions would appear which were not representative of the fortunes of the companies involved.

Consider the computation of a simple average for three stocks A, B, and C having prices of $30, $50, and $70 respectively. Calculations for this average are shown in Exhibit 2–1. Then assume that stock B

EXHIBIT 2–1
CALCULATION OF A SIMPLE STOCK PRICE AVERAGE

Stock	Price	
A	30	
B	50	
C	70	
Sum :	150	
Divisor :	3	
Average:	50	(150 ÷ 3)

AVERAGES AND INDEXES

EXHIBIT 2–2
DISTORTIONS IN AN AVERAGE CAUSED BY A STOCK SPLIT

Stock	Price	
A	30	
B	25	
C	70	
Sum :	125	
Divisor :	3	
Average:	41.67	(125 ÷ 3)

splits 2-for-1. Exhibit 2–2 shows the outcome recomputed using post split prices. Because of the split the average dropped significantly but there was no fundamental change in the value of issue B to shareholders. Thus the average calculated as shown is erroneous.

To prevent such discontinuities, two alternatives are possible. One is to adjust the price of stock B by multiplying by the split ratio before computing the average. The second alternative, and the one generally implemented, is to adjust the divisor so that the average after the split equals the average before the split. In the example above if the divisor is reduced to 2.5, the average after the stock split is identical to the average before the stock split. This calculation is shown in Exhibit 2–3.

EXHIBIT 2–3
CALCULATION OF THE AVERAGE USING AN ADJUSTED DIVISOR

Stock	Price	
A	30	
B	25	
C	70	
Sum :	125	
Divisor :	2.50	
Average:	50	(125 ÷ 2.5)

A similar discontinuity in the average takes place on those occasional instances when changes are made in the stocks comprising the average. Once again the divisor is adjusted so that continuity is maintained.

It is characteristic of averages that the higher the price of a component stock the greater the influence it will have on the calculation. Consider a simple average of three stocks having a relatively wide range in prices; namely, $20, $110, and $200. The average is calculated in Exhibit 2–4.

STOCK INDEX OPTIONS

EXHIBIT 2–4
CALCULATION OF A SIMPLE AVERAGE CONTAINING A HIGH-PRICED ISSUE AND A LOW-PRICED ISSUE

Stock	Price
A	20
B	110
C	200
Sum :	330
Divisor :	3
Average:	110 (330 ÷ 3)

Exhibit 2–5 shows the affect of a five percent change in the price of the cheapest issue. The average increases by 0.3 percent. Exhibit 2–6 shows the affect of a five percent change in the price of the most expensive issue. The average increases by 3.03 percent. Thus the impact on the average caused by a five percent change in the high-priced component is more than ten times the impact caused by a five percent change in the low-priced issue. In fact, with a little arithmetic it can be shown that the low-priced issue would have to increase by fifty percent to equal the impact on the average of a five percent change in the high-priced issue.

If high priced issues have an inordinate amount of influence on an average, it follows that a stock split will reduce that stock's influence.

EXHIBIT 2–5
AFFECT ON THE AVERAGE OF A 5% (1 POINT) MOVE IN THE LOW-PRICED ISSUE

Stock	Price
A	21
B	110
C	200
Sum :	331
Divisor :	3
Average:	110.33 (331 ÷ 3)

The increase in the average is $\dfrac{110.33 - 110}{110} = 0.3\%$

AVERAGES AND INDEXES

EXHIBIT 2-6
AFFECT ON THE AVERAGE OF A 5% (10 POINT) MOVE IN THE HIGH-PRICED ISSUE

Stock	Price
A	20
B	110
C	210
Sum :	340
Divisor :	3
Average:	113.33 (340 ÷ 3)

The increase in the average is $\dfrac{113.33 - 110}{110} = 3.03\%$

This is demonstrated in Exhibit 2–7 and Exhibit 2–8. Assume stock B trading at $60 triples in price to $180 after which it is split 3-for-1. The average is now computed using a price $60 and the divisor is reduced so that the average after the split equals the average before the split.

Whereas on the upside stock B originally influenced the average by a move of 120 points, on the downside the average can only be influenced by 60 points assuming the worst case condition that stock B goes bankrupt. In fact even if stock B did drop to zero after the split, its influence is so diminished that the average would still be higher than it was when it included B before the split!

EXHIBIT 2-7
AFFECT ON AN AVERAGE OF A SINGLE STOCK TRIPLING IN PRICE

Initial		Stock B Triples in Price	
Stock	Price	Stock	Price
A	20	A	20
B	60	B	180
C	200	C	200
Sum :	280	Sum :	400
Divisor :	3	Divisor :	3
Average:	93.33	Average:	133.33

STOCK INDEX OPTIONS

EXHIBIT 2–8
AFFECT OF BANKRUPTCY ON THE AVERAGE AFTER THE DIVISOR WAS ADJUSTED FOR A 3-FOR-1 SPLIT IN STOCK B

Stock B Splits 3-for-1		Stock B Goes Bankrupt	
Stock	*Price*	*Stock*	*Price*
A	20	A	20
B	60	B	0
C	200	C	200
Sum :	280	Sum :	220
Divisor :	2.10	Divisor :	2.10
Average:	133.33	Average:	104.76

DOW JONES INDUSTRIAL AVERAGE

The Dow Jones Industrial Average is not an optionable index. Nevertheless it was selected as the representative average to be discussed in detail because of its great popularity and widespread use. The Dow was a candidate when the exchanges were considering the various indexes for options listing. However, Dow Jones & Co., publishers of the index, refused to grant permission to allow the Dow to be in any way associated with a speculative vehicle such as options or futures. The American Stock Exchange responded by developing its own index, the Amex Major Market Index, which closely matches the Dow's performance. Calculation is the same but the components are slightly different.

The Dow Jones Industrial Average is probably the most widely quoted of all the averages. Part of its popularity can be attributed to its long history, having been calculated in one form or another since 1884. A second reason for its great popularity is the spotlight it receives daily in *The Wall Street Journal.* But over and above these factors, the DJIA is a useful and important indicator and has withstood the test of time for this reason.

The DJIA is calculated as a true average, computed by adding the prices of all 30 component stocks and dividing that sum—not by 30—but by 1.194. This divisor reflects the adjustments required by splits, dividends, substitutions, mergers, and others over the years.

On April 27, 1984 the sum of the closing prices of the 30 Dow

AVERAGES AND INDEXES

stocks was 1,395.875. If one were to initiate the average on that date, this sum would be divided by 30 and the resulting level of the index would be 46.529. This compares with the closing price of the Dow on that date of 1,169.07 which is the sum of the stock prices divided by the adjusted divisor (1,395.875 ÷ 1.194). Thus, one of the oft-cited criticisms of the Dow: its level has little meaning out of context.

In fact, some observers complain that the Dow can no longer precisely be called an average because the index level is so distant from the average price. When the divisor reaches 1.000, every point move in an individual "Dow" stock will cause a one point move in the average.

At current levels, a one point increase in the price of each of the component stocks would cause the Dow to rise slightly more than 25 points. From another perspective, a one point increase in the Dow is equivalent to a $0.04 increase in each individual issue.

Attributes and Shortcomings

Averages in general and the Dow in particular have as a stock market indicator a few strengths and many weaknesses. Although it is difficult to prove all of the allegations, in sum it appears that the majority of the evidence supports the critics. The astute investor should abandon the Dow and establish the same familiarity and comfort level with one of the more representative indexes.

Strengths

Only three positives of any significance characterize the Dow as a good choice for an indicator. The strengths are as follows:

1. The Dow is simple to calculate. In the computer age, however, this attribute has little significance.

2. The average is timely. All of the component issues are actively traded. Thus, when the market moves suddenly and sharply, new prices are quickly established in all the Dow stocks. As a result, the Dow reflects short term price moves more quickly and more accurately than indexes sampling a larger number of stocks.

3. The Dow, while limited in its composition, still represents a large segment of the market. The 30 Dow companies represent about 25 percent of the total market value of all stocks traded on the New York Stock Exchange and about 20 percent of the value of all stocks traded in the United States.

16
STOCK INDEX OPTIONS

Weaknesses

The list of negatives for the Dow as an indicator is somewhat longer. So adverse are these criticisms that they probably eliminate the Dow as a contender for a good market indicator. The weakness are as follows:

1. The sample size is too small. An average of only 30 stocks cannot possibly give insight into the movement of the market as a whole. For example, none of the smaller companies are included. In addition, industry group representation is limited. The Value Line Investment Survey has identified more than 90 different industry groups. With regard to diversification, the Dow stocks only represent 20 of these groups. Therefore the Dow does not represent all segments of U.S. industrial activity.

2. The procedure for calculating the DJIA does not take into account small stock dividends. This causes a definite downward bias but because it has not been researched fully, its impact is not known.

3. Because of the weighting method high priced issues have greater influence on the average than low priced issues. There is no sound rationale for this weighting scheme.

4. The optimum procedure for accommodating stock splits is not adjustment of the divisor, the methodology used in calculating the DJIA. This procedure regularly introduces an upward bias in the average, a shortcoming compounded by the fact that stocks tend to split at times when their importance on the average is at a historical high.

5. Whenever a stock is split, its influence on the average is systematically reduced. Successful companies characterized by a pattern of increasing stock prices followed by a stock split are regularly awarded a diminished importance in the Dow. At the same time, those companies which go nowhere regularly inherit increased importance. In summary the Dow does not properly indicate the long term upward trend.

6. The Dow is advertised as an indicator of performance in the industrial sector. Nevertheless, two stocks fall outside that classification; namely, AT&T which is a utility and American Express which is a financial issue.

STOCK INDEXES

The purpose of an index is generally the same as that of an average. In its simplest form an index is an average stated with reference to a base value which is generally set at 100 at some prior point in history. Although averaging may be used in the calculation of the index, weight-

AVERAGES AND INDEXES

ing schemes are more generally encountered. This different method of calculation is chosen to eliminate some of the shortcomings inherent in simple averaging.

When devising an index, the first step is establishment of the base period. This may be an arbitrary selection or it may be set at an important market juncture. Stock prices in the index for that date are then averaged and normalized by dividing through by the average. This quotient (one) is then multiplied by the factor selected to be the index base value. This number is usually 100 but it may also be the average value of the prices of the components in the index on the base period date. The calculations for creating an index are shown in Exhibit 2-9.

To determine the value of the index in subsequent periods, the prices of the component issues are again averaged. This average is then divided by the base value established in the base period. The final step is multiplication by the constant factor. This calculation is shown in Exhibit 2-10.

Weighted Indexes

Virtually all of the popular indexes are weighted by the number of shares outstanding for each of the component issues. Such weighting accomplishes two things. First it makes the index responsive to the total value of the issues involved. Second, it eliminates the sensitivity of the index to stock splits since the product of stock price times number of shares outstanding remains constant.

EXHIBIT 2-9
CALCULATION OF A SIMPLE STOCK PRICE INDEX
(base period)

Stock	Price	
A	20	
B	50	
C	200	
Sum :	270	
Divisor :	3	
Average:	90	
Index :	100	(Index $= \dfrac{90}{90} \times 100 = 100$)

STOCK INDEX OPTIONS

EXHIBIT 2–10
AFFECT ON THE INDEX ASSUMING ALL STOCKS DOUBLE IN VALUE
(subsequent period)

Stock	Price	
A	50	
B	100	
C	400	
Sum :	540	
Divisor :	3	
Average:	180	
Index :	200	(Index $= \dfrac{180}{90} \times 100 = 200$)

Exhibit 2–11 shows the calculation of a simple capitalization-weighted stock price index. The calculation is the same as for the simpler index except that before averaging, each stock price is multiplied by the number of shares outstanding. Exhibit 2–12 shows the calculation of the index at a future period after all stocks double in price. Note that index is computed by dividing the current aggregate market value by the base value from the base period. Exhibit 2–13 shows how stock splits are accommodated by this form of index calculation. Stock B, of which there were originally 2,000,000 shares priced at $100 splits 2-for-1. The result is 4,000,000 shares priced at $50.

EXHIBIT 2–11
CALCULATION OF A SIMPLE CAPITALIZATION WEIGHTED STOCK PRICE INDEX
(base period)

Stock	Price	Shares Outstanding	Value
A	20	1,000,000	$ 20,000,000
B	50	2,000,000	100,000,000
C	200	3,000,000	600,000,000
Aggregate Market Value			$720,000,000

$$\text{Index} = \dfrac{720,000,000}{720,000,000} \times 100 = 100$$

AVERAGES AND INDEXES

EXHIBIT 2–12
AFFECT ON THE INDEX ASSUMING DOUBLE IN VALUE
(subsequent period)

Stock	Price	Shares Outstanding	Market Value
A	40	1,000,000	$ 40,000,000
B	100	2,000,000	200,000,000
C	400	3,000,000	1,200,000,000
Aggregate Market Value			$1,440,000,000

$$\text{Index} = \frac{1{,}440{,}000{,}000}{720{,}000{,}000} \times 100 = 200$$

The market value of stock B remains constant and the affect on the index is unchanged.

NEW YORK STOCK EXCHANGE COMPOSITE INDEX

The NYSE Composite Index is an optionable index. Although not the most widely used index (the S&P 500 probably enjoys this status) it is a popular index and has been very well received. Because of the number of stocks included in the index and because its composition cuts across all industry lines, the NYSE Composite Index is one of the broadest and most representative indicators. It was therefore selected as the example index to be discussed here in detail.

EXHIBIT 2–13
IMPACT OF A STOCK SPLIT ON THE INDEX
(subsequent period with split)

Stock	Price	Shares Outstanding	Market Value
A	40	1,000,000	40,000,000
B	50	4,000,000	200,000,000
C	400	3,000,000	1,200,000,000
Aggregate Market Value			$1,440,000,000

$$\text{Index} = \frac{1{,}440{,}000{,}000}{720{,}000{,}000} \times 100 = 200$$

20
STOCK INDEX OPTIONS

The NYSE Composite Index is a broad-based capitalization-weighted index which includes all 1,500+ common stocks listed on the New York Stock Exchange. It includes the common stocks of most major U.S. corporations as well as the stocks of numerous multinational firms.

The method of computation is as follows:

$$\text{current NYSE index} = \frac{\text{current aggregate market value}}{\text{adjusted base market value}} \times \text{base value}$$

The current aggregate market value is the summation of the product of the share price times the number of shares outstanding for all stocks listed. The adjusted base market value is the market value as of the base date of December 31, 1965 adjusted for capitalization changes over time. The base value is 50 which was reasonably close to the average price of all common stocks listed on the NYSE as of the base date.

On the base date the aggregate market value was approximately $500 billion, a number which also set the base market value. Therefore the index calculation as of December 31, 1965 was

$$\text{current NYSE index} = \frac{\$500 \text{ billion}}{\$500 \text{ billion}} \times 50$$
$$= 50$$

Recently the aggregate market value was approximately $1,500 billion and the base market value adjusted for mergers, additions, deletions, and so forth was $800 billion. Substituting these numbers:

$$\text{current NYSE index} = \frac{\$1,500 \text{ billion}}{800 \text{ billion}} \times 50$$
$$= 93.75$$

Attributes and Shortcomings

The NYSE Composite Index is not the subject of a great deal of controversy. The sample size is large and all industry groups are represented. Since it is capitalization-weighted it is free from distortion caused by the weighting scheme. A change in the price of a large company will affect the index more than a proportionate change in the price of a

AVERAGES AND INDEXES

small company. Thus it is not possible as it is with the Dow, for the NYSE Composite Index to move contrary to aggregate market value.

BROAD-BASED VERSUS NARROW-BASED INDEXES

Of the 13 optionable indexes available, six are broad-based; that is, there are a large number of stocks in the index and it is designed to reflect the overall market. Seven of the indexes are narrow-based; that is, there are a small number of stocks in the index. They are concentrated in a particular industry or market sector and the index is designed to be highly representative of that particular group.

The contract specifications for broad-based and narrow-based index options are similar but not identical. The differences can be ascertained by examining the terms in Apendix C. For many investors the most important difference is the margin requirement (it is higher for narrow-based index options).

Broad-Based Indexes

There are six broad-based optionable indexes as shown in Exhibit 2-14. Later in the chapter the similarities and differences will be examined in detail; however, for now it is sufficient to say that while there is some overlap, there is sufficient variation in the component stocks and the method of calculating the index that some care is required when selecting an index for a particular purpose.

A brief summary of each index follows. A full description including method of calculation, component issues, and a historical price chart is given in Appendix A.

Amex Major Market Index: A price-weighted average of 20 well-known blue chip stocks designed to measure the market performance of major U.S. industrial corporations. Stocks were selected with the

EXHIBIT 2-14
BROAD-BASED OPTIONABLE INDEXES

Amex Major Market Index
Amex Market Value Index
New York Stock Exchange Composite Index
Pacific Stock Exchange Technology Index
S&P 100 Index
S&P 500 Index

STOCK INDEX OPTIONS

intention of replicating the Dow Jones Industrial Average (15 issues are common to both indexes).

Amex Market Value Index: A capitalization-weighted index of the 800+ common stocks, ADRs, and warrants listed on the American Stock Exchange. It is designed to measure the collective performance of a large group of midrange growth oriented companies. The Amex Market Value Index is unique in its treatment of dividends. Stock dividends are treated as if reinvested. Therefore the index reflects the total return of its components.

New York Stock Exchange Composite Index: A capitalization-weighted index designed to measure the changes in the aggregate market value of the 1,500+ common stocks listed on the New York Stock Exchange.

Pacific Stock Exchange Technology Index: A price-weighted average of 100 securities representing a broad spectrum of companies principally engaged in manufacturing or service related products within advanced technology fields.

S&P 100 Index: A capitalization-weighted index designed to measure changes in the market value of 100 stocks for which options are currently listed on the CBOE.

S&P 500 Index: A capitalization-weighted index designed to measure changes in the aggregate market value of 500 stocks representing all major industries in approximately the same proportion to their representation on the New York Stock Exchange.

Narrow-Based Indexes

There are seven narrow-based optionable indexes (NBIs) as shown in Exhibit 2–15. Each index covers stocks in a particular industry group except for the Pacific Stock Exchange Technology Index which includes stocks based on the nature of the company's activities rather than their particular specialty.

As of this writing the narrow-based indexes have not been an outstanding success. In fact three entries—the S&P Computer & Business Equipment Index, the S&P Integrated International Oil Index, and the S&P Telephone Index—were discontinued because of a lack of investor interest. Nevertheless, it may be premature to discount the viability of the concept. Their brief existence has not been in an optimum market environment being a period when even equity options were languishing. If their popularity improves, the list should expand rapidly as dozens more have already been proposed by the various exchanges.

AVERAGES AND INDEXES

EXHIBIT 2–15
NARROW-BASED OPTIONABLE INDEXES

Amex Computer Technology Index
Amex Oil and Gas Index
Amex Transportation Index
NYSE Telephone Index
Philadelphia Stock Exchange Gaming/Hotel Index
Philadelphia Stock Exchange Gold/Silver Index
S&P Transportation Index

A brief summary of each index follows. A full description including method of calculation, component issues, and a historical price chart is given in Appendix A.

Amex Computer Technology Index: A capitalization-weighted index of 30 stocks representing a cross-section of widely-held U.S. corporations involved in various phases of the computer industry.

Amex Oil and Gas Index: A capitalization-weighted index of 30 stocks representing a cross-section of widely-held U.S. corporations involved in various phases of the oil and gas industry.

Amex Transportation Index: A price-weighted average of 20 stocks representing widely-held and actively traded corporations involved in a number of diversified transportation systems.

NYSE Telephone Index: A capitalization-weighted index of the eight common stocks of the companies which comprised the "old" AT&T; that is, AT&T before the divestiture.

Philadelphia Stock Exchange Gaming/Hotel Index: A capitalization-weighted index of nine stocks designed to represent a cross section of widely held U.S. corporations involved in various phases of the gaming and hotel industries.

Philadelphia Stock Exchange Gold/Silver Index: A capitalization-weighted index of seven stocks designed to represent a cross section of widely-held U.S. corporations involved primarily in the mining of gold/silver.

S&P Transportation Index: A capitalization-weighted index of 20 stocks in companies which are a major factor in the U.S. transportation industry.

IMPORTANT INDEXES WITHOUT LISTED OPTIONS

Thus far 14 different indexes have been discussed, the 13 optionable indexes plus the Dow Jones Industrial Average; however, these repre-

STOCK INDEX OPTIONS

sent only a small portion of the total number of indexes which have been developed. Brokerage firms, investment advisers, and publishers maintain numerous other indexes which have varying degrees of usefulness and popularity.

Four of these non-optionable indexes are important in that they are widely followed and they measure a different aspect of the overall market. These indexes are the Dow Jones Industrial Average (already discussed), the NASDAQ-OTC Price Index, the Value Line Composite Average, and the Wilshire 5000 Equity Index.

Even though options are not available for these indexes, they may be useful in other ways and it is interesting to put them in perspective with other indexes. For example, the Value Line Composite Average (as well as the NYSE Composite Index, the S&P 100 and the S&P 500) have futures contracts trading on various exchanges. Therefore investors not satisfied with the risk/reward profile of options, or with the correlation of optioned indexes to specific portfolios, may wish to consider operations in the futures markets. A summary of each index follows. A full description including method of calculation, component issues, and a historical price chart, is given in Appendix B.

Dow Jones Industrial Average: A price-weighted average of 30 "blue chip" stocks chosen as representative of the broad market and

EXHIBIT 2-16
CALCULATION OF A SIMPLE
GEOMETRIC STOCK PRICE INDEX

Stock	Base Period Price	Subsequent Period Price	Price Ratio
A	30	32	32/30 = 1.06
B	50	55	55/50 = 1.10
C	70	73	73/70 = 1.04
Geometric Average	:—		1.07*
Index Level	100		107**

* $\sqrt[3]{1.06 \times 1.10 \times 1.04}$

** The geometric average times the index level in the base period (1.07 × 100).

AVERAGES AND INDEXES

American Industry. The Dow is discussed in complete detail on page 14.

NASDAQ-OTC Price Index: A capitalization-weighted index of approximately 3,600 domestic OTC common stocks listed on the National Association of Securities Dealers Automated Quotation (NASDAQ) system.

Wilshire 5000 Equity Index: A capitalization-weighted index which represents the dollar value in billions of dollars of all actively traded common stocks in the United States including all NYSE and Amex issues plus every OTC issue for which a quotation is available.

Value Line Composite Average: An equally weighted *geometric* average expressed in index form of approximately 1,700 stocks followed by the Value Line investment advisory including NYSE, Amex, and OTC issues. A geometric average is computed by taking the nth root of the product of the price changes of the n stocks (in this case 1,700) in the sample. An example calculation is shown in Exhibit 2–16.

Using this technique, equal percentage fluctuations in the prices of different stocks have equal impact on the index. Because the Value Line Composite is not weighted by price or capitalization, and because the number of components is large, the index is excellent at reflecting price change of the typical stock.

3

COMPARING BROAD-BASED INDEXES

INTRODUCTION

There are three perspectives from which the interrelationship between indexes can be viewed. The first is graphical and is accomplished by preparing an overlay of the price history of one index with that of another. The second approach—divergence analysis—is a quantification of the evidence presented in the graphs. The technique compares percentage changes in the various indexes for major market swings. The third approach, also numerical, measures the degree to which two indexes move in concert and is called correlation.

When using index options the investor can never escape two difficult decisions. The first is to make a market prediction (direction, magnitude, and duration) and the second is to identify the index most likely to achieve the projection. As was discussed earlier, the various indexes are calculated differently. Further, each measures different markets or limited segments of a particular market. As a result, the indexes are not in lock step and particular care is required when choosing an index to be certain that their options fulfill the particular need. The objective of the three comparisons—graphic, divergence, and correlation—is to assist in selecting the best index for its intended application.

GRAPHIC JUXTAPOSITION

Charting is one of the best ways to gain insight into the comovement between indexes. A first approach would be to line up all the indexes as is done in Exhibit 3–1 and to compare the wiggles. This approach

EXHIBIT 3-1
NINE BROAD-BASED INDEXES IN JUXTAPOSITION

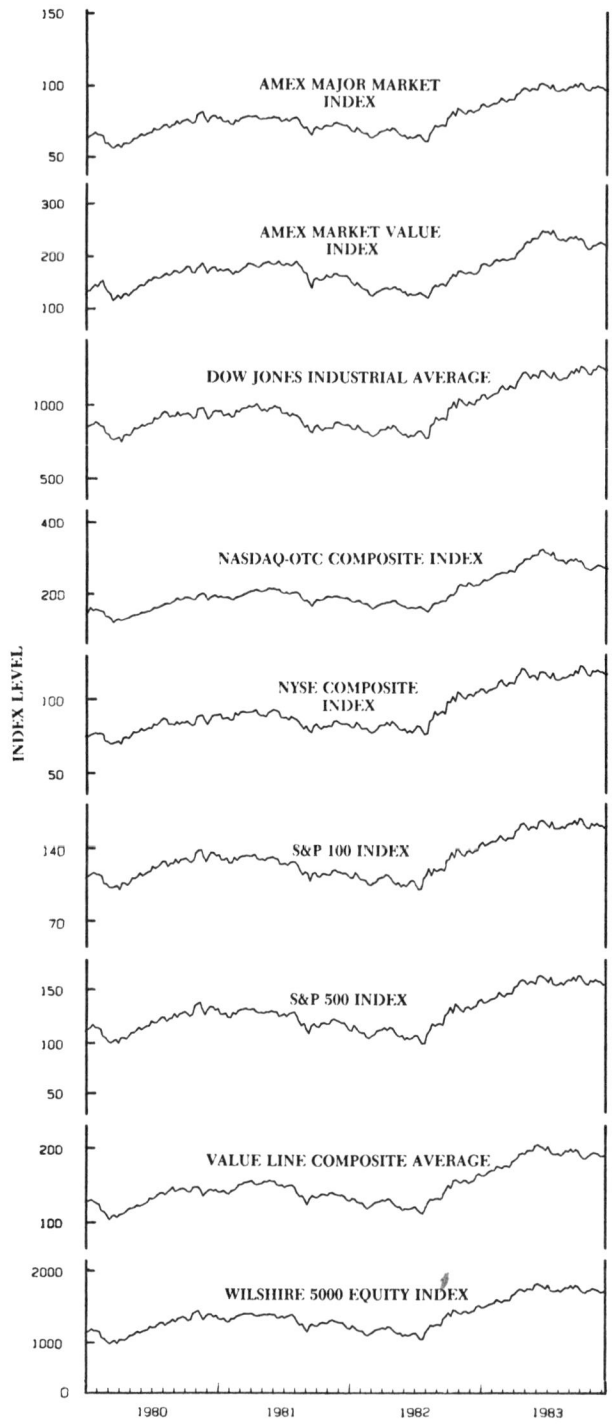

COMPARING BROAD-BASED INDEXES

is less than satisfactory, however, because the current levels of the various indexes are significantly different. As a result, plots of the indexes cannot all be drawn on graphs having the same scale factor. Therefore the magnitude of various excursions, while appearing equivalent, may be considerably different when considered in terms of percentage change which is the most revealing measure.

Various techniques are available to minimize distortions when comparing indexes at different levels. One approach is to use a ratio (logarithmic) scale. Labeling with a transformed numbering system produces a grid such that equal distances represent equivalent percentage price changes. This technique is widely employed and is a valid method of presentation.

A second approach is to compare the logarithms of the index levels. The beauty of this approach is that the charts are scaled linearly. When using this technique the indexes are reduced to terms which are difficult to relate to. Thus, the transformation would not be widely appreciated and might introduce new areas of misunderstanding.

Another technique, and the one which will be used in the remainder of this discussion, is to re-index every average setting each equal to the same base value at the beginning of the historic period to be considered. A negative to this approach is, once again, that the raw index number, the quoted value with which everyone is familiar, is altered and this may cause confusion in the interpretation.

As an example of this method of presentation consider the Amex Major Market Index (XMI) and the Amex Market Value Index (XAM). The XMI consists of 20 stocks, 15 of which are included in the Dow Jones Industrial Average. The goal in constructing the XMI was to replicate the Dow without actually copying it. On the other hand, the XAM is composed of all the issues traded on the American Stock Exchange. Because listing requirements for the Amex are less stringent in terms of company size, capitalization, number of shareholders, and so forth, the Amex Market Value Index represents issues considerably more speculative than the Amex Major Market Index. It should be anticipated that the two indexes would behave quite differently.

The Amex Major Market Index and the Amex Market Value Index are plotted together in Exhibit 3-2. A four year history was chosen because it covers a market cycle including a period of very weak prices (1982) and a period of very strong prices (1983). The base value of 100 was chosen arbitrarily.

The chart clearly shows the greater volatility of the more speculative index. Both the advances and the declines tend to be more exaggerated. Note, however, the correspondence in the peaks and troughs of both indexes.

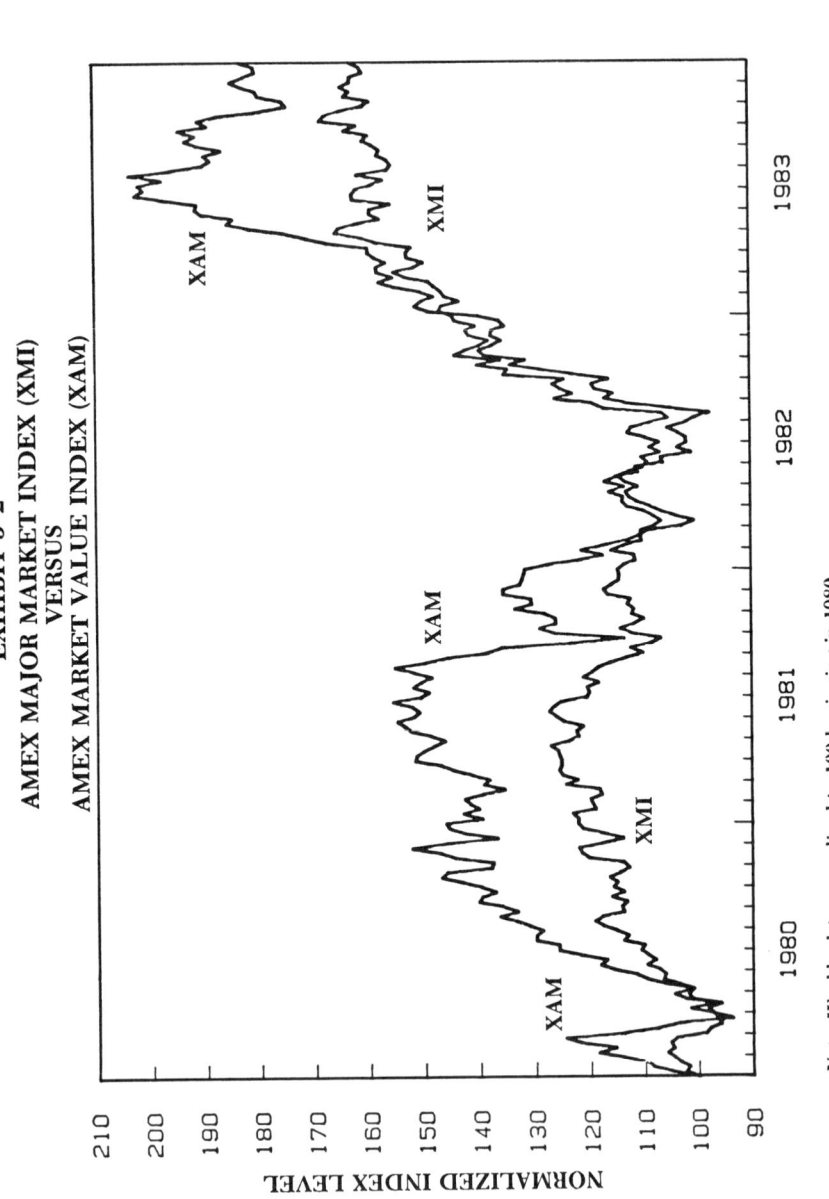

EXHIBIT 3-2*
**AMEX MAJOR MARKET INDEX (XMI)
VERSUS
AMEX MARKET VALUE INDEX (XAM)**

Note: Weekly data normalized to 100 beginning in 1980.

COMPARING BROAD-BASED INDEXES

The following charts compare price movements for the majority of widely followed broad-based market indexes using the same graphic approach. Rather than overlay each index with every other index, one index was chosen as the standard of comparison. Although the S&P 500 would have been a good choice for this standard because it is widely used throughout the investment industry for performance measurement, the S&P 100 was selected as the reference to be used in this text because options on that index are so popular. The relationship between the S&P 100 and the S&P 500 is shown in Exhibit 3-3. For all practical purposes the graphs coincide and the indexes are interchangeable. Since both indexes are weighted in the same manner and sample the highest capitalization stocks, the similarity should be expected.

Exhibit 3-4 shows the Amex Major Market Index versus the S&P 100. While some deviation is apparent it is not significant. Future divergences could probably not be predicted with sufficient accuracy to influence an investment strategy.

Exhibit 3-5 shows the Amex Market Value Index versus the S&P 100. From data on indexes thus far presented it would be expected that these plots would resemble those for the Amex Major Market Index versus the Amex Market Value Index shown in Exhibit 3-2. This is in fact the case.

Exhibit 3-6 shows the NASDAQ-OTC Index versus the S&P 100. Differences here should have been anticipated given the vastly different universe from which the component issues were selected.

The Value Line Composite Average versus the S&P 100 is shown in Exhibit 3-7. The similarity here is somewhat unexpected given the major differences in the components and the method of construction of the two indexes. The similarity, however, cannot be depended upon when formulating an investment strategy. As will be shown in later discussions, the Value Line Composite Average has been a maverick in the past and is likely to repeat that performance in the future.

Finally, Exhibit 3-8 shows the Wilshire 5000 Equity Index versus the S&P 100. Since the composition of this index is vastly different from any of the indexes thus far encountered, prediction of wide divergences would not be illogical. There is high correspondence, however, explained because New York Stock Exchange issues comprise 87% of the total Wilshire 5000 Index value.

Two other indexes were also examined graphically, the NYSE Composite Index and the Dow Jones Industrial Average, both in reference to the S&P 100. The graphs matched so closely that no significant information was revealed. Therefore they are not illustrated here.

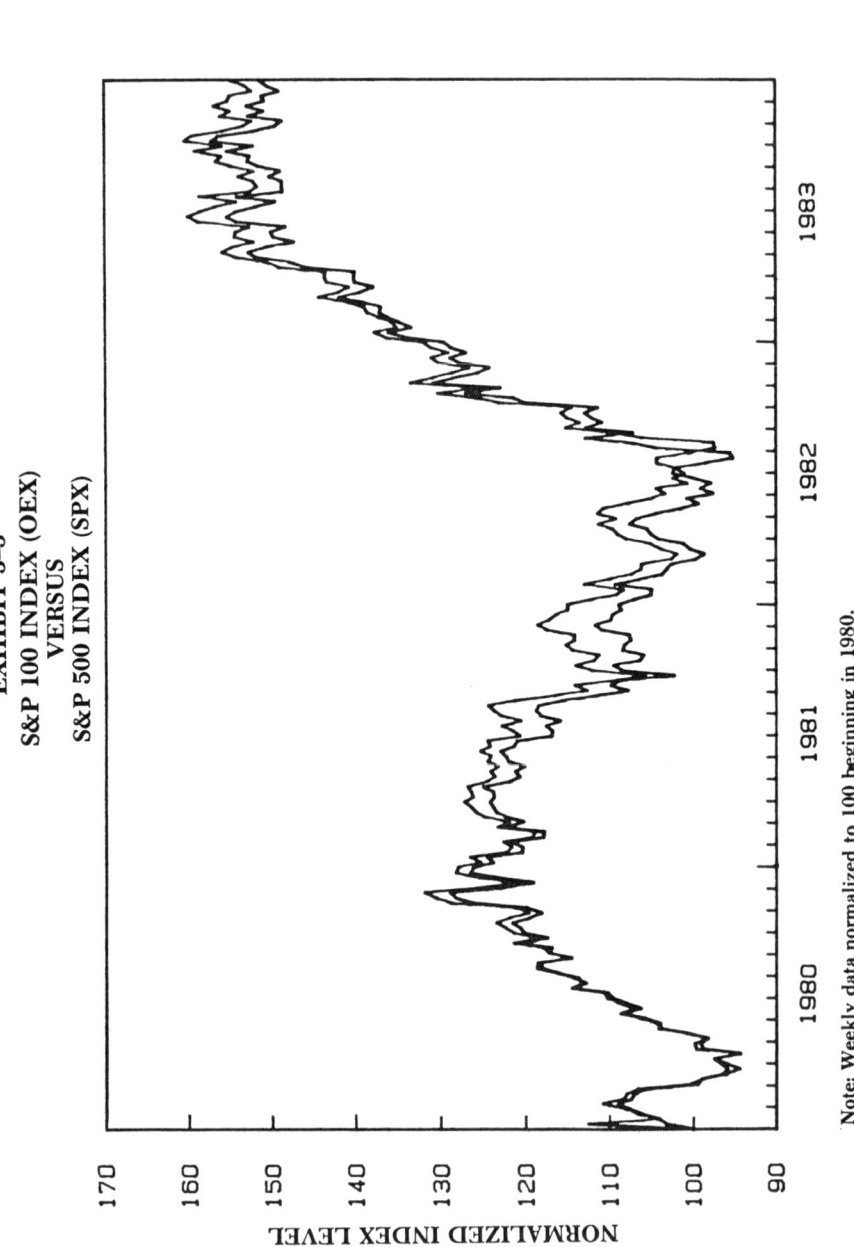

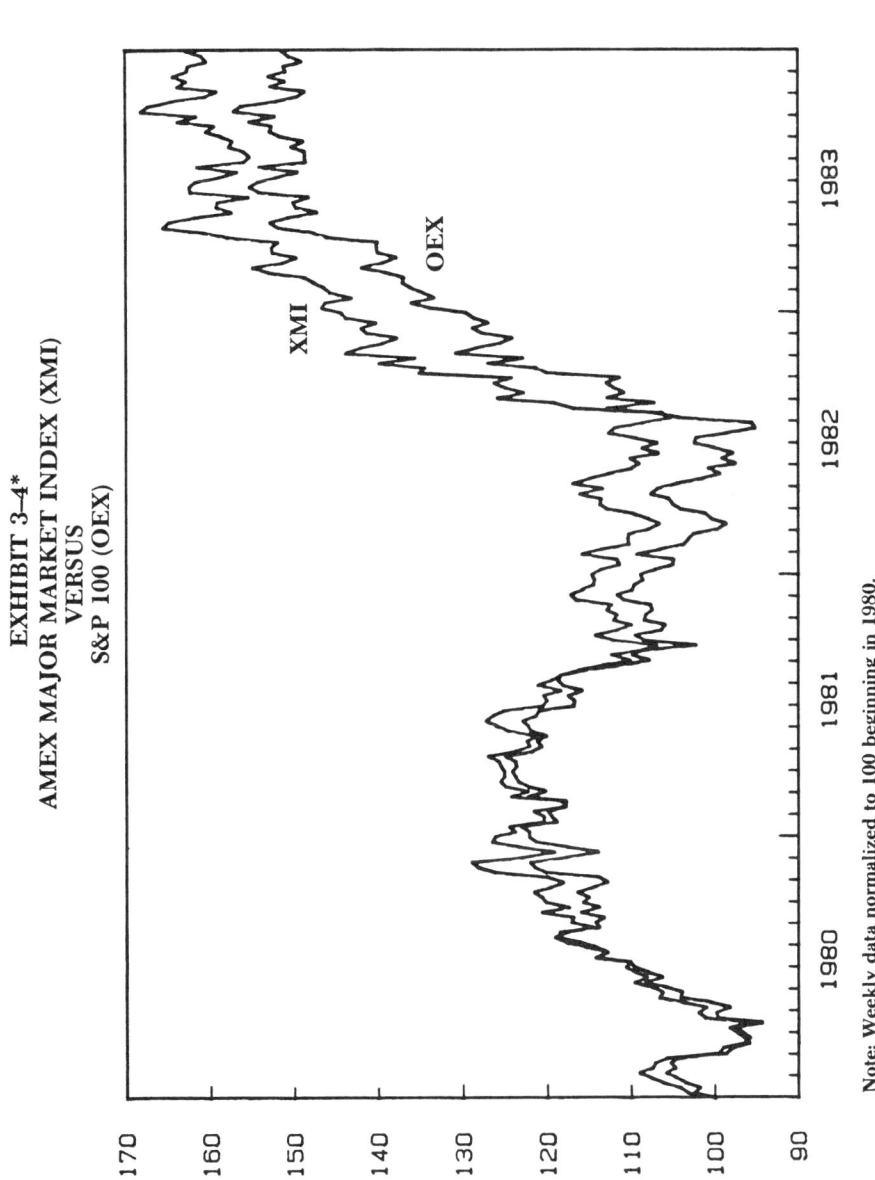

EXHIBIT 3–4*
AMEX MAJOR MARKET INDEX (XMI)
VERSUS
S&P 100 (OEX)

Note: Weekly data normalized to 100 beginning in 1980.

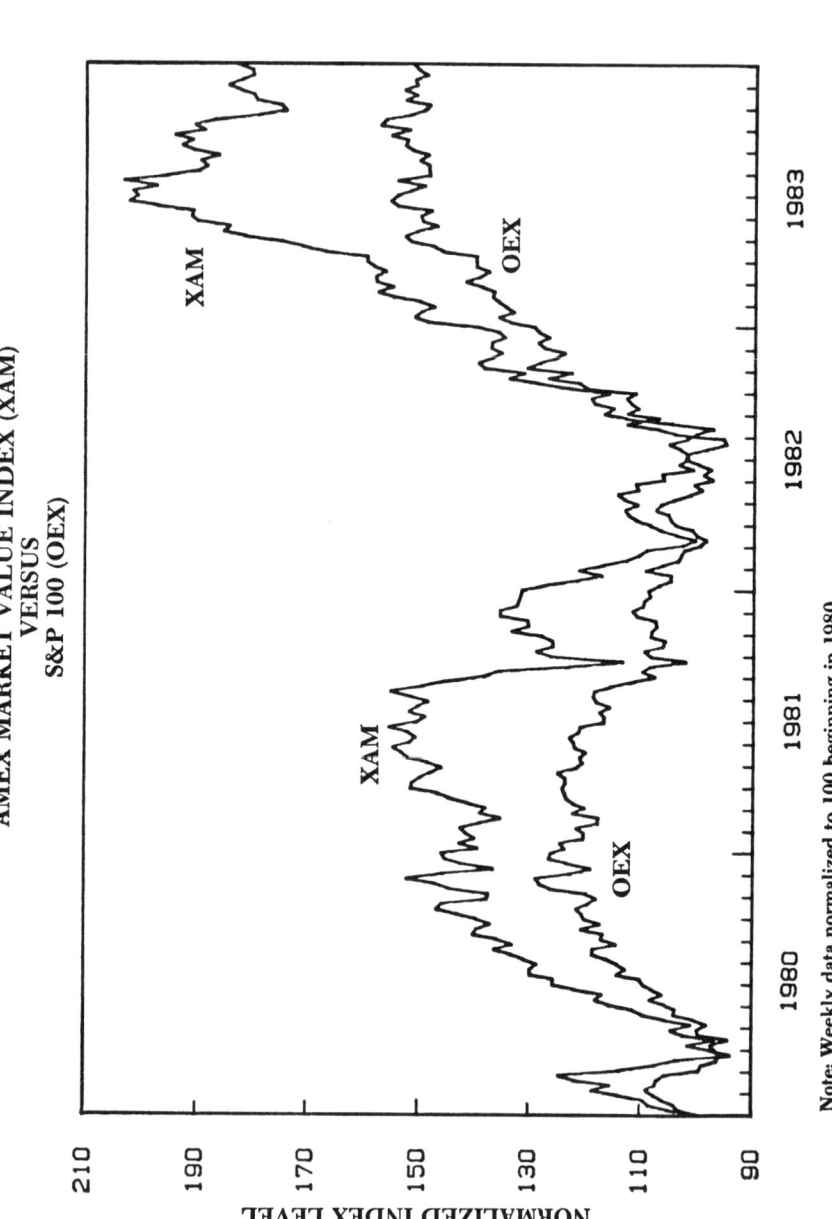

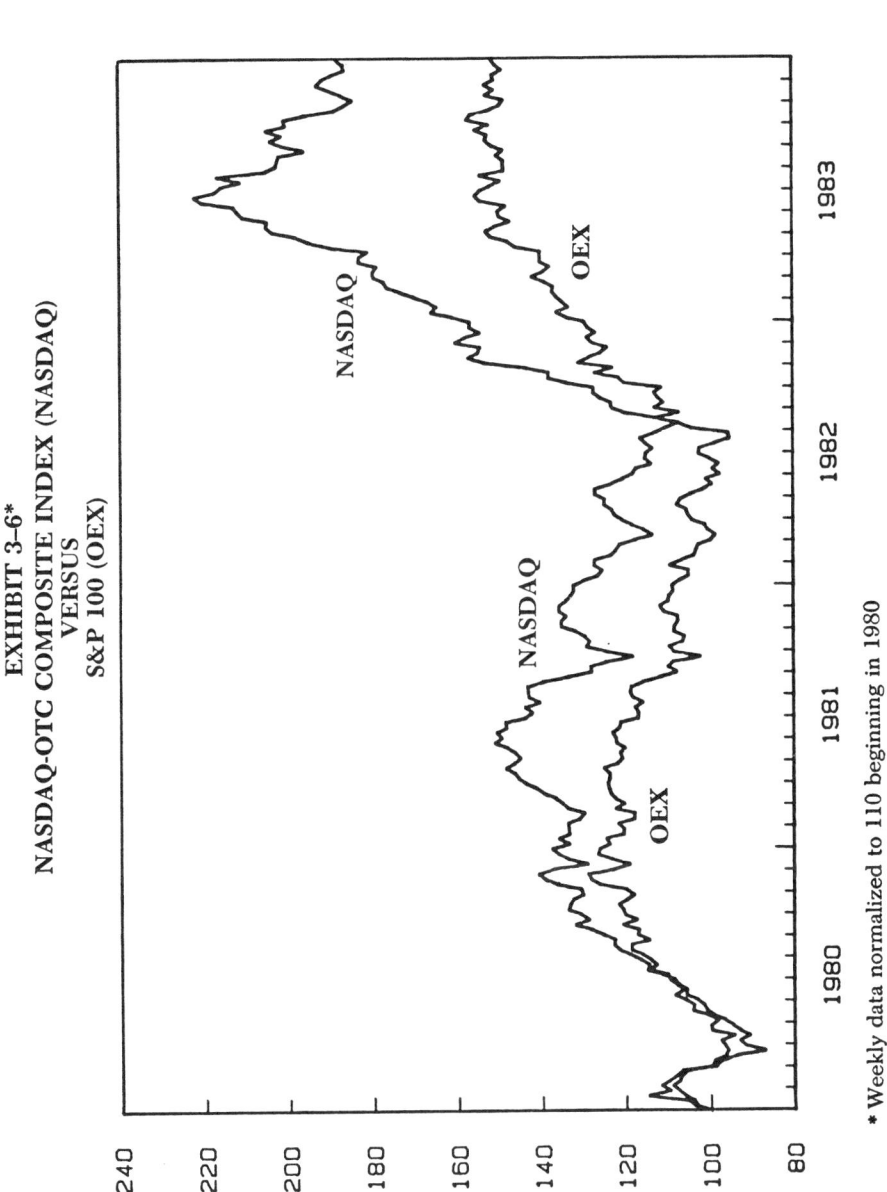

EXHIBIT 3-6*
NASDAQ-OTC COMPOSITE INDEX (NASDAQ)
VERSUS
S&P 100 (OEX)

* Weekly data normalized to 110 beginning in 1980

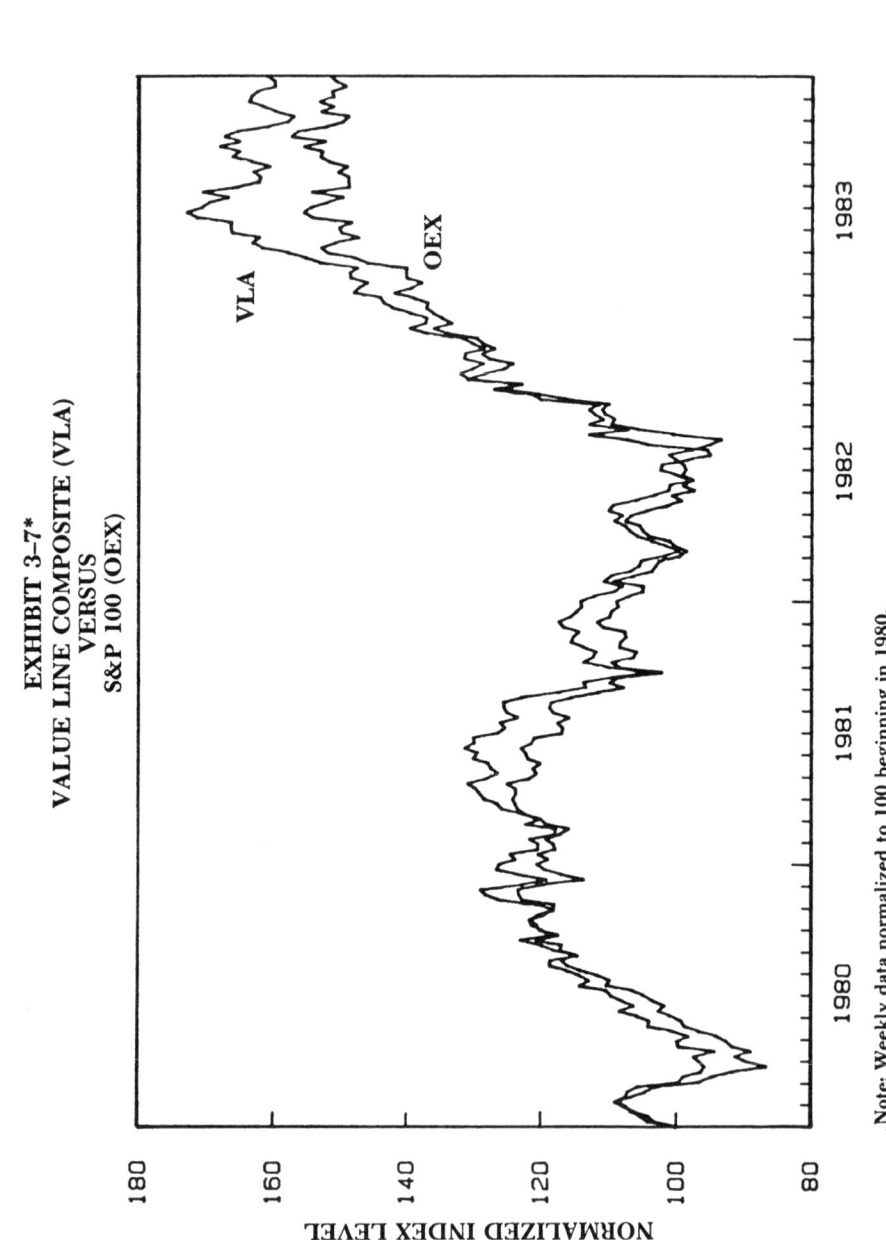

EXHIBIT 3-7*
VALUE LINE COMPOSITE (VLA)
VERSUS
S&P 100 (OEX)

Note: Weekly data normalized to 100 beginning in 1980.

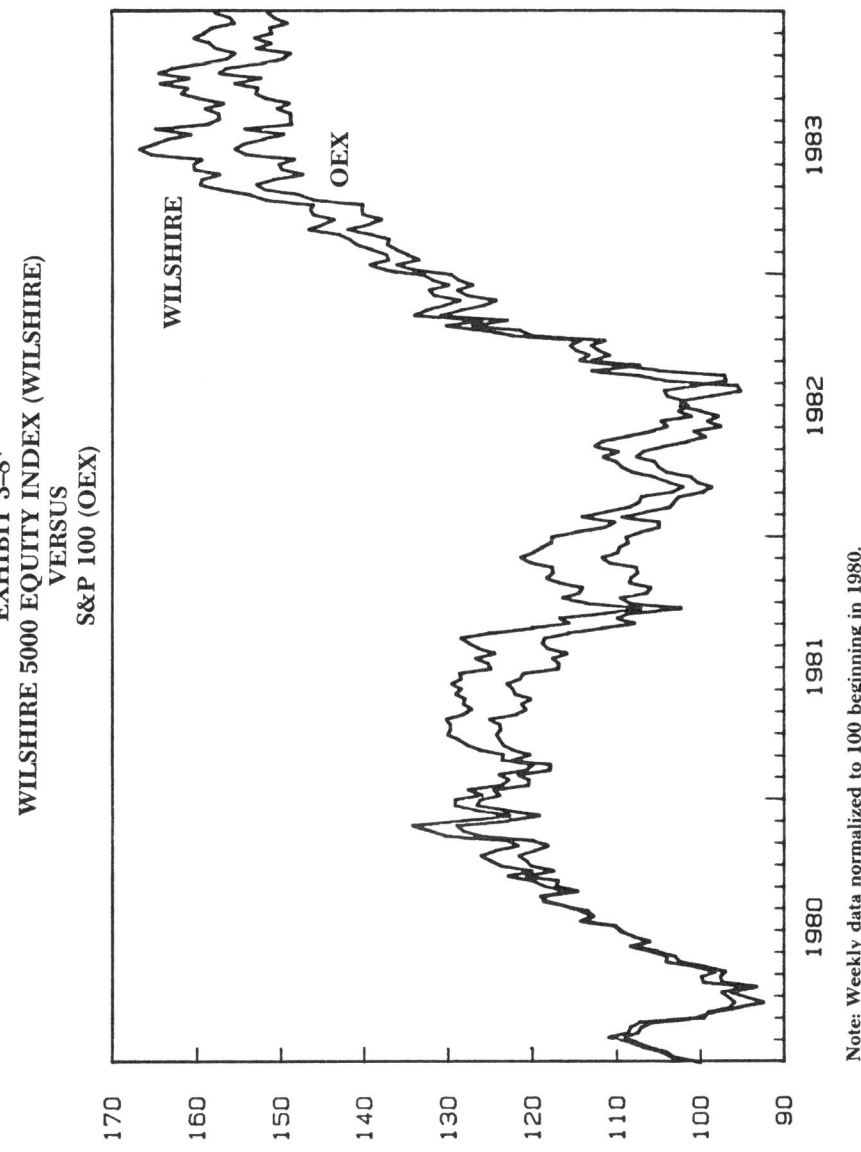

EXHIBIT 3-8*
WILSHIRE 5000 EQUITY INDEX (WILSHIRE)
VERSUS
S&P 100 (OEX)

Note: Weekly data normalized to 100 beginning in 1980.

COMPARING BROAD-BASED INDEXES

CYCLICAL PERCENTAGE CHANGES

The information which the graphs display visually can be conveyed numerically by tabulating the percentage change in the various indexes in different market phases. For the four year period under consideration—1980 through 1983—all of the broad-based indexes made the four major moves as shown in Exhibit 3-9. Although in close proximity, the peaks and troughs did not generally coincide, however. In addition, the path from top to bottom was considerably bumpier in certain of the indexes.

Percentage changes for nine major broad-based indexes for the four major phases occurring in 1980 through 1983 are given in Table 3-1. For the time period selected, the nine broad-based indexes moved in concert. The magnitude of the moves was substantially different, however, because of the differences in construction and composition of the indexes. It is premature to draw other conclusions. The relative movement between indexes in one market cycle will not necessarily be duplicated in other market cycles. In fact, an examination of longer term data shows that predicting which index will move fastest and farthest at any market juncture is virtually impossible.

Complete divergence is even possible, the maverick in the group being the Value Line Composite Average. For example, in early 1978 the Dow Jones Industrial Average dropped 24.3 percent while the

TABLE 3-1
CYCLICAL PERCENTAGE CHANGES FOR
THE MAJOR BROAD-BASED INDEXES

	Cycle Phase			
Index	I	II	III	IV
Amex Major Market Index	− 9.4	+32.6	−17.3	+ 59.7
Amex Market Value Index	−24.6	+65.6	−37.3	+108.4
Dow Jones Industrial Average	−14.8	+33.7	−23.1	+ 62.9
NASDAQ-OTC Market Index	−23.8	+72.9	−28.8	+106.7
NYSE Composite Index	−16.0	+42.6	−26.5	+ 66.0
S&P 100	−13.4	+36.6	−26.2	+ 65.0
S&P 500	−16.1	+39.7	−26.2	+ 64.3
Value Line Composite Average	−20.2	+51.5	−28.7	+ 84.5
Wilshire 5000	−16.7	+45.1	−27.7	+ 71.9

Note: Based on weekly closing prices

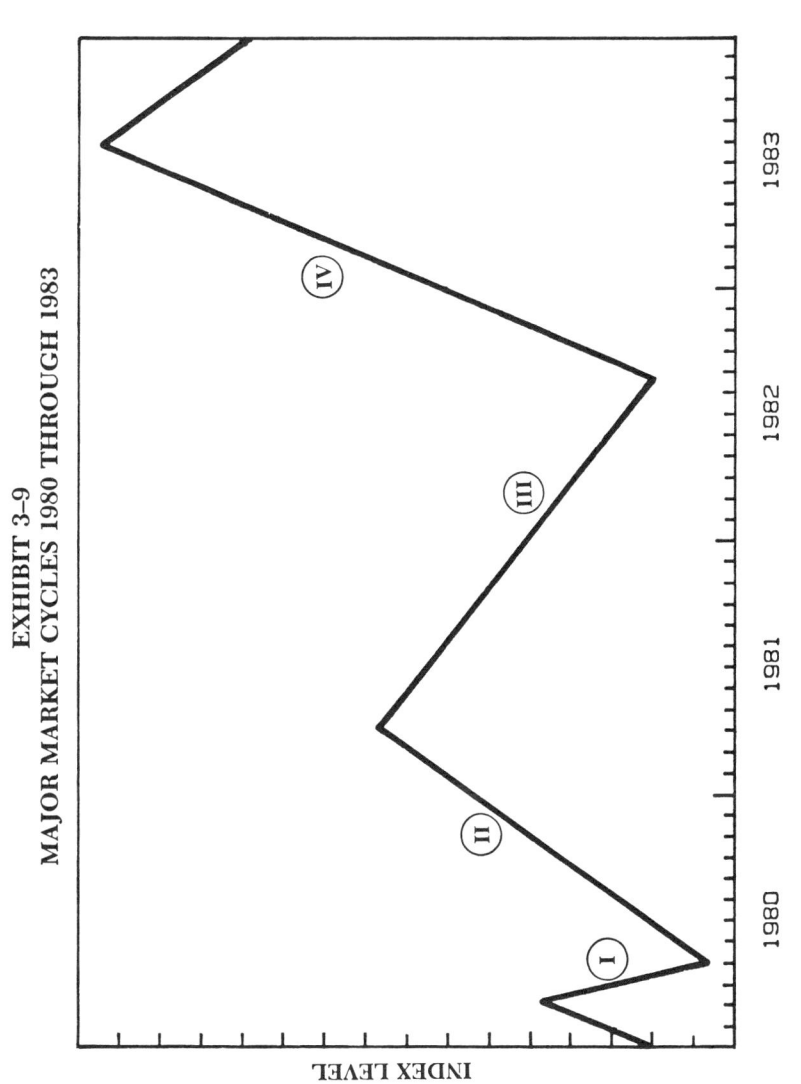

STOCK INDEX OPTIONS

Value Line Composite Average *advanced* 1.2 percent. In early 1981 the S&P 100 dropped 4.4 percent while the Value Line Composite Average *advanced* 7.5 percent.

Most of the broad-based indexes are equivalent in that they concentrate in high quality issues and the largest capitalization issues are weighted most heavily. Examples would include the Amex Major Market Index, the Dow Jones Industrial Average, the NYSE Composite Index, the S&P 100, and the S&P 500. The tendency to track one another should be less evident in the Amex Market Value Index, the NASDAQ-OTC Index, the Value Line Composite Average, and the Wilshire 5000.

CORRELATION COEFFICIENT

The correlation coefficient is a mathematical measure describing the degree of association or interdependence between two variables, in this case the returns on market indexes. Correlation is best appreciated by an understanding of its derivation and the complexities of the calculations which it entails. However, the meaning and importance of the coefficient can be conveyed through less rigorous analysis and that is the approach to be taken here.

In following two indexes, if the advances and declines of one are mirrored exactly by the second, there is perfect positive correlation. If, on the other hand, movements in one index are always contrary to movements in the other, perfect negative correlation is exhibited. Of course these examples represent extremes. In the real world actual indexes are generally well correlated.

The concept of correlation is illustrated pictorially in Exhibit 3–10. Figure 1 is a plot of a single point, the return in hypothetical index B versus the return on hypothetical index A. Figure 2 is a scatter diagram of the returns on these indexes for many periods. The tendency for the points to fall on a straight line is indicative of high correlation.

Figure 3 is a scatter diagram of the returns for many periods for two hypothetical indexes, A and C. The dispersion of the points is indicative of low correlation.

Figure 4 is a scatter diagram of the returns for many periods for two hypothetical indexes, A and D. When index A advances index D declines and vice versa. This is an example of negative correlation.

Because of the nature of the mathematics involved, the correlation coefficient can assume values ranging from −1 to +1. Correlation coefficient values near +1 (such as .985) imply a very strong positive associa-

COMPARING BROAD-BASED INDEXES

EXHIBIT 3-10
CORRELATION

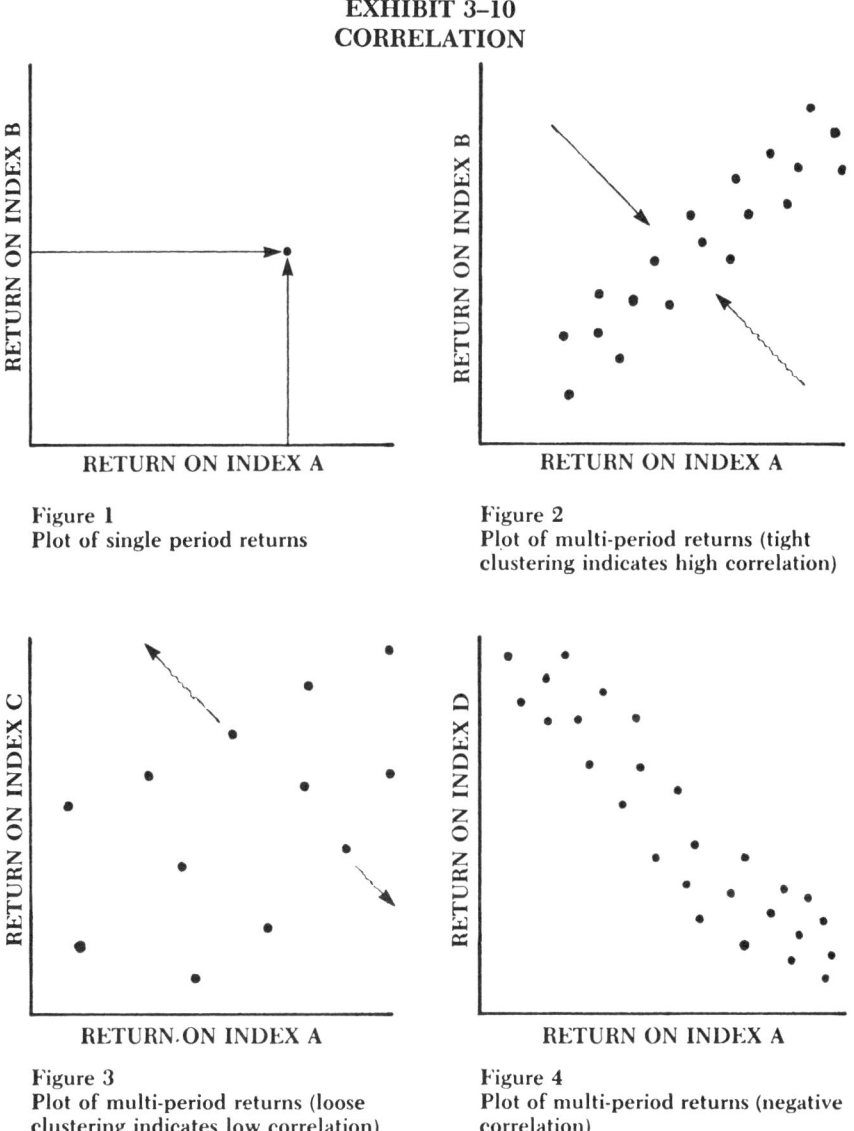

Figure 1
Plot of single period returns

Figure 2
Plot of multi-period returns (tight clustering indicates high correlation)

Figure 3
Plot of multi-period returns (loose clustering indicates low correlation)

Figure 4
Plot of multi-period returns (negative correlation)

tion while values near −1 (such as −.995) imply a very strong negative association.

The correlations between several of the widely followed broad-based indexes were calculated using weekly data from 1980 through 1983, a period exhibiting major advances and declines in the overall market. Results are tabulated in Exhibits 3–11 through 3–16.

EXHIBIT 3-11
ANNUAL CORRELATION COEFFICIENTS*
AMEX MAJOR MARKET INDEX WITH:

Index	1980	1981	1982	1983
Amex Major Market Index	1.000	1.000	1.000	1.000
Amex Market Value Index	.942	.795	.903	.746
Dow Jones Industrial Average	.968	.981	.996	.967
NASDAQ-OTC Market Index	.920	.809	.924	.656
NYSE Composite Index	.955	.939	.972	.919
S&P 100	.969	.969	.964	.948
S&P 500	.948	.947	.979	.936
Value Line Composite Average	.923	.894	.947	.833
Wilshire 5000	.944	.933	.965	.886

* Calculations based on weekly closing prices.

EXHIBIT 3-12
ANNUAL CORRELATION COEFFICIENTS*
AMEX MARKET VALUE INDEX WITH:

Index	1980	1981	1982	1983
Amex Major Market Index	.942	.795	.903	.746
Amex Market Value Index	1.000	1.000	1.000	1.000
Dow Jones Industrial Average	.949	.842	.930	.814
NASDAQ-OTC Market Index	.966	.897	.957	.934
NYSE Composite Index	.974	.893	.969	.941
S&P 100	.974	.785	.900	.906
S&P 500	.961	.855	.961	.925
Value Line Composite Average	.954	.937	.975	.983
Wilshire 5000	.976	.923	.976	.964

* Calculations based on weekly closing prices.

EXHIBIT 3-13
ANNUAL CORRELATION COEFFICIENTS*
DOW JONES INDUSTRIAL AVERAGE WITH:

Index	1980	1981	1982	1983
Amex Major Market Index	.968	.981	.996	.967
Amex Market Value Index	.949	.842	.930	.814
Dow Jones Industrial Average	1.000	1.000	1.000	1.000
NASDAQ-OTC Market Index	.951	.805	.933	.680
NYSE Composite Index	.968	.944	.984	.950
S&P 100	.974	.967	.967	.961
S&P 500	.963	.954	.988	.958
Value Line Composite Average	.978	.907	.961	.885
Wilshire 5000	.962	.943	.978	.919

* Calculations based on weekly closing prices.

EXHIBIT 3–14
ANNUAL CORRELATION COEFFICIENTS*
NYSE COMPOSITE INDEX WITH:

Index	1980	1981	1982	1983
Amex Major Market Index	.955	.939	.972	.919
Amex Market Value Index	.974	.893	.969	.941
Dow Jones Industrial Average	.968	.944	.984	.950
NASDAQ-OTC Market Index	.989	.854	.966	.852
NYSE Composite Index	1.000	1.000	1.000	1.000
S&P 100	.997	.936	.948	.992
S&P 500	.993	.993	.999	.998
Value Line Composite Average	.972	.918	.991	.977
Wilshire 5000	.999	.995	.999	.994

* Calculations based on weekly closing prices.

EXHIBIT 3–15
ANNUAL CORRELATION COEFFICIENTS*
S&P 100 WITH:

Index	1980	1981	1982	1983
Amex Major Market Index	.969	.943	.964	.948
Amex Market Value Index	.974	.785	.900	.906
Dow Jones Industrial Average	.974	.967	.967	.961
NASDAQ-OTC Market Index	.981	.699	.907	.810
NYSE Composite Index	.997	.936	.948	.992
S&P 100	1.000	1.000	1.000	1.000
S&P 500	.990	.965	.952	.996
Value Line Composite Average	.968	.817	.930	.949
Wilshire 5000	.994	.919	.941	.979

* Calculations based on weekly closing prices.

EXHIBIT 3–16
ANNUAL CORRELATION COEFFICIENTS*
S&P 500 WITH:

Index	1980	1981	1982	1983
Amex Major Market Index	.948	.947	.979	.936
Amex Market Value Index	.961	.855	.961	.925
Dow Jones Industrial Average	.963	.954	.988	.958
NASDAQ-OTC Market Index	.979	.794	.959	.838
NYSE Composite Index	.993	.993	.999	.998
S&P 100	.990	.965	.952	.996
S&P 500	1.000	1.000	1.000	1.000
Value Line Composite Average	.965	.879	.986	.968
Wilshire 5000	.992	.980	.997	.990

* Calculations based on weekly closing prices.

STOCK INDEX OPTIONS

For the period under consideration the indexes were all positively correlated and generally highly correlated. Based on the graphic data and the cycle studies in the preceding sections, this should have been anticipated. The highest correlations occur between indexes of similar composition and construction; namely, the Amex Major Market Index, the Dow Jones Industrial Average, the New York Stock Exchange Composite Index, the S&P 100 and the S&P 500. For all of these indexes, large capitalization issues selected from the same universe of stocks have a major weighting; thus, the high correlation.

Even the Value Line Composite Average exhibits high correlation with the above indexes. While it is true that the Value Line Composite Average contains most of the high capitalization issues in those indexes, many smaller issues and many OTC issues are included. In addition, the weighting scheme is vastly different. To conclude that the high correlation will always prevail is erroneous. For example, data from a longer historical record shows that the Value Line Composite exhibited negative correlation with the Dow, the S&P 500 and the NYSE Composite in 1972.

Low correlations appear between the look-alike indexes and the indexes of distinctly different composition; namely, the NASDAQ-OTC Index and the Amex Market Value Index. This fact was also foreshadowed by the graphic data. Note, for example in 1981 the low correlation between the Dow and the Amex Market Value Index (.842) and the Dow and the NASDAQ-OTC Index (.805). Again in 1983 note similar low correlations between these indexes. Late 1983 was a particularly troublesome period for many money managers. High quality Dow type stocks were holding well masking a decline of devastating proportions in secondary issues in general and in OTC stocks in particular.

USING THE COMPARISON MEASURES

Speculators, having made decisions regarding the nature of upcoming market moves, can draw conclusions from the historical record as to which is the best index in which to operate given the particular outlook. However, without a definite opinion as to where the action is going to occur, historical data will not prove very useful.

Hedgers, on the other hand, should try to locate an index which matches movements in the portfolio being hedged. It is unlikely that the composition of the index and the portfolio will be identical. There-

COMPARING BROAD-BASED INDEXES

fore it is unrealistic to expect that the hedge will perform flawlessly. Except for the Amex Market Value Index, the indexes and averages do not include dividends. Therefore when evaluating performance of a portfolio, dividends should be subtracted out so that comparisons are made on an equivalent basis.

4

INDEX OPTION BASICS

INTRODUCTION

In most respects index options are identical to listed stock options. They are traded in a similar manner on the major exchanges. Many of the same investment strategies can be deployed. Margin requirements, although different in the details of the calculation, are similar.

As stated in the preface, for purposes of this book it is assumed that the reader is familiar with listed stock options. The remainder of chapter four discusses index options using the concepts and terminology of stock options without preliminary preparation or explanation. For those readers uncomfortable with the details of stock options, an abbreviated discussion is included as a supplement preceding the Appendixes. For readers wishing to pursue stock options in depth, a thorough bibliography is included in the Appendix.

DEFINITION

A stock index option is a contingent claim on the value of the underlying index. Index option contracts are essentially the same size as stock option contracts. The index number can be viewed as the price of one share of an underlying stock. Looked at in this light, each index option contract covers 100 "shares."

HISTORY

To insure that this new product would be successful, the various exchanges took great care in choosing the underlying indexes. Factors complicating the selection process were competition from other ex-

STOCK INDEX OPTIONS

changes (commodity exchanges were already trading stock index futures) and negotiations with the publishers of the indexes who considered them proprietary. Consideration was given not only to existing indexes but also to possible new ones as well. The intent was to make the options as useful and versatile as possible and hopefully very popular. First consideration was given to the major indexes, particularly those whose purpose it is to indicate the trend of the overall market. These have come to be known as broad-based indexes. Later on, consideration was given to indexes characterizing a particular industry group or segment of the market. These are now called narrow-based indexes or sub-indexes.

The first index options began trading March 11, 1983. They were for a newly conceived index, the CBOE 100 (the name was subsequently changed to the S&P 100), an index of 100 stocks for which stock options were trading on the Chicago Board Options Exchange. Additional indexes were introduced periodically after that date for both new and existing indexes.

The first sub-index was the Amex Computer Technology Index introduced August 26, 1983. The most recent additions, a group of four, were listed simultaneously on March 20, 1984. Included were the Amex Transportation Index, the NYSE Telephone Index, the S&P Telephone

TABLE 4-1
CHRONOLOGY OF INDEX OPTION LISTINGS

Mar 11, 1983	S&P 100 Index Options
Apr 29, 1983	Amex Major Market Index Options
Jul 1, 1983	S&P 500 Index Options
Jul 8, 1983	Amex Market Value Index Options
Aug 26, 1983	Amex Computer Technology Index Options
Sep 9, 1983	Amex Oil & Gas Index Options
Sep 19, 1983	S&P Integrated International Oil Index Options
Sep 23, 1983	NYSE Composite Index Options
Sep 28, 1983	S&P Office & Business Equipment Index Options
Dec 19, 1983	Philadelphia Stock Exchange Gaming/Hotel Index Options
Dec 19, 1983	Philadelphia Stock Exchange Gold/Silver Index Options
Jan 13, 1984	Pacific Stock Exchange Technology Index Options
Mar 20, 1984	Amex Transportation Index Options
	NYSE Telephone Index Options
	S&P Telephone Index Options
	S&P Transportation Index Options

INDEX OPTION BASICS

Index, and the S&P Transportation Index. The sequence of listings for all the index options is given in Table 4-1. The popularity of the sub-indexes did not meet expectations and for most contracts volume and open interest failed to materialize. As a result there were fatalities and three index option contracts were delisted. These are tabulated in Table 4-2.

TABLE 4-2
CHRONOLOGY OF INDEX OPTION DELISTINGS
(final contract expiration)

May 18, 1984	S&P Integrated International Oil Index Options
	S&P Office & Business Equipment Index Options
June 15, 1984	S&P Telephone Index Options

CURRENT OFFERINGS

As of this writing there are option contracts for 13 different stock indexes. Six are for broad-based indexes and seven are for narrow-

TABLE 4-3
INDEXES WITH LISTED OPTIONS
GROUPED BROAD-BASED VERSUS NARROW-BASED

Broad-Based Indexes

Amex Major Market Index
Amex Market Value Index
New York Stock Exchange Composite Index
Pacific Stock Exchange Technology Index
S&P 100 Index
S&P 500 Index

Narrow-Based Indexes

Amex Computer Technology Index
Amex Oil & Gas Index
Amex Transportation Index
NYSE Telephone Index
Philadelphia Stock Exchange Gaming/Hotel Index
Philadelphia Stock Exchange Gold/Silver Index
S&P Transportation Index

STOCK INDEX OPTIONS

based indexes. The various exchanges have proposed many new offerings as well but their introduction will depend on many factors including enthusiasm by the investment community and the general public, the overall market climate, and restrictions imposed by regulatory authorities. Table 4–3 shows the underlying indexes grouped according to their classification as broad-based or narrow-based. Table 4–4 shows the underlying indexes grouped according to the exchange where the options are traded.

As with equity options, trading for index options is reported daily in major newspapers and weekly in *Barron's*. Exhibit 4–1 is the listing from *The Wall Street Journal* for Wednesday, May 30, 1984. Trading for the same date as reported in *The New York Times* is shown in Exhibit 4–2.

TABLE 4–4
INDEXES WITH LISTED OPTIONS
GROUPED BY EXCHANGE WHERE TRADED

American Stock Exchange

Amex Computer Technology Index
Amex Major Market Index
Amex Market Value Index
Amex Oil & Gas Index
Amex Transportation Index

Chicago Board Options Exchange

S&P 100 Index
S&P 500 Index
S&P Transportation Index

New York Stock Exchange

NYSE Composite Index
NYSE Telephone Index

Pacific Stock Exchange

PSE Technology Index

Philadelphia Stock Exchange

PHLX Gaming/Hotel Index
PHLX Gold/Silver Index

EXHIBIT 4–1

Listed Options Quotations

Wednesday, May 30, 1984

Closing prices of all options. Sales unit usually is 100 shares. Security description includes exercise price. Stock close is New York or American exchange final price.

Index Options

Chicago Board

S&P 100 INDEX

Strike Price	Calls–Last June	July	Aug	Puts–Last June	July	Aug
140	11	9¾	....	1/16	⅜	¾
145	5⅛	7⅛	8¼	⅜	1 5/16	1 13/16
150	1 13/16	3⅞	5¼	2¼	3⅜	3⅞
155	½	1 13/16	2¾	5¾	6½	6½
160	1/16	11/16	1¼	10¾	11	9¾
165	1/16	¼	⅝	15½	14½	16½
170	....	1/16	¼	21½	....	....
175	....	....	1/16	....	....	....

Total call volume 210,997 Total call open int. 452,840
Total put volume 215,682 Total put open int. 306,087
The index: High 150.66; Low 147.19; Close 149.26, +0.33

S&P 500 INDEX

Strike Price	Calls–Last June	Sept	Puts–Last June	Sept
150	....	....	1½	3⅞
155	....	....	4⅞	....
160	....	....	10	....
165	....	....	15	....

Total call volume 0 Total call open int. 355
Total put volume 82 Total put open int. 280
The index: High 151.43; Low 148.68; Close 150.35, +0.06

American Exchange

MAJOR MARKET INDEX

Strike Price	Calls–Last June	July	Aug	Puts–Last June	July	Aug
105	3⅜	4⅜	5⅛	⅜	15/16	1 5/16
110	9/16	1 11/16	2⅞	2¾	3¼	3½
115	1/16	7/16	1 1/16	7⅜	7⅜	7⅜
120	1/16	⅛	½	....	....	....

Total call volume 17,294 Total call open int. 34,949
Total put volume 17,202 Total put open int. 27,515
The index: High 108.77; Low 106.07; Close 107.73, +0.39

AMEX MARKET VALUE INDEX

Strike Price	Calls–Last June	July	Aug	Puts–Last June	July	Aug
195	....	6⅛	....	....	2½	3⅛
200	1¼	3½	....	3⅜	5⅛	5¾
205	¼	1⅝	....	8	7¾	....
210	⅛	⅞	....	12	....	....
215	....	....	....	17	....	....

Total call volume 439 Total call open int. 1,959
Total put volume 698 Total put open int. 1,678
The index: High 197.51; Low 195.43; Close 197.00, −0.49

COMPUTER TECHNOLOGY INDEX

Strike Price	Calls–Last June	July	Aug	Puts–Last June	July	Aug
80	....	6⅛	....	....	½	1
85	2⅛	4	4⅞	1¼	2 7/16	....
90	½	1⅞	3	4¾	5¾	....
95	1/16	⅝	....	....	....	....

Total call volume 3,173 Total call open int. 9,113
Total put volume 2,817 Total put open int. 4,578
The index: High 86.34; Low 83.50; Close 85.39, +0.93

OIL & GAS INDEX

Strike Price	Calls–Last June	July	Aug	Puts–Last June	July	Aug
110	6⅞	....	....	....	½	....
115	2	....	....	11/16	1¼	....
120	⅜	1⅜	....	4¾	....	....
125	....	....	....	....	9¼	....

Total call volume 163 Total call open int. 1,179
Total put volume 56 Total put open int. 362
The index: High 116.49; Low 114.85; Close 114.89, −1.57

N.Y. Stock Exchange

NYSE OPTIONS INDEX

Strike Price	Calls–Last June	July	Aug.	Puts–Last June	July	Aug.
85	2 3/16	3⅛	3½	7/16	1	1 5/16
90	3/16	15/16	1⅜	3⅝	3⅝	4⅝
95	1/16	⅛	⅜	9	....	....
100	1/16	1/16	⅛	....	....	....

Total call volume 13,562. Total call open int. 66,217.
Total put volume 21,662. Total put open int. 39,405.
The index: High 86.95; Low 85.55; Close 86.46, +0.01

Philadelphia Exchange

GAMING/HOTEL INDEX

(No Trades)

Total call volume 0 Total call open int. 104
Total put volume 0 Total put open int. 14
The index: High 78.05; Low 75.91; Close 77.70, +1.07

GOLD/SILVER INDEX

Strike Price	Calls–Last June	July	Aug	Puts–Last June	July	Aug
100	....	....	....	⅛	....	....
105	7⅜	....	....	7/16	....	....
110	3½	....	....	1 7/16	....	....
115	1¼	3¾	....	4⅝	3⅛	....
120	½	1⅝	....	....	....	....
125	⅛	1	....	....	....	....

Total call volume 185 Total call open int. 2,286
Total put volume 97 Total put open int. 1,007
The index: High 113.12; Low 110.47; Close 110.47, −1.93

Pacific Exchange

TECHNOLOGY INDEX

Strike Price	Calls–Last June	July	Aug	Puts–Last June	July	Aug
95	4¾	....	....	⅝	....	....
100	1 9/16	3	5½	2	4½	....
105	9/16	2	....	8⅜	7¼	....
110	⅛	⅝	....	....	....	....
115	....	....	¾	....	....	....

Total call volume 302 Total call open int. 1,024
Total put volume 236 Total put open int. 1,028
The index: High 99.46; Low 96.61; Close 98.94, +0.82

Source: *The Wall Street Journal,* May 31, 1984. Copyright 1984 by Dow Jones and Company, Inc. Reprinted by permission. All rights reserved.

EXHIBIT 4–2

Trading in Stock Options

WEDNESDAY, MAY 30, 1984

Index Options

Chicago

S. & P. 100

Option & NY Close	Strike Price	Calls-Last June	Calls-Last July	Calls-Last Aug	Puts-Last June	Puts-Last July	Puts-Last Aug
SP100	...140	11	9¾	r	1-16	⅜	¾
149.26	.145	5⅛	7⅛	8¼	⅜	1 5-16	1 13-16
149.26	.150	1 13-16	3⅞	5¼	2¼	3⅜	3⅞
149.26	.155	½	1 13-16	2¾	5¾	6½	6½
149.26	.160	1-16	11-16	1¼	10¾	11	9¾
149.26	.165	1-16	¼	⅝	15½	14½	16½
149.26	.170	r	1-16	¼	21½	r	r
149.26	.175	r	r	1-16	r	r	r

Total call vol. 186,218 Call open int. 434,208
Total put vol. 239,991 Put open int. 325,131

American

Major Market Index

Option & NY Close	Strike Price	Calls-Last June	Calls-Last July	Calls-Last Aug	Puts-Last June	Puts-Last July	Puts-Last Aug
MMIdx	105	3⅜	4⅜	5⅛	⅜	15-16	1 5-16
107.73	.110	9-16	1 11-16	2⅞	2¾	3¼	3½
107.73	.115	1-16	7-16	1 1-16	7⅜	7⅜	7⅜
107.73	.120	1-16	⅛	½	r	r	r

Total call vol. 17,294 Call open int. 34,949
Total put vol. 17,218 Put open int. 27,999

Market Value Index

Option & NY Close	Strike Price	Calls-Last June	Calls-Last July	Calls-Last Aug	Puts-Last June	Puts-Last July	Puts-Last Aug
AMIdx	195	s	2⅝	r	s	2½	3⅛
197.00	.200	1¼	3½	r	3⅜	5⅛	5¾
197.00	.205	¼	1⅝	r	8	7¾	r
197.00	.210	⅛	⅞	r	12	r	r
197.00	.215	r	r	r	17	r	r

Total call vol. 439 Call open int. 1,959
Total put vol. 698 Put open int. 1,680

Computer Technology Index

Option & NY Close	Strike Price	Calls-Last June	Calls-Last July	Calls-Last Aug	Puts-Last June	Puts-Last July	Puts-Last Aug
CTIdx	.. 80	s	6⅛	r	s	½	1
85.39	...85	2⅛	4	4⅞	1¼	2 7-16	r
85.39	...90	½	1⅞	3	4¾	5¾	r
85.39	...95	1-16	⅝	r	r	r	r

Total call vol. 3,173 Call open int. 9,113
Total put vol. 2,817 Put open int. 4,599

New York

N.Y.S.E. Composite Index

Option & NY Close	Strike Price	Calls-Last June	Calls-Last July	Calls-Last Aug	Puts-Last June	Puts-Last July	Puts-Last Aug
NY Idx	..85	2 3-16	3⅛	3½	7-16	1	1 5-16
86.46	...90	3-16	15-16	1⅜	3⅝	3⅝	4⅝
86.46	...95	1-16	⅛	⅜	9	r	r
86.46	..100	1-16	1-16	⅛	r	r	r

Total call vol. 13,562 Call open int. 66,217
Total put vol. 21,662 Put open int. 39,405

Pacific

Technology Index

Option & NY Close	Strike Price	Calls-Last June	Calls-Last July	Calls-Last Aug	Puts-Last June	Puts-Last July	Puts-Last Aug
HT Idx	.. 95	4¾	r	r	⅝	r	r
98.94	..100	1 9-16	3	5½	2	4½	r
98.94	..105	9-16	2	r	8⅜	7¼	r
98.94	..110	⅛	⅝	r	r	r	r

Total call vol. 302 Call open int. 1,033
Total put vol. 236 Put open int. 1,036

Source: *The New York Times,* May 31, 1984. Copyright 1984 by The New York Times Company. Reprinted by permission. All rights reserved.

INDEX OPTION BASICS

BASIC CHARACTERISTICS OF INDEX OPTIONS

Complete specifications for each of the index option contracts are given in Appendix C. Although there is some variation from contract to contract they are all basically similar. The purpose of this section is to summarize the characteristics which they share in common.

Contract Value

Each contract represents $100 (the index multiplier) times the current value of the index. For example, the S&P 500 stock index was recently at a level of 160. The dollar value of the index is $16,000 ($100 × 160). The total exercise price is $100 times the exercise price.

Exercise Prices

Exercise prices are set at five point intervals and new strike prices are introduced as the index advances and declines.

Premiums

Premiums are expressed in terms of points and fractions per unit of the index. Each point represents $100. The minimum fraction is $\frac{1}{16}$ for options trading below 3 and $\frac{1}{8}$ for options trading above 3. For example a premium of 1 $\frac{3}{16}$ represents $100 × 1 $\frac{3}{16}$ = $118.75

Expiration Cycles

When initially introduced, index options were assigned the standard three, six, and nine month expirations matching those of stock options; however, from the very beginning investor interest concentrated in the nearby expiration months. The response of the exchanges to this lopsided demand was similar although not uniform but in late 1983 monthly expirations were introduced.

Currently all Amex index options have monthly expirations with a maximum of three months trading at any time. The NYSE issues have expirations in the three nearby months superimposed on a quarterly cycle. The PSE Technology Index has monthly expirations with a maximum of four months trading at any time. The two PHLX indexes have monthly expirations superimposed on a quarterly cycle. On the CBOE, the S&P 100 is monthly extending up to four months. The S&P 500 is on the standard quarterly cycle. Finally, the S&P Transpor-

STOCK INDEX OPTIONS

tation Index is monthly extending out for three months. All contracts expire on the Saturday following the third Friday of the expiration month.

Contract specifications in Appendix C are correct as of this writing, but, since this is a transition period, the expiration months available should be checked before a transaction is attempted.

Cash Settlement

The most unusual feature of index options is the settlement procedure. Unlike stock options, when an index option is exercised no physical security changes hands. It would be impractical or impossible to deliver a package of securities representing the same components and same weighting as the index. Instead, the index option holder who exercises receives a cash payment. The amount of the payment is the difference between the exercise price of the option and the closing value of the index on the day of exercise multiplied by $100. In effect, the exercising holder receives the amount by which the option is in-the-money.

In cash settlement the amount received is *not* the exercise price times $100. Assume the holder of a NYSE Index February 95 call option issues exercise instructions when the index closes at 98. The cash settlement is not $9500 but rather $(98 - 95) \times (\$100) = \$300$. This arithmetic may seem foreign to investors experienced with stock options. However, when exercising a stock option stock is received and if this stock is immediately sold, the outcome is the equivalent to a cash settlement. As an example, consider the owner of an XYZ call option with an exercise price of 95. With the underlying stock at 98, exercise instructions are issued. Stock is purchased from the writer for $9500 and sold on the market for $9800, a $300 difference. This is identical to the cash settlement outcome with index options.

Margin Requirements

Margin calculations for index options are similar but not identical to those for stock options. It should be noted also, that the calculation is not the same for both broad-based and narrow-based index options.

For all option purchases—and this applies uniformly to options on stock as well as to options on the indexes and sub-indexes—the premium must be paid in full.

Differences arise in option sales which are opening transactions. First, since covered writing is not possible with index options because the underlying asset cannot be held long, margin is always required.

INDEX OPTION BASICS

Second, the margin for broad-based index options is less than the margin for narrow-based index options.

Margin calculations for naked sub-index options and stock options are the same. The requirement is 30% of the index value plus or minus the amount by which the index is in- or out-of-the-money. The premium received can be applied against the margin requirement. The minimum margin is $250 per contract.

For naked broad-based index options the margin requirement is 100% of the premium plus 10% of the current index number times the index multiplier ($100). This is reduced by the amount which the option is out-of-the-money, but not to an amount that reduces the margin requirement to less than the premium plus 2% of the current index number times the index multiplier.

COMPARING INDEX OPTIONS AND STOCK OPTIONS

It has been stated repeatedly that familiarity with stock options is the key ingredient in understanding index options. Although the differences between the two option types are few, they are important—extremely so under certain circumstances.

Table 4–5 is a listing of the principal similarities and differences between index options and stock options. When new positions involving index options are contemplated it would be prudent to review details of these differences so that an unexpected implication does not destroy an otherwise good strategy.

TABLE 4–5
COMPARING INDEX OPTIONS AND STOCK OPTIONS

Similarities

certificateless trading
fungible
margin account transaction
standardized terms
stockbroker executed

Differences

expiration cycles
margin requirements
settlement (cash versus delivery)
tax consequences

STOCK INDEX OPTIONS

THE OEX PHENOMENON

The CBOE pioneered index options and they did their homework well. They earned success and the current rewards are justly deserved; however, the current popularity of the OEX options cannot all be attributed to the skill and cunning of exchange planners. Several other factors have been important in assuring success of the product.

For starters, the CBOE was first on the index option bandwagon. The major options exchange launched a significant new product. Interest focused immediately on the CBOE and their initial entry.

Second, the product fills a definite need. It has great appeal for speculators and it is a simple tool to employ. The same statement is applicable to hedgers as well. The product provides a host of powerful new strategies which are readily implemented.

Third, the exchange zeroed in on the right index. While they may have made a success of other indexes, the S&P 100 was an outstanding choice. The index is not controversial, and since it tracks the S&P 500, the index is familiar. It did not need to establish a trading history or attract a new following.

Fourth, there are hedge opportunities for the S&P 100 options nonexistent with other index options. Since futures contracts exist for both the S&P 100 and the S&P 500 indexes, traders—both upstairs and downstairs—can accommodate and facilitate large trades because they can hedge the positions. They can offset risk by appropriate purchases and sales in the futures markets. These transactions are easily implemented because the futures markets are also very liquid.

This optimum set of circumstances feeds on itself, a Catch-22 in reverse. The conceptually good product caught the fancy of floor traders, investment professionals, institutions, and the public. Increased interest created increased volume and reduced bid-asked spreads. Traders could assume large positions knowing that if they were wrong they could exit quickly near the last price quoted without distorting the markets. Gradually a product evolved which is an ideal vehicle. It is volatile, it is liquid, it has tremendous depth, and the spreads are small.

The popularity of OEX options has influenced the equity option market-negatively, most observers would agree. However, this should be regarded as evolution, be it good or bad. The ideal characteristics of the OEX market have diverted interest from equity options to index options. As of this writing (May 1984) volume in equity options has diminished while volume in the S&P 100 options continues to hit new highs.

INDEX OPTION BASICS

While it is true that index options have siphoned activity from equity options, the final chapter on this subject has probably not been written. Current judgments about the damage to equity options are being made following a period of poor market performance. The Dow dropped from a high of 1287 in November 1983 to a low of 1140 in February 1984. This was followed by a stagnant market trading within a narrow range between February 1984 and May 1984. Bear markets and market doldrums frequently create inactivity. The odds are that everything will change in the next market upswing.

5

APPLICATIONS

INTRODUCTION

This chapter is intended to be the focus of the book. It concentrates on the strategies and techniques used to make index options perform. The preceding chapters and those which follow contain the supporting evidence—definitions, rules, regulations, and procedures.

The chapter is organized as follows. The two broad strategy classifications are introduced at the outset; however, that discussion is terminated temporarily for a brief diversion into risk and its components. To use index options most effectively a sophisticated knowledge of risk is required. Such terms as systematic risk, unsystematic risk, residual risk, and nondiversifiable risk are generally not familiar to investors. A clear understanding of these aspects of risk, however, will assist in the selection and implementation of the various strategies.

BASIC STRATEGIES

Index option strategies can be divided into two major classes: those concerned with trading or speculation and those concerned with hedging and the control of risk. Strategies with index options are nearly identical to strategies with stock options and experienced stock option investors should be very comfortable with them. Index option strategies should be viewed as extensions of existing strategies rather than as the introduction of major new investment techniques.

INTRODUCTION TO RISK AND RETURN

Many investments are made without much consideration of the risk involved. For example, people are eager to put a substantial portion

STOCK INDEX OPTIONS

of their assets into a residence even though real estate values are known to gyrate rather annoyingly.

Securities also are frequently purchased without specific awareness or consideration of the risk involved. Often the objective is investment and savings with a very long term time horizon so that risk, especially in the near term, may not be particularly important.

When using index options, however, risk cannot be disregarded. In fact, all strategies utilizing index options involve either the voluntary assumption of risk or an attempt to control, modify, or reduce risk of an existing position.

The concept of risk is not easy to explain or to understand. Most people have a general feel for risk and usually equate it with exposure to loss; however to be precise, the definition must be somewhat more comprehensive.

Generally a complex factor cannot be understood thoroughly until it can be measured and quantified. So it is with risk. Academicians and investment professionals define risk as uncertainty of future return. This definition permits risk to be stated in numerical terms and makes possible a host of statistical computations. For purposes of this discussion, the formal definition of risk, that is, uncertainty of future return, will be adopted; however, a discussion of numerical methods for describing risk are beyond the scope of this text.

RETURN CONCEPTS

Return is a more precise word for describing yield or growth. It is the difference in total value of an investment at the end of a measurement interval compared to its value at the beginning of the interval. For some investments such as treasury bills the return can be predicted rather accurately. There is little uncertainty of future return and thus the risk is low. For other investments, new issues for example, the return is much less assured. It can be very large, negligible, or even negative. There is great uncertainty as to future returns and thus the risk is high.

Risk and return are very much interrelated. On average, in diversified portfolios over the long term, high risk is rewarded with high returns. That is why historically an investment in common stocks has outperformed an investment in treasury bills.

If the relationship were otherwise it would soon correct itself. Investors would not hold positions for which they were inappropriately compensated. Money would flow from the high risk area to the low risk

APPLICATIONS

area in search of higher returns. Prices of the low risk securities would be bid up making high future returns less likely. The risky securities being abandoned would drop in value setting the stage for higher future returns. Through this process the expected risk/reward pattern would be reestablished.

RISK CONCEPTS

To derive maximum benefit from index options it is necessary to have an in-depth understanding of risk and its components. Then the interrelationship between risk and index options can be identified, permitting the most intelligent application of these instruments.

It is no secret that stocks in general move in tandem. When the market declines there is a tendency for all stocks to drop and when the market advances there is a tendency for all stocks to rise. Similarly it is readily observed that ownership of a single stock entails greater risk than ownership of a multistock portfolio. Diversification reduces risk.

Risk Decomposition

Risk of stock ownership has been studied extensively and is one of the frontiers of research in finance. One of the basic tenets of modern portfolio and capital marked theory is that price variability (risk) of common stock ownership can be separated into parts, in particular, two components. These are termed systematic risk and unsystematic risk.

Systematic Risk

Systematic risk is that part of total risk attributable to the overall influence of the market. It describes the tendency for stock prices to move up and down together. Systematic risk is also called market risk or nondiversifiable risk. Stocks have varying degrees of sensitivity to market movements and thus different levels of market risk.

On average, systematic risk accounts for about 35 percent of the price variability of individual common stocks. For some issues, however, market risk can account for as much as 50 to 70 percent of price variability. Systematic risk accounts for nearly all the uncertainty in well-diversified portfolios.

STOCK INDEX OPTIONS

Unsystematic Risk

Unsystematic risk is that part of total risk attributable to a particular firm and its industry group. It pertains to the business risk aspects of individual stocks. Unsystematic risk is also called diversifiable risk, unique risk, specific risk, or residual risk.

Unlike market risk, company risk can be reduced and for all practical purposes eliminated. When securities are combined to form a portfolio, unsystematic risk is lowered and if the portfolio contains a sufficient number of issues, unsystematic risk is diversified away. Thus with adequate and proper diversification, the sole source of uncertainty about a portfolio's rate of return is the degree of systematic or market risk.

Risk Unbundling*

An investor holding a single stock has several alternatives available for reducing risk. As previously mentioned, diversification will reduce company—but not market—risk. A second strategy for risk control is to write call options against the position. Using call options as a hedge is not satisfactory in all respects, however, as it provides only partial protection in a major downswing. A third alternative is to buy put options; however, put options for a single issue may provide more insurance than is necessary because the hedge protection encompasses both market risk and company risk.

Index options offer two additional alternatives for risk control. Since these options are affected only by the market risk component of a position, they offer definite advantages over stock options in certain circumstances. Selling index calls provides partial protection against market risk while buying index puts provides total protection against market risk.

These concepts are illustrated graphically for a single stock in Exhibit 5-1. Figure 1 depicts the total risk of a position as a combination of systematic risk (SR) and unsystematic risk (UR). Figure 2 shows the extent of risk protection provided by the sale of an equity call option or the purchase of an equity put option. Figure 3 shows the extent of risk protection provided by the sale of an index call or the purchase of an index put. Clearly, the investor adept at selecting undervalued securities will optimize results by utilizing index rather than equity options.

---

*This discussion relies heavily on arguments presented in *Option Strategies and Stock Index Futures*, a publication of the Kansas City Board of Trade.

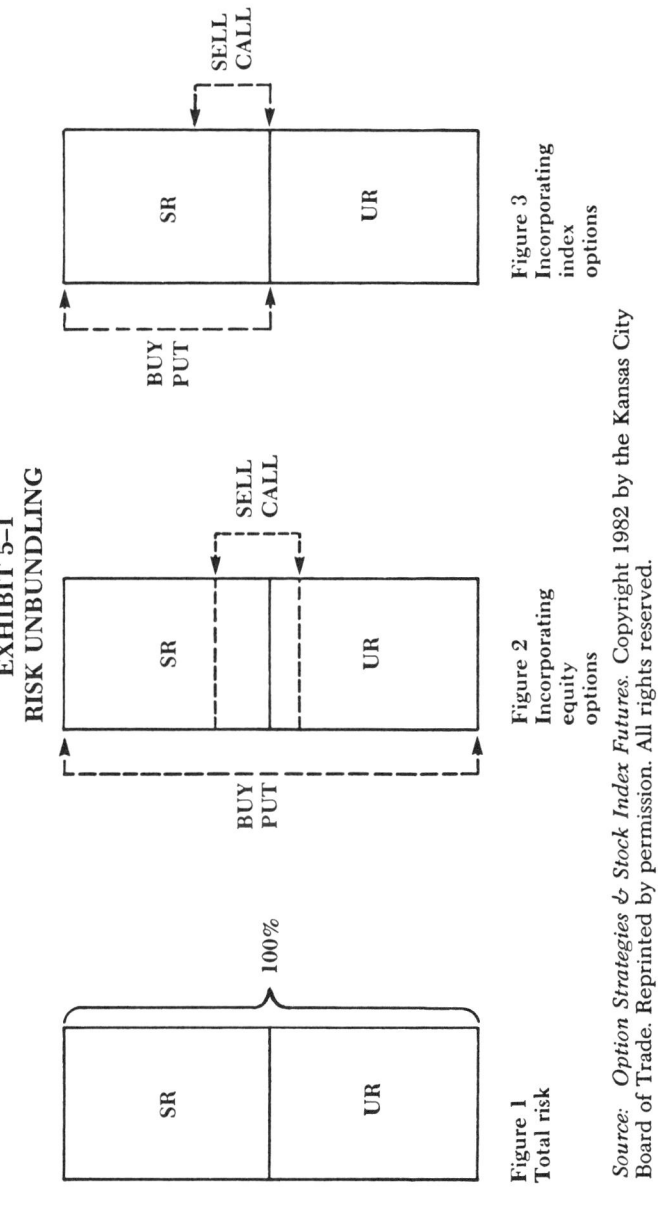

**EXHIBIT 5-1
RISK UNBUNDLING**

Figure 1
Total risk

Figure 2
Incorporating equity options

Figure 3
Incorporating index options

Source: Option Strategies & Stock Index Futures. Copyright 1982 by the Kansas City Board of Trade. Reprinted by permission. All rights reserved.

STOCK INDEX OPTIONS

SPECULATIVE/TRADING STRATEGIES

These strategies involve the purchase or sale of options unhedged; that is, without offsetting positions in other securities. The objectives are as follows:

1. Seek leveraged profits in strongly trending markets.
2. Establish market positions prior to receiving funds necessary for cash payment.
3. Capitalize on perceived changes in market volatility.

A speculator preparing to use index options must make several decisions. First, is the strategy bullish or bearish; that is, are higher prices or lower prices anticipated. Second, where is the price action going to occur? Will it be in the broad based market, the blue chip market, or in secondary issues. The selection may be narrowed even further; that is, to specific industry sectors (technology stocks) or industry groups (computers, gold/silver, gaming/hotel, oil and gas, telephone, or transportation). The investor must also have an opinion as to the extent or magnitude of the move as well as a prediction as to the time factor.

The investor must also determine if individual stocks or portfolios of stocks are better suited to the investment objective. Finally it must be determined if options or a collection of options on individual stocks is a more appropriate means of meeting the investor's objectives.

SPECULATIVE/TRADING STRATEGY I

Investor Status:	Aggressively bullish.
Objective:	To capitalize on a major market advance.
Analysis:	Identify the markets or market sectors most likely to participate in a sharp sustained rise.
Action:	Buy index call options.
Implementation:	A healthy market upswing implies an advance in the broad-based indexes *and* the narrow-based indexes. If the advance is predicted for large capitalization blue chip stocks, investments should be restricted to the NYSE Composite Index, the Amex Major Market Index, the S&P 100 Index, or the S&P 500 Index. If the advance is predicted for secondary stocks, investments should be considered in the Amex Market Value Index or perhaps the PSE Technology Index.
Risk:	If the anticipated advance fails to materialize, the loss on the call options purchased is 100 percent of the capital invested.

APPLICATIONS

SPECULATIVE/TRADING STRATEGY II

Investor Status:	Moderately bullish.
Objective:	To profit from a gradual upward trending market.
Analysis:	Identify the markets or market sectors most likely to follow the rising scenario.
Action:	Sell (write) index put options.
Implementation:	A moderately rising market implies an advance in the broad-based indexes and selective advances in the sub-indexes. Put options are sold in anticipation of capturing the premium received as profit. Call purchases are not considered because the advance may not be sufficient to recover premium costs.
Risk:	Selling put options is equivalent to speculation that the market will advance. A market reversal could cause losses which are a large multiple of the initial capital committed to the put writing program.

SPECULATIVE/TRADING STRATEGY III

Investor Status:	Anticipates market doldrums.
Objective:	To capture as profit decaying option premiums under conditions of low market volatility with minimal assumption of risk.
Analysis:	Identify the market sectors or industry groups most likely to stagnate or remain stationary.
Action:	Sell index option straddles (short puts and short calls).
Implementation:	Selling a straddle means selling a put and selling a call usually in the same index, at the same exercise price, and with identical maturity months.* The profit profile (at expiration) is "tent" shaped and because premiums are received from the sale of two options, profits are generous and are produced even if the index has fairly wide excursions.
Risk:	If the index moves sharply within the time frame of the straddle, losses can quickly consume the original margin deposit.

* Margin is required for both sides of the transaction.

STOCK INDEX OPTIONS

SPECULATIVE/TRADING STRATEGY IV

Investor Status:	Anticipates major market move but uncertain as to direction.
Objective:	To capitalize on increasing market volatility.
Analysis:	Identify the market sectors or industry groups most likely to spearhead any major market change.
Action:	Buy index option straddles (long puts and long calls).
Implementation:	Buying a straddle means buying a put and buying a call usually in the same index, at the same exercise price, and with identical maturity months.* The profit profile (at expiration) is "V" shaped. To establish this straddle requires the purchase of two different options. Therefore, the penalty is severe if the index remains unchanged or within a narrow trading range. If the index changes abruptly within the time frame of the straddle, profits can be multiples of the original investment.
Risk:	If the index fails to change abruptly within the time frame of the straddle, losses could consume as much as 100 percent of the original capital invested.

*The full purchase price of both options must be deposited.

SPECULATIVE/TRADING STRATEGY V

Investor Status:	Moderately bearish.
Objective:	To profit from a gradual downward trending market.
Analysis:	Identify the markets or market sectors most likely to follow the falling scenario.
Action:	Sell (write) index call options.
Implementation:	A moderately declining market implies a decline in the broad-based indexes and selective declines in the sub-indexes. Call options are sold in anticipation of capturing the premium received as profit. Put purchases are not considered because the decline may not be sufficient to recover premium costs.
Risk:	Selling call options is equivalent to speculation that the market will decline. A market reversal could cause losses which are a large multiple of the initial capital committed to the call writing program.

APPLICATIONS

SPECULATIVE/TRADING STRATEGY VI

Investor Status:	Aggressively bearish.
Objective:	To capitalize on a major market decline.
Analysis:	Identify the market sectors or industry groups most likely to participate in a sharp sustained decline.
Action:	Buy index put options.
Implementation:	An across-the-board market downturn implies a decline in broad-based indexes *and* the narrow-based indexes. If the decline is predicted for large capitalization blue chip stocks, put purchases should be restricted to the NYSE Composite Index, the Amex Major Market Index, the S&P 100 Index, or the S&P 500 Index. If the decline is predicted for secondary stocks, put purchases should be considered in the Amex Market Value Index or perhaps the PSE Technology Index.
Risk:	If the anticipated decline fails to materialize, the loss on the put options purchased is 100 percent of the capital invested.

SPECULATIVE/TRADING STRATEGY VII

Investor Status:	Awaiting receipt of funds earmarked for equity investing.
Objective:	To become fully invested under the prevailing conditions rather than at a future date.
Analysis:	Identify the market sectors or industry groups most likely to perform like the equity whose purchase has been delayed.
Action:	Buy index call options.
Implementation:	The total value of the index represented by the calls purchased should approximate the amount of the anticipated cash influx. In addition, conditions of Speculative/Trading Strategy I apply.
Risk:	If the market remains flat or declines, the total option premium—100 percent of the capital invested—is lost. This loss can be viewed as a form of insurance against missing a major purchase opportunity.

STOCK INDEX OPTIONS

Omission of any of these steps does not necessarily imply that the investor has neglected homework. In fact, one of the justifications for index options is to eliminate the necessity for some of this research. Nevertheless, the investor should be aware of the tradeoffs which are possible.

Only when all this information has been assembled is it possible to zero in on specific option; however, the hard work is not yet finished. It is still necessary to determine the exercise price and the expiration date. As explained in Chapter 6, however, this process can be relatively painless with proper selection of an advisory service.

HEDGING STRATEGIES

These strategies involve index option positions in conjunction with other securities. Basically they should be viewed as insurance or a form of risk control. The objectives are as follows:

1. Insulate portfolios from marketwide price movements.
2. Earn premium income to supplement dividend income.
3. Cushion moderate stock price declines.
4. Stabilize returns in volatile markets.
5. Hedge individual stocks when stock options are unavailable for that issue.

The hedger's homework is equally as difficult as the speculator's. The selection process is again twofold; first determination of the appropriate index and second selection of the specific option. By the very nature of the activity, this investor is a market timer and must determine market junctures and predict the magnitude of market moves. The hedger must also estimate the degree to which the portfolio under consideration tracks the various indexes.

The hedger also has alternatives other than index options. For example, instead of hedging, a portion of the portfolio could be liquidated. If margin is used, the debit balance could be adjusted. And finally, stock options on the various issues in the portfolio could be utilized.

There is no simple algorithm to derive all the solutions to either the speculator's problems or the hedger's problems. In some cases one approach might be clearly superior; in others, several approaches may be equivalent.

HEDGE STRATEGY I

Investor Status:	Long a diversified portfolio of common stocks. Moderately bullish.
Objective:	To tailor portfolio risk by adding option positions in anticipation of higher total returns resulting from captured option premiums.
Analysis:	Identify the market sectors or industry groups most likely to match movement in the portfolio being hedged.
Action:	Sell (write) index call options.
Implementation:	Selling index call options in conjunction with a diversified portfolio is similar to covered call writing with individual stocks. Upside potential of the portfolio is sacrificed in return for option premiums if the market is unchanged and a cushion against loss if the market declines. Selling (writing) put options is not advised. The increased exposure to loss is out of proportion to the original objectives of the stock portfolio.
Risk:	The index and the portfolio do not necessarily move in unison. If the index advanced and the portfolio declined, losses would occur on both sides of the transaction. Similarly, if the index declined and the portfolio advanced, profits would be greater than anticipated.

HEDGE STRATEGY II

Investor Status:	Long a diversified portfolio of common stocks. Anticipates market doldrums.
Objective:	To tailor portfolio risk by adding option positions in anticipation of higher total returns resulting from captured option premiums.
Analysis:	Identify the market sectors or industry groups most likely to stagnate or remain stationary.
Action:	Sell (write) index call options.
Implementation:	The factors which apply here are the same as those in Hedge Strategy I. Writing index call options against a portfolio is roughly equivalent to writing covered options against individual stocks.
Risk:	The risks involved in selling index call options in conjunction with a diversified portfolio were discussed in Hedge Strategy I. Briefly stated, a divergence between movement in the portfolio and the index can be either beneficial or detrimental. Worst case occurs when the portfolio is down and the index is up. The optimum outcome occurs when the portfolio is up and the index is down.

STOCK INDEX OPTIONS

HEDGE STRATEGY III

Investor Status:	Long a diversified portfolio of common stocks. Moderately bearish.
Objective:	To tailor portfolio risk by adding option positions in anticipation of higher total returns resulting from captured option premiums.
Analysis:	Identify the market sectors or industry groups most likely to match movement in the portfolio being hedged.
Action:	Sell (write) index call options.
Implementation:	Selling call options in conjunction with a diversified portfolio is similar to covered call writing with individual stocks. Upside potential of the portfolio is sacrificed in return for option premiums if the market is unchanged and a cushion against loss if the market declines. Put options are not purchased because the impending decline may not be sufficient to recover premium costs.
Risk:	The index and the portfolio do not necessarily move in unison. If the index advanced and the portfolio itself declined, losses would occur on both sides of the transaction. Similarly, if the index declined and the portfolio advanced, profits would be greater than anticipated.

HEDGE STRATEGY IV

Investor Status:	Long a diversified portfolio of common stocks. Aggressively bearish.
Objective:	Protect portfolio from impending decline.
Analysis:	Identify the market sectors or industry groups most likely to match movement in the portfolio being hedged.
Action:	Buy index put options to offset loss on the stock holdings.
Implementation:	Puts should be purchased representing a total index value approximating that of the portfolio. A more precise method adjusts the number of puts purchased in accordance with the beta of the portfolio being hedged.
Risk:	Put premiums are not negligible. Therefore buying puts is a form of insurance which can be fairly expensive. For the hedge to work perfectly the index and the portfolio must decline in unison. If the index selected does not mirror the portfolio's performance, the puts may overprotect (result in hedge profits) or underprotect (result in hedge losses).

APPLICATIONS

HEDGE STRATEGY V

Investor Status:	Portfolio contains one stock only (or is concentrated in relatively few positions).
Objective:	Hedge against market risk.
Analysis:	Identify the index most likely to represent the market risk of the position held.
Action:	Buy at-the-money or in-the-money index put options.
Implementation:	Holding a single issue implies confidence by the investor in the ability to select stocks which will outperform the market. Because of the absence of diversification, however, both market risk and company risk are encountered. Puts are introduced when similar confidence is lacking in the ability to time markets or predict market direction. If the price of the stock subsequently declines as part of a general market downturn, but by a smaller percentage than the market, the investor will gain from this strategy, provided that the stock outperforms the market by more than the cost of the puts plus transaction costs. If the stock and the index both decline, but the stock does not outperform the index by more than the cost of the puts, the investor will sustain a loss. If the stock rises more than the market in a rally, the gain on the long stock position will exceed losses on the option provided that the stock position outperforms the index by more than the cost of the put premium.
Risk:	The bond between the stock and the index is very elastic and difficult to estimate with precision. In addition the proportion of systematic and unsystematic risk in the stock position may change dramatically as time passes. Since the two positions have a life of their own they can move independently. It is therefore possible that the hedge will not work and that losses will develop on both the stock and the put.

EXAMPLE TRANSACTIONS

Although 12 different strategies were defined in the sections on speculating and hedging, many share common characteristics. Therefore, rather than give an example for every strategy, only a few samples have been solved. From these it should be possible to prepare an analysis for a particular strategy which an investor may be contemplating. To simplify the tables, transaction costs have not been included; however, they are significant and should be included for a complete picture.

STOCK INDEX OPTIONS

The examples were calculated using prices prevailing in the marketplace in mid-May 1984.

Speculative Call Purchase

Assume an investor is bullish on precious metals and has capital available to speculate on this opinion. How this might be accomplished with Philadelphia Stock Exchange Gold/Silver Index options is shown in Example 5–1. The investment outcome is calculated for various projections in the index price level. The profit profile is typical for call options purchased at-the-money. Risk is limited to dollars invested and if the index does advance, the returns are highly leveraged. Note that the index must advance to 123.50 (7.4%) for the investment to break even.

The profit profile is a worst case representation. If the index drops before the options expire and the investor reevaluates the precious metals outlook, the options could probably be sold with some time value remaining, diminishing the loss somewhat. If the index advances sharply before expiration and the investor decides to take profits, the options could probably be sold at prices higher than the intrinsic value shown in the example.

EXAMPLE 5–1
CALL OPTION SPECULATIVE PURCHASE

Security Statistics
(May 1984)

Index: XAU
Index Level: 115.00
Call Option: Sept 115 (IC)

Option Price: 8½
Expiration : 4 months

Strategy

Buy 1 XAU Sep 115 call @ 8½ = $850

Profit Profile
(At Expiration)

Index change	−10%	0%	+10%	+20%
Index level	103.50	115.00	126.50	138.00
Call price	0	0	11½	23
Call profit (loss)	($850)	($850)	$300	$1,450

APPLICATIONS

Protective Puts

An investor concerned about an imminent decline in the market has several alternative courses of action; however, all have major shortcomings. The portfolio could be liquidated but considering both exit and reentry, transaction costs could be prohibitive. If the portfolio is large, the selling pressure could by itself depress share prices.

If available, puts could be purchased for the individual issues; however, these puts will be expensive, reflecting volatility of the underlying stocks. Time costs are also incurred as the investor must select the puts carefully and direct the purchase transaction.

The most attractive alternative is to use index puts as portfolio insurance. Transaction costs and time costs are lower and, as explained elsewhere, they may also afford certain tax advantages.

An important question with a simple but not obvious answer is how many puts are required to hedge a specific portfolio. When buying puts, the underlying value of the purchase is the number of options times the index level times the multiplier ($100). For example, if the index level were 90, the purchase of five at-the-money puts would hedge a portfolio worth $45,000 (5 × 90 × $100). In other words, to determine the number of puts to purchase, divide the portfolio value by 100 times the index level. This methodology also assumes that the beta of the portfolio is unity. The analysis for portfolios when beta is other than unity is treated later in this section.

Example 5–2A shows detailed calculations for a $45,000 portfolio hedged with puts. This example assumes that the option is held until expiration and that proceeds from the sale or exercise of the option equate to its intrinsic value. If the decline occurred rapidly the option could probably be sold at a higher price, thus reducing the cost of the insurance. On the upside, if market strength was recognized prior to expiration, it might be possible to sell the puts with some time value remaining, thus recovering part of the initial cost.

Tax considerations may also lower the true cost of the puts. For example, they may have served to protect a portfolio during the transition from a short-term to a long-term holding period. Thus tax consequences could overshadow put costs.

Ideally, one transaction in puts could provide protection for an entire portfolio at low execution costs. For large portfolios, put purchases could be spread across several expiration months and exercise prices to prevent buying pressure from influencing option levels.

In the previous example it was assumed that the overall portfolio movements would match those of the market. More precisely it was

STOCK INDEX OPTIONS

EXAMPLE 5-2A
PROTECTIVE PUTS
PORTFOLIO BETA = 1.00

Security Statistics
(May 1984)

Portfolio Value:	$45,000	Put Option:	Dec 90 (XR)
Portfolio Beta :	1.00	Put Price :	3
Index :	NYA	Expiration :	7 months
Index Level :	90.00		

Strategy
Buy 5 NYA Dec 90 puts @ 3 = $1,500

Profit Profile
(At Expiration)

Index change	−10%	0	+10%
Index level	81.00	90.00	99.00
Portfolio value	$40,500	$45,000	$49,500
Put price	9	0	0
Portfolio profit	($4,500)	0	$4,500
Put profit	$3,000	($1,500)	($1,500)
Net profit	($1,500)	($1,500)	$3,000

assumed that the portfolio beta was equal to 1.00. Determining the number of protective puts to purchase when the portfolio beta is other than unity requires an intermediate step—calculation of the weighted average portfolio beta.

Assume a hypothetical portfolio containing three issues having the dollar value and respective betas as shown below.

HYPOTHETICAL PORTFOLIO

Issue	Dollar Value	Stock Beta
A	$15,000	.90
B	$22,000	1.50
C	$25,000	1.70

Portfolio beta is the weighted average of the betas of the individual components.

PORTFOLIO WEIGHTED AVERAGE BETA

$$\frac{(15,000)(.90) + (22,000)(1.50) + (25,000)(1.70)}{15,000 + 22,000 + 25,000} = \frac{89,000}{62,000} = 1.44$$

APPLICATIONS

Assume that S&P 100 is selected as the index most likely to correlate with the portfolio being hedged. With OEX at 155.00, each put option with a 155 strike hedges $15,500 of equity and four puts hedge 4 × $15,500 or $62,000 in equity. Since the portfolio weighted average beta is 1.44, it requires 1.44 × 4 = 5.76 or roughly 6 puts with a 155 strike to properly hedge the portfolio.

Before preparing the profit profile, gains and losses for the portfolio must be calculated for the projected ±10 percent change in the S&P 100 index.

PORTFOLIO LOSS

Stock	Initial Value	Stock Beta	Market Change	Stock Loss
A	$15,000	.90	−10%	$1,350
B	$22,000	1.50	−10%	$3,300
C	$25,000	1.70	−10%	$4,250
			Total loss	$8,900

A similar set of calculations would show a $8,900 gain for a 10 percent advance in the S&P 100 index.

Example 5–2B shows how the index puts adjusted for beta protected the hypothetical portfolio. A slight amount of overprotection was afforded because theoretically only 5.76 puts were required but for a practical implementation, six were actually necessary.

"Covered" Call Writing

As explained earlier, covered call writing cannot be accomplished with index options. It can, however, be approximated by selling index call options having an underlying aggregate market value equal to that of the portfolio being hedged.

Example 5–3 shows how a $45,000 portfolio might incorporate NYSE Composite Index options. Assuming the beta of the portfolio is 1.0, selling five calls having a strike price of 90 would hedge the portfolio on a covered basis (5 × 90 × $100 = $45,000).

Straddle Sales

The straddle sale consists of a short position in puts and a short position in calls, both having the same strike price and the same expiration date. Investors sell straddles in anticipation of a dull market wherein premiums can be captured from both wasting assets.

EXAMPLE 5-2B
PROTECTIVE PUTS
PORTFOLIO BETA = 1.44

Security Statistics
(May 1984)

Portfolio Value:	$62,000	Put Option:	Aug 155 (TK)
Portfolio Beta :	1.44	Put Price :	3½
Index :	OEX	Expiration :	3 months
Index Level :	155.00		

Strategy

Buy 6 OEX Aug 155 puts @ 3½ = $2,100

Profit Profile
(At Expiration)

Index change	−10%	0%	+10%
Index level	139.50	155.00	170.50
Portfolio value	$53,100	$62,100	$70,900
Put Price	15½	0	0
Portfolio profit	($8,900)	0	$8,900
Put profit	($7,200)	($2,100)	($2,100)
Net profit	($1,700)	($2,100)	$6,800

EXAMPLE 5-3
"COVERED" CALL WRITING

Security Statistics
(May 1984)

Portfolio Value:	$45,000	Call Option:	Dec 90 (LR)
Portfolio Beta :	1.00	Call Price :	6
Index :	NYA	Expiration :	7 months
Index Level :	90.00		

Strategy

Sell 5 NYA Dec 90 calls @ 6 = $3,000

Profit Profile
(At Expiration)

Index change	−10%	0	+10%
Index level	81.00	90.00	99.00
Portfolio value	$40,500	$45,000	$49,500
Call price	0	0	9
Portfolio profit	($4,500)	0	$4,500
Call profit	$3,000	$3,000	($1,500)
Net profit	($1,500)	$3,000	$3,000

APPLICATIONS

EXAMPLE 5-4
STRADDLE SALE

Security Statistics
(May 1984)

Index : OEX		Put Price : 3½
Index Level: 155.00		Call Price : 6
Call Option: Aug 155 (HK)		Expiration: 3 months
Put Option : Aug 155 (TK)		

Strategy

Sell 1 OEX Aug 155 put @ 3½ = $350
Sell 1 OEX Aug 155 call @ 6 = $600

Profit Profile
(At Expiration)

Index change	−10%	−6.1%	0%	+6.1%	+10%
Index level	139.50	145.55	155.00	164.46	170.50
Put price	15½	9½	0	0	0
Call price	0	0	0	9½	15½
Profit put	($1,200)	($600)	$350	$350	$350
Profit call	$600	$600	$600	($350)	($950)
Net profit	($600)	0	$950	0	($600)

Example 5-4 shows the outcome for a straddle sale in OEX options. The profit profile is tent-shaped and is profitable if the index is within +6.1% of the entry level. Severe losses accrue if the index moves beyond the upper or lower breakeven points.

Although the outcome may appear promising, the reader is cautioned that a simple program of selling straddles on a regular basis will not provide consistent profits let alone a high rate of return. Generous profits some of the time will be annihilated by substantial losses at other times. Protective strategies implemented as the market moves adversely are likely to result in whipsaws. This strategy is reliable only for investors having proven ability to predict future market movements.

Straddle Purchases

The straddle purchase consists of a long position in puts and a long position in calls, both having the same strike price and the same expiration date. Investors purchase straddles in preparation for a market move of major proportions with direction uncertain.

STOCK INDEX OPTIONS

EXAMPLE 5-5
STRADDLE PURCHASE

Security Statistics
(May 1984)

Index	: OEX	Put Price :	3½
Index Level:	155.00	Call Price :	6
Call Option :	Aug 155 (HK)	Expiration:	3 months
Put Option :	Aug 155 (TK)		

Strategy

Buy 1 OEX Aug 155 put @ 3½ = $350
Buy 1 OEX Aug 155 call @ 6 = $600

Profit Profile
(At Expiration)

Index change	−10%	−6.1%	0%	+6.1%	+10%
Index level	139.50	145.55	155.00	164.46	170.50
Put price	15½	9½	0	0	0
Call price	0	0	0	9½	15½
Profit put	$1,200	$600	($350)	($350)	($350)
Profit call	($600)	($600)	($600)	$350	$950
Net profit	$600	0	($950)	0	$600

Example 5-5 shows the outcome for a straddle purchase in OEX options. The profit profile is V-shaped with a loss resulting if the index is within +6.1% of the entry level. Once reaching this level premium costs have been recovered and profits on the winning option can be substantial.

Various advisers have great faith in this strategy as a means of regularly extracting profits from the market. When the numbers are tabulated, however, the reasons for this optimism are not obvious. The index must move more than 6 percent before profits accrue. In those instances when such a move does not occur, the losses are considerable. Prospects for investors using this strategy without above average timing ability are not encouraging.

6

OPTION EVALUATION

SELECTING THE BEST OPTION

In the preceding chapters the thought process necessary to approach index option investments was unfolded. Information on indexes was presented to permit a determination of approximate relative behavior. Information on index options was presented to show the relationship to stock options and to show the ease with which transactions could be effected. Finally, information on strategies was presented to show the scope of potential applications, the similarity to strategies already possible with equity options, and new strategies unique to index options.

The information supplied thus far brings the investor to the following point in the investment decision process. A market judgment has been made, a strategy selected, an index targeted, the number of options required to accomplish the objective calculated, and an approximate time frame established. The final step is to select the specific option (exercise price and expiration month) to operate in. At this time the option valuation should also be considered. Is it mispriced and by how much? What price is satisfactory?

OPTION MODELS

Option theory is well advanced and mathematical models have been derived to determine fair option value. Most stock option users have heard about the Black-Scholes model. Information about the model was published in the academic literature and is now accessible to the public in many forms. Several programs are available at reasonable prices for analysis of equity options on a microcomputer.

Unfortunately, other special mathematical models are required to

STOCK INDEX OPTIONS

evaluate index option premiums. This is because of the nature of the dividends on the stocks within the index. The dividend credit is a varying amount paid continually on the component stocks throughout the life of the index option. This is in contrast to the underlying stock in an equity option where the dividend is periodic and typically of constant magnitude.

FAIR VALUE

The task of option selection is further complicated by an option pricing concept known as fair value. The public is generally unaware of the concept of fair value and if there is an awareness it is not necessarily understood and is frequently ignored.

Option fair value is concerned with the price at which an option *should* trade in the market place as opposed to the price at which it *does* trade. In the option markets large numbers of sophisticated well financed buyers and sellers compete for contracts and thus set prices. Any profitable situation or strategy is quickly recognized and soon funded until the exceptional potential disappears.

If writing options gave investors a meaningful edge, sellers would literally come out of the woodwork. If buying options produced greater than expected profit, money would concentrate in that strategy. In the liquid highly visible listed option markets this is the process which is operative. The price adjusts until neither buyer nor seller has any advantage.

If options are priced fairly both buyers and sellers will be disappointed. For the buyer, the occasional winner will just offset the frequent losses from the cost of the options. For the seller the occasional large losses will offset the frequent premium proceeds. For both buyer and seller the reward is canceled by what is sacrificed. When either has an edge, investors and speculators concentrate in that position until the edge disappears. Formally stated, fair value is the price at which the expected profit for both the buyer and the writer is equal to zero.

Assuming the investor is average in predictive ability, then incorporating options in an investment program will not enhance performance. Without a reliable method for estimating the future price of the underlying asset, the only way to make money consistently in an options program is to buy undervalued options and to sell overvalued options. Any investment scheme with options which does not address valuation should be questioned seriously.

OPTION EVALUATION

Unfortunately, there is no simple way of determining fair value—or for that matter other option parameters such as price and leverage projections. There are no rules of thumb or simple algebraic expressions universally applicable to option evaluation. Options are complex instruments and they lend themselves to analytical techniques incorporating advanced financial and mathematical theory.

The foregoing does not preclude the use of options by rational thinkers. An investor adept at predicting price moves (magnitude, direction, and timing) can enhance overall performance through appropriate option transactions. For equity owners index options are the easiest and simplest way to alter the risk/reward characteristics of a portfolio.

SCOPE OF UNDERTAKING

Anyone considering the use of options (index options or stock options) on more than an occasional basis is cautioned to map out in advance a total investment plan. First, the true nature of options, that is, option theory, should be explored beyond the elementary and often misleading material supplied by the brokerage firms and the various exchanges. Second, the scope of an option analysis program should be well understood.

A successful program requires extreme care in the selection of the option; however, difficulties can arise for several reasons. First, the number of options to scan is overwhelming. Second, even though closing prices might indicate that the option is attractive, the index level may have changed significantly since the last option traded. Thus the quotes may not be indicative of the prices at which future transactions could be executed. Finally, professional traders have the options under continuous surveillance also using powerful evaluation tools. It should be expected that they would absorb the best option deals. And because of their low transaction costs, they will also soak up options marginal or unattractive to the commission paying public.

Alternative Information Sources

The foregoing cautions were not intended to define insurmountable hurdles. Their purpose was to properly define the magnitude and complexity of the problem at hand. To help with the information gathering process three routes are available to investors. The alternatives are microcomputer software, computer data bases, and investment advisory services.

STOCK INDEX OPTIONS

Computer Software

Programs for modeling index options have been prepared by a few investment firms and securities industry consultants. Such programs, however, are not designed for public consumption and are not readily accessible.

Two software packages, the Commodity Options Trading System (COTS)[1] and Optionview Plus[2], are available which permit owners of personal computers to conduct relatively sophisticated analysis routines. Literature describing the programs is available from the software developer directly. Considering the utility and popularity of index options, evaluation programs should be in widespread demand. Both investment publications and computer publications should be monitored carefully for announcements of additional software.

Computer Data Bases

Another alternative is to communicate with a computer data base. These services provide timely screens not only of attractive puts and calls but also of various strategies such as spreads, straddles, covered writes, and others.

A list of the primary sources of computerized data is given in Appendix F. Unfortunately, such services are expensive and appeal primarily to investment professionals, especially exchange members who have at their disposal significant amounts of capital and who can trade with minimal commissions. Once again the investor must estimate carefully the potential profit of a strategy balanced against the time and cost of its implementation.

Advisory Services

The final alternative is an investment advisory service. In concept they should be able to summarize attractive positions and provide data in printed form at reasonable cost. The primary objection to this route is the delay in receiving information; however, attractive option positions are often available for extended periods.

At this writing at least five advisory services are available which cover index options; these are listed in Appendix G. These services vary in the scope and depth of index option coverage; however, one

---

[1] Software Options, Inc.
19 Rector Street
New York, NY 10006

[2] Star Value Software
12218 Scribe Drive
Austin, TX 78759

OPTION EVALUATION

service, *Value Line Options,* is remarkably comprehensive. It provides sufficient information for investors to comfortably operate in index option markets (as well as stock option markets) without access to proprietary mathematical models, a computer, or a data base.

Value Line Options is published 48 times a year on the first four Mondays of each month. It comes in two sections. Part A (The Option Strategist) is a commentary on current events in the options market. It includes a feature article covering a number of topics ranging from trading strategies to new products. It also includes news items affecting particular options or their underlying stocks and a listing of selected options recommended for various strategies. Part B (Option Evaluation Section) gives extensive statistics for *every* listed stock option and index option. All told, approximately 8,000 different options are evaluated. The cost of the service is $285 per year.

VALUE LINE OPTION EVALUATION

As stated earlier, the Value Line coverage of index options (as well as equity options) is extensive and thorough. The analysis includes fair value and other information which is very valuable; however, before examining a sample of the statistics in the Value Line data array it is necessary to understand their methodology and nomenclature.

The Value Line approach to determining fair value (or, using their terminology, normal value) relies on empirical rather than theoretical projections. The current option price is viewed in relationship to its historical price under like conditions. If the issue was not traded, similar issues are examined.

Value Line then assigns a price curve (track) to the option projecting prices at which it would trade if it were normally valued. The deviation between the estimated price and the traded price is the amount which the option is overvalued or undervalued. Value Line has observed that there is a tendency for options to remain off the projected track. Hence, they do not project that the option will return to normal value immediately. In fact, their model slowly adjusts the determination of normal price to match the traded price thus taking into account persistence of sentiment which has influenced its value.

Figure 6–1 is a sample of the statistics from *Value Line Options* dated May 28, 1984 (prices are as of May 22, 1984). The array contains data for all puts and calls trading in the S&P 100 index. A brief explanation will assist in interpreting this data.

Line ① gives the name of the index (S&P 100), the current yield

STOCK INDEX OPTIONS

FIGURE 6-1
VALUE LINE OPTION EVALUATION

—OPTION BUYER—

	Description of Each Security	Recent Market Price	Est. Normal Price	Change Per Point	Performance Rank / Relative Volatility	Current Leverage +10% -10%
(1)						
(2)	S&P 100 Index (4.7% yield) CBO					
	OEX units	152.35			3	50%
	Jun 175 FO	.06	.01	4 (-)	9999	+990%-100%
	170 FN	.06	.05	7 -	9999	+990 -100
	165 FM	.06	.16	13 -	9999	+990 -100
	160 FL	.44	.53	27 2	8900	+990 -100
	155 FK	1.56	1.61	42 2	3900	+720 -100
	150 FJ	4.00	4.05	58 2	1650	+340 -100
	145 FI	8.25	7.89	73 2	770	+175 -95
	140 FH	13.00	12.50	84 (2)	490	+115 -85
	Jul 175 GO	.06	.27	5 -	9999	+990 -95
	170 GN	.13	.53	9 -	9999	+990 -95
	165 GM	.56	1.04	19 2	5700	+925 -95
	160 GL	1.38	1.97	30 2	3300	+580 -95
(3)	155 GK	3.13	3.57	44 (3)	2100	+335 -90
	150 GJ	5.88	6.03	58 (2)	1250	+210 -90
	145 GI	9.50	9.36	70 (2)	720	+140 -85
	Aug 175 HO	.19	.60	7 1	9200	+990 -90
	170 HN	.38	1.02	12 1	6400	+910 -90
	165 HM	.94	1.73	21 2	3600	+600 -90
	160 HL	2.19	2.87	33 2	2200	+370 -90
	155 HK	4.13	4.61	45 2	1650	+250 -85
	150 HJ	6.88	7.05	58 2	1100	+175 -85
	145 HI	10.50	10.23	69 (2)	680	+125 -75
(4)	P Jun 140 RH	.06	.04	12 -	9999	-100 +990
	P 145 RI	.13	.22	26 -	9999	-100 +990
	P 150 RJ	.94	1.05	42 2	5200	-100 +990
	P 155 RK	2.50	3.61	59 2	1500	-100 +410
	P 160 RL	7.65	7.84	75 1+	610	-100 +200
	P 165 RM	12.65	12.68	89 2	410	-95 +120
	P 170 RN	17.65	17.66	97 (3)	320	-80 +85
	P 175 RO	23.00	22.65	91 (3)	300	-55 +65
	P Jul 145 SI	.56	1.16	27 2	6600	-95 +990
	P 150 SJ	1.88	2.58	42 2	2800	-95 +595
	P 155 SK	4.25	5.10	58 2	1300	-95 +320
	P 160 SL	7.88	8.72	74 2+	620	-95 +190
	P 165 SM	13.00	13.08	83 2	430	-80 +115
	P 170 SN	17.75	17.82	92 (3)	330	-70 +85
	P 175 SO	NEW	22.71	96 -	280	-60 +65
	P Aug 145 TI	.94	1.91	28 1	4100	-90 +825
	P 150 TJ	2.50	3.53	43 2	2200	-90 +430
	P 155 TK	4.88	6.04	57 3	1200	-90 +270
	P 160 TL	8.13	9.45	73 2+	620	-90 +180
	P 165 TM	13.00	13.54	83 2	420	-80 +115
	P 170 TN	NEW	18.08	87 -	330	-65 +80
	P 175 TO	NEW	22.85	93 -	280	-60 +65

Source: Value Line Options, May 28, 1984. Copyright 1984 by Value Line, Inc. Reprinted by permission. All rights reserved.

OPTION EVALUATION

on the index (4.7%), and an abbreviation for the exchange where the options are traded (CBO). Line ② gives the index ticker symbol (OEX), the index level (152.35), a performance rank (3) and a relative volatility (50%). The performance rank, ranging from 1 (highest) down to 5 (lowest), is Value Line's assessment of the probable relative investment performance. The volatility is the overall risk expressed as a percentage of the risk of the typical common stock. Line ③ gives parameters for the July calls with an exercise price of 155 including the symbol (GK), the recent market price (3.13), the estimated normal price (3.57), the change per point (44), the performance rank (3), the relative volatility (2100), and the current leverage (+335%, −90%). The change per point is the estimated number of pennies that the normal price and the quoted price of the option would change if the price of the underlying index changed by one point. With this number subscribers can estimate option value as the index level varies. Performance rank is Value Line's figure of merit and relative volatility is the risk measure. The current leverage projections show the expected percent price changes in the option for a quick 10% rise or a quick 10% decline in the index. Adjacent lines give the option parameters for calls at other strike prices. Line ④ beginning with a "p" starts coverage of put options.

Appendix D contains data from *Value Line Options* for all 13 optionable indexes. The issue was dated May 28, 1984 analyzing prices as of May 22, 1984. Note once again that every option—all puts, all calls, all strike prices, and all expirations—are included. (Each issue of Value Line Options also contains similar data for *all* stock options as well. Options on the 13 indexes are only a small part of the total Value Line coverage.) No other service provides information as complete or as thorough. Approximatley 500 different index options are analyzed—every valid option on the date of evaluation. Once again, the Value Line data array is unusually complete.

7

SPECIAL CONSIDERATIONS

INTRODUCTION

By now it should be clear that index options are modeled after stock options in most respects. Almost without exception what applies to listed stock options also applies to index options. There are, however, a few subtleties which can trap the uninformed investor. The purpose of this chapter is to explore some of the unique aspects of index options, some of the special pitfalls, and some of the important differences between stock and index options.

The most unusual facets of index options include timing risk, unpredictable tracking of the underlying asset, and cash settlement. Other differences, although less extreme, are still important; they include margin requirements, taxes, and variations in covered writing techniques.

LIQUIDITY

To incorporate the various index option strategies into an investment program and to capitalize on the subtleties among the indexes, one critical factor was assumed—that the transactions could indeed be executed, unconstrained by market conditions. Unfortunately such is not the case. The liquidity of the options is frequently less than ideal, particularly if consideration is given to distant options or options at strike prices above or below the current market.

A small investor may be able to execute a handful of options with little or no difficulty. A substantial investor may not have this flexibility. As a rule of thumb it takes between five and ten contracts to hedge

STOCK INDEX OPTIONS

each $100,000 of portfolio equity. Current data on trading suggest that the alternatives, in choice of indexes as well as stock prices and expiration months, may be more apparent than real.

Table 7-1 shows the volume of trading for index options on May 11, 1984. This is a representative day in the market. The Dow was down 10.05 points on a volume of nearly 83 million shares—nothing unusual, nothing spectacular. (It was, however, the day on which trading in S&P 100 options hit an historic high; namely, 390,040 contracts). While the data is no substitute for trading experience, it provides information from which several conclusions can be drawn.

For the broad-based indexes, the S&P 500 is the laggard. Volume and open interest figures suggest that operations in the vehicle should be avoided. The remaining broad-based indexes have varying degrees of liquidity, but unfortunately it is not distributed evenly throughout the range of strike prices and expiration months.

As for the narrow-based indexes, volume and open interest figures are disappointing. The Amex Computer Technology Index has a meaningful open interest but for the other narrow-based indexes it is quite low. Although the exchanges have applied for listing of dozens of additional sub-indexes, volume figures discussed here plus the fact that

TABLE 7-1
LIQUIDITY IN INDEX OPTIONS
DAILY VOLUME FRIDAY
MAY 11, 1984 WITH OPEN INTEREST

Index	Total Call Volume	Total Put Volume	Total Call Open Interest	Total Put Open Interest
Amex Computer Technology Index	3,406	3,253	10,132	7,287
Amex Major Market Index	16,376	12,719	30,741	39,029
Amex Market Value Index	354	509	2,464	2,632
Amex Oil & Gas Index	38	53	592	889
Amex Transportation Index	190	627	1,976	1,262
NYSE Composite Index	10,952	10,157	58,903	59,986
NYSE Telephone Index	0	0	0	0
PSE Technology Index	104	92	1,420	1,379
PHL Gaming/Hotel Index	0	0	195	144
PHL Gold/Silver Index	171	137	1,939	720
S&P 100 Index	173,654	216,386	369,465	459,228
S&P 500 Index	5	0	246	274
S&P Transportation Index	51	29	929	454

SPECIAL CONSIDERATIONS

three sub-index options have already been delisted, suggest that it will be some time before these new sub-indexes debut.

A quick determination of the liquidity of an index option can be obtained from the Value Line advisory service. Referring to the sample in Appendix D, whenever the option performance rank is shown in parentheses it indicates an inactively traded option.

Specifically, Value Line designates as inactive options meeting any of the following three conditions. First, an option that has traded in the past is inactive if it has an open interest of fewer than 25 contracts. Second, an option is classified as inactive if it has traded less than a total of 100 contracts over the last 10 market days. Third, if the option has had more than three days of zero trading before it accumulates 100 contracts of trading, it is also designated as inactive. A perusal of the data quickly reveals how many contracts are in place but not really useful.

SENTIMENT AND ARBITRAGE

When hedging individual stocks with options, the relationship between the stock price and the option price is generally predictable and relatively easy to ascertain. Option theory is well advanced and the tools necessary to analyze the stock/option prices are widely disseminated. The market is efficient and misaligned prices provide profitable arbitrage opportunities which are targeted by professional investors.

For example, when a stock option is overpriced, an arbitrageur will buy the underlying common stock and sell the option until the normal relationship returns. Both positions are then closed, consummating a very low risk transaction. Similarly, when a stock option is underpriced, an arbitrageur will buy the option and sell short the underlying common until the normal relationship returns. Both positions are then closed, again consummating a very low risk transaction. Undervalued stock options are purchased relentlessly and overvalued stock options are sold relentlessly until any price disparity disappears.

The forces which keep listed stock options in line cannot necessarily be applied to index options. Therefore sentiment factors or others as poorly defined may keep index options out of line price wise for extended periods. For example, assume that options in the Amex Major Market Index are identified as overpriced. The options can be sold short but that is a risky proposition if the market moves higher. The other half of an arbitrage transaction cannot be implemented because it would require purchase of the 20 component stocks in the index

STOCK INDEX OPTIONS

in their proper proportion. Obviously hedging the S&P 500 would entail even further difficulty. Thus overvalued or undervalued option price relationships might persist indefinitely.

PORTFOLIO TRACKING

Speculators are faced with the problem of being in the right index at the right time. Hedgers have a similar dilemma; they must equate the performance of an index with their portfolio in some future time period.

Most portfolios do not have the same composition and weighting as any of the standard indexes. There is the constant threat that diversification of the individual portfolio is inadequate or imperfect. In addition, as the market gyrates, group rotation or strength in particular sectors may cause mismatch between indexes and typical portfolios.

Precisely stated, the problem is to determine the future correlation between the portfolio being protected and the index under consideration. An extremely conservative portfolio or an undiversified portfolio may not be well hedged by any of the indexes available. Likewise, an extremely volatile portfolio may not be fully protected by index options. It must be recognized in advance that hedging portfolios is an imperfect process. Unless the selection and weighting of the components in the portfolio match perfectly those in the index, the hedge outcome will be flawed.

A typical hedge position involves the purchase of put options to offset portfolio losses in a predicted decline. The option selected may not provide complete protection. The resulting loss must be viewed in light of the rationale for hedging in the first place. Presumably it is easier and cheaper to buy puts than to liquidate a portfolio. It is also less time consuming. Also tax considerations may mandate holding positions for long term capital gains. All these factors must be weighed in conjunction with the possibility of an inefficient or ineffective hedge.

TIMING RISK

The cash settlement feature of stock index options introduces a special risk not present when using options requiring delivery of stock. The risk is caused by the time lag between actual exercise of an index option and receipt of notification of that exercise.

Exercise of an index option is possible at any time before expiration.

SPECIAL CONSIDERATIONS

The value of the cash settlement is based on the closing level of the index on the day that the option is exercised. However, writers of index options will not be notified of their obligation to pay cash in settlement of the option exercise until the following business day.

As a consequence, writers who are hedged, that is, have established offsetting positions in stocks or other index options, may endure a period when they are temporarily unintentionally unhedged. They face risk of an unfavorable price move on the unhedged position during the period when important information awaits dissemination.

If the options were sold to hedge a large portfolio of stocks the potential for damage in the reaction time necessary to reestablish the hedge may not be large. However, in spread positions an adverse move in the unhedged leg may entail far greater risk than initially envisioned.

COMMISSIONS

Commissions levied for the purchase and sale of index options are equivalent to those for equity options. Although the formulas and rates are different at various brokerage firms, they are generally based on the money involved; that is, the total dollars debited or credited in the transaction.

When exercise or assignment occurs with equity options, securities are transferred and normal stock commissions are charged. When index options are exercised or assigned, settlement is for cash; however, a commission is charged for implementing the transaction. For one major full service brokerage firm the fee was $50 per contract.

COVERED WRITING

With stock options covered call writing is a position which is clearly defined. A covered writer sells calls on shares of stock already owned. Such stock placed with the broker eliminates margin requirements for the option position. Covered writing is not currently permitted with index options. Although theoretically possible, practical considerations prevent a neat and tidy implementation.

Realistically it is impossible to maintain a portfolio containing exactly the same stocks as the underlying index. Conceivably this could be accomplished for a sub-index containing relatively few issues; however, constructing a portfolio to reproduce the relative stock positions in a value weighted index would be even more difficult. Also, attempts

STOCK INDEX OPTIONS

at covered writing are always thwarted by timing risk—the risk that the value of the securities will change significantly during the lag between the time the option was exercised and the time notification of the assignment was received. This risk is reduced significantly if the portfolio is widely diversified.

As a consequence of these considerations, writing positions in index options cannot be covered for margin purposes, and are therefore subject to applicable margin requirements. Such a restriction is necessary because index options are settled in cash and call writers cannot provide in advance for their potential settlement obligations by acquiring and holding the underlying securities. The risk is always present that the value of the portfolio will not increase as much as the index.

The covered writing posture can be approximated by carefully selecting the stocks in the portfolio to be hedged. An alternative is to write index options against a mutual fund, such as an index fund, which strives to achieve equivalency to a popular index. One such possibility is The Equity Income Fund S&P 500 Index, a unit investment trust sponsored by Merrill Lynch, Dean Witter, Prudential-Bache, and Shearson/American Express. This fund replicates the S&P 500 and can be acquired easily, requiring a minimum purchase of 1,000 units at approximately $1.00 each.

The objectives of covered writing with index options are generally the same as those for covered writing with stock options; namely, to earn premium income to supplement dividend income, to cushion moderate price declines, and to stabilize returns in volatile markets.

A Note about Covered Writing

Covered writing is often promoted as a means of supplementing portfolio income with option premiums; however, such a description is less than accurate. It implies that a desirable attribute is somehow gained without cost or sacrifice. The option premium is an advantage only if the underlying stock is unchanged or lower. When the stock advances, the option inhibits overall performance. Further, option premiums are never income. Closing transactions or option expirations result in short term gains or losses.

A typical option writing program is managed as follows. The basic requirement is a large diversified portfolio of optionable stocks. Options are written (sold) on a one-for-one basis on each of the stocks.

If the stock declines, the option expires worthless. The premium is garnered and another option is written on the same stock. Taxwise there is an unrealized loss on the stock and a short-term gain on the option. If the underlying stock price is unchanged, the outcome is

SPECIAL CONSIDERATIONS

similar. The premium on the option sold is profit and after expiration a replacement option is written. Taxwise, there is a short-term gain on the option. If the stock advances and the option is in-the-money, the option is not sold at a loss. Assignment is permitted and the stock is delivered from the portfolio. For tax purposes, the stock is sold at the exercise price. The option premium received increases the amount realized by the writer on the sale of the stock.

The covered writing strategy outlined earlier is misleading in that it camouflages actual developments within the portfolio. For example, an astute manager can maintain an option writing portfolio without ever realizing a loss. Since options are always permitted to be assigned, no losses are ever realized on the option portion of the portfolio. The only occasion to realize a loss is if options are sold repetitively on a declining issue. A subsequent rebound may cause assignment at an exercise price below the original purchase price of the stock; however, these losses can be avoided by never rolling down. Stocks which have declined are held in the portfolio with unrealized losses.

Investors using index options in a "covered writing" scenario may find the strategy more revealing than writers using equity options. That is because in a rising market the options will be exercised but settlement will be for cash which of course will be a loss. These account debits should quickly cause the investor to question the description of the strategy which is defined as "income" producing.

An investor involved in covered writing or contemplating such a program should explore the validity of the strategy theoretically. From this perspective covered writing is not a lucrative undertaking. The investor should also verify the historical returns produced by this strategy. This can be accomplished relatively easily by checking the performance of the so-called option income funds. Several of these funds are available and have track records in excess of six years. The results confirm the theoretical predictions.

ESCROW LETTERS

It is possible for investors maintaining bank custodial accounts to use those assets to cover short positions in broad-based index options. The mechanism is an escrow letter issued by a bank or trust company. Requirements for short calls are as follows:

1. The bank/trust company must hold securities of at least 10 different issuers having a total market value equaling or exceeding the current index value times the index multiplier.

STOCK INDEX OPTIONS

2. The bank/trust company must commit to pay the exercise settlement amount plus commissions.
3. None of the 10 or more deposited securities can represent more than 15% of the total collateral.
4. Each deposited security must be traded on a national securities exchange and substantially meet the listing requirements of the NYSE or AMEX or be traded over-the-counter and be included on the Federal Reserve Board's list of OTC marginable stocks.

The escrow letter for use with short puts is similar to the one for short calls except that the required collateral is cash or cash equivalents having an aggregate market value at least equal to the "aggregate exercise price" times the number of contracts. Cash equivalents are defined as securities issued or guaranteed by the United States or its agencies, negotiable bank certificates of deposit, or bankers acceptances issued by banking institutions in the United States and payable in the United States.

THE SPECTER OF MANIPULATION

On April 19, 1984 a series of events occurred on the NYSE and the CBOE which caused certain traders great consternation, which gave the press material for some sensational journalism, and which triggered investigations by the CBOE, the NYSE, and the SEC. In particular, large block trades in stocks which are components of the S&P 100 Index were transacted in a short period of time late in the day. These trades were of such consequence that they impacted the S&P 100 Index causing it to move from a level just below 155 to a level just above 155. Ordinarily, these transactions would not have attracted much attention but a related series of transactions occurred in an expiring OEX index options contract which caused substantial losses for some CBOE floor traders and, of course, windfall profits for some other participants in the events.

Professional investors, especially exchange members with low transaction costs, regularly maintain short positions in out-of-the-money options with a limited life, say a day or so. These options trade at only $1/8$ or $1/16$, but if the position is large enough and if the options do expire worthless, profits can be handsome indeed. While no one would claim that this strategy is riskless, on the day in question many professional traders learned to their chagrin that under the right circumstances the outcome can be devastating.

SPECIAL CONSIDERATIONS

The low for the S&P 100 Index on that day was 154.34. The OEX April 155 options were expiring and many traders calculated that they would be out-of-the-money at the close. Therefore large short positions were established at $\frac{1}{16}$ ($.0625) or $6.25 per contract. They were accommodated by other parties eager to make large scale purchases of the options. The late afternoon trading in large blocks of stock making up the S&P 100 caused the index to close at 155.78. Since settlement was for cash, each contract was worth $78. Those who sold the options at $6.25 lost nearly $72 per contract.

Naturally the traders who got burned were miffed and the press seized the opportunity to expound on manipulation and plotted killings in the market. Although results of the various investigations are not complete, it appears at the time of this writing that nothing irregular actually occurred. The transactions were straightforward, routine, and legal. However, a combination of circumstances caused the impact to be larger than it might otherwise have been.

What really happened is as follows. A little-known New York-based securities firm was closing an arbitrage position known as a reverse conversion (short stock, long calls, and short puts). To do so required purchase of the shares previously sold short and they elected to effect these transactions with market-on-close orders. To fill these orders the specialists made their existence known on the floor of the exchange. Savvy traders there analyzed the situation, put two and two together, and assumed speculative positions in OEX April 155 calls. Their prognostications turned out to be correct and as a result they profited handsomely.

Knowledgeable commentators maintain that manipulation of the OEX is impossible and that the events described above were a fluke. The circumstances were unusual because Thursday April 19, 1984 was the day before a holiday (Good Friday) and trading was unusually light. The second important factor was the nature of the orders to buy the stocks involved. The third important factor was the proximity of the index to the option exercise price. The option possessed tremendous leverage which was activated by only a small advance in the index.

At least for the OEX it is agreed that a stock purchase campaign designed by a manipulator would be too risky to justify profits which might accrue in the options market. The issues involved are too large, too liquid, and too visible to make such an undertaking worthwhile. However, implications for some of the other indexes are less clear. Undoubtedly findings from the ongoing investigations will result in the establishment of new controls and surveillance techniques.

SUPPLEMENT

OPTION FUNDAMENTALS

INTRODUCTION

This book is written at a level which assumes a basic knowledge of listed stock options. The point was made repeatedly that stock options and index options are very similar. An understanding of one implies an understanding of the other; however, because the subject is complex a brief review of stock options is included here for reference.

Any intelligent discussion of options is necessarily involved. It must navigate through puts and calls, buyers and writers, and a host of specific terminology. The following discussion includes numerous diagrams and the reader should learn to think in these terms. Diagrams are often the simplest and quickest way to visualize the outcome of a complex option strategy.

OPTION DEFINITION

An option is a contract allowing purchase or sale of an asset (common stock) at a specified price within a specified period of time. For every option there is a buyer—the person who acquires the option—and a writer, the person who sells or grants the option. It always takes two parties to consummate an option transaction

CALL OPTIONS

A call is an option to buy. It is a privilege but not an obligation to buy at a particular price for a specified period of time. The price at

STOCK INDEX OPTIONS

which the stock will change hands is known as the exercise price or the strike price.

Call Buyers

The purchaser of a call option has contracted to buy the stock at the exercise price no matter how far the stock may subsequently advance.

Figure 1 of Exhibit S–1 shows graphically the outcome for an option purchase. It is a plot of profit expressed in dollars as a function of the price of the underlying stock. In this example it was assumed that the stock price was at the exercise price when the transaction was entered.

At expiration if the stock is unchanged or lower, it could be purchased on the market cheaper than it could be obtained by exercising the option. The option would not be exercised and the original cost of the call would be the loss on the position.

If the stock advances, the option privilege permits purchase at the exercise price with the opportunity to sell in the marketplace at the prevailing higher price. The actual price of the call reflects this increase in value. Profits can be realized by closing the options position without initiating the exercise procedure.

Options are frequently touted as having limited risk and unlimited potential; this statement is true but certainly misleading. Expressed as a percentage, the risk is 100 percent or total loss.

Call Writers

The call option writer is obligated to deliver stock at the exercise price irrespective of the level which the stock price may reach. The writer's profit profile is shown in Figure 2 of Exhibit S–1. If the stock price is unchanged when the option expires, the writer retains the proceeds from the sale of the options.

Similarly, if the stock declines, the buyer will not exercise the option and the writer retains the proceeds. If the stock advances the option will be exercised. The writer must purchase stock in the market at the (high) prevailing market price and sell it to the person exercising the option at the (low) exercise price. The writer's loss position will be reflected in the option price but it is not necessary to wait for assignment to establish the loss. The option writer can buy back (cover) the position and terminate the obligation. Since the assignment procedure involves two stock commissions (sale of the stock and subsequent

OPTION FUNDAMENTALS

**EXHIBIT S–1
PROFIT PROFILES FOR CALL OPTION TRANSACTIONS**

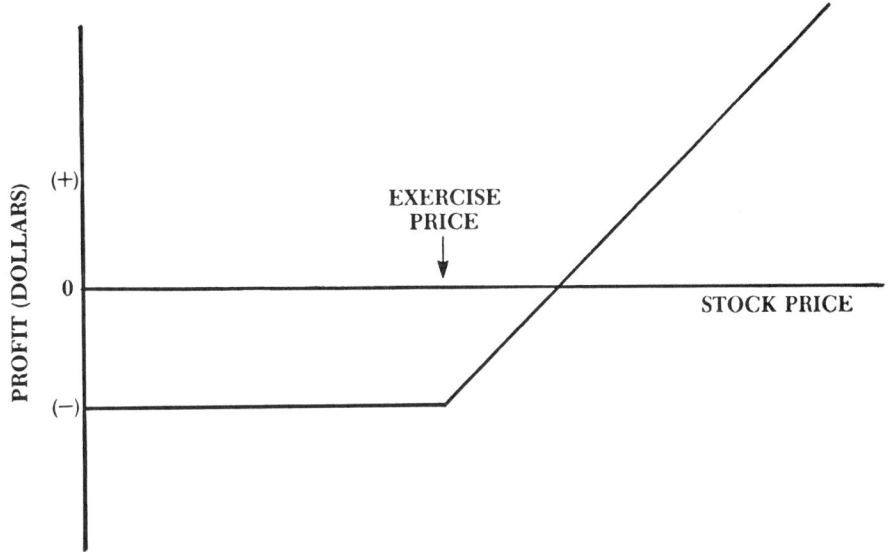

Figure 1

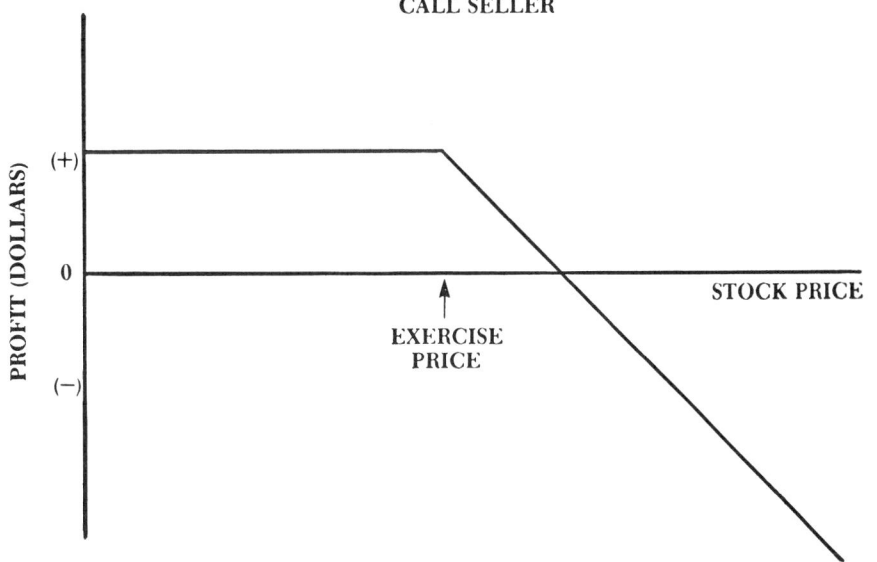

Figure 2

STOCK INDEX OPTIONS

repurchase), transaction costs are less when the option is covered through an offsetting buy transaction.

Option Diagram for Calls

A different perspective of relative pricing is presented in Exhibit S–2, the call option diagram. The curve shows how, at some period during the life of the option, the price of the call will respond to changes in the price of the underlying stock. The shaded area is the option premium which is the value of the option over and above its value if it were converted into stock.

Exhibit S–3 is the call option diagram labeled with selected option terminology. An option is said to be at-the-money when the stock price equals the exercise price. An option is out-of-the-money when the stock price is below the exercise price. Finally an option is in-the-money when the stock price exceeds the exercise price.

The intrinsic value is the value of the option if it were converted into stock. If the stock is at the exercise price or below, the option would never be exercised. It would be cheaper to buy the stock outright. Therefore the option is worthless and its intrinsic value is zero. When the option is in-the-money it can be used with the dollar amount

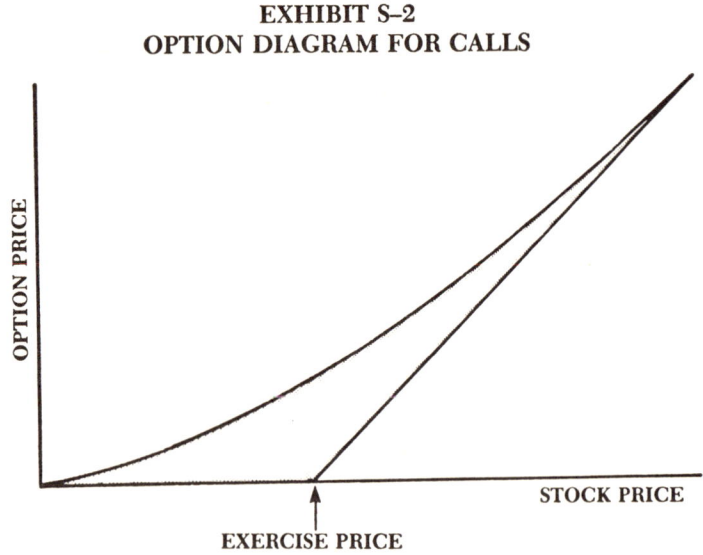

**EXHIBIT S–2
OPTION DIAGRAM FOR CALLS**

OPTION FUNDAMENTALS

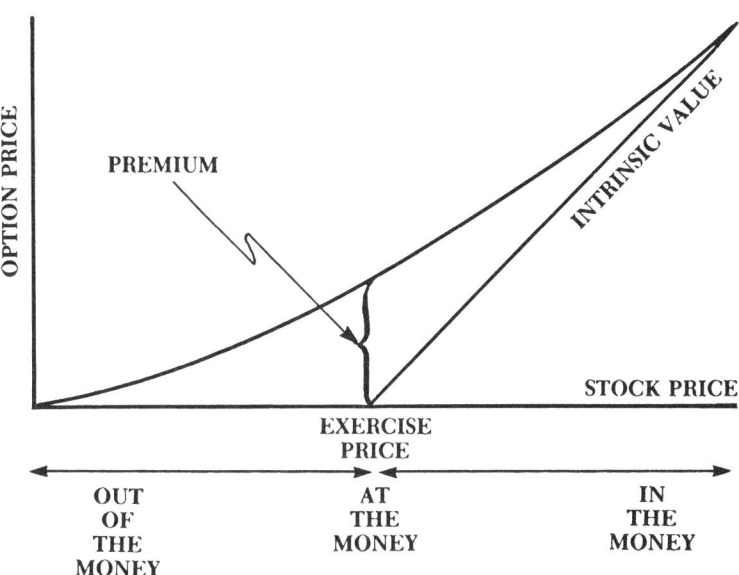

EXHIBIT S-3
OPTION TERMINOLOGY

of the exercise price to acquire stock. Therefore the options have intrinsic value which, of course, increases with increasing stock prices. For example, consider a call option with an exercise price of $20. If the stock rises to $30, the option plus $20 enables purchase of the $30 stock; therefore, the option has an intrinsic value of $10.

Even though an option may be well out-of-the-money it will still retain premium. Options have tremendous leverage and a good price move in the common stock can result in a multifold increase in the price of an option. For this reason even options well out-of-the-money exhibit some premium because of their speculative value.

DETERMINANTS OF PREMIUM LEVELS

The factors which determine option premiums have been identified and studied thoroughly. There are five such factors and fortunately all can be measured and quantified. The most significant is the relationship of the stock price to the exercise price. The other factors are stock volatility, time until expiration, the stock dividend, and the prevailing level of interest rates.

STOCK INDEX OPTIONS

Relationship of Stock Price to Exercise Price

The affect of the first factor, the relationship of the stock price to the exercise price, is clear from an examination of the option diagram. Options well out-of-the-money or options well in-the-money exhibit very low premiums. The highest premium occurs when the stock is at the exercise price.

Out-of-the-money options exhibit low premiums because there is only a small (but still finite) chance that the stock will move far enough and fast enough to give the option intrinsic value prior to expiration. In-the-money options exhibit low premiums because the price (which includes high intrinsic value) is a large percentage of the underlying stock price. Thus the option has lost one of its most desirable characteristics; namely, leverage.

Time until Expiration

The second factor which is important in option pricing is time. Options possess leverage and if the underlying stock advances the percentage increase in the option can be significantly larger. The shorter the option's life the less the likelihood that the leverage will be operative and the less premium the buyer will be willing to pay. The longer the time remaining the higher the premium.

Stock Volatility

The third factor which is important in option pricing is volatility. If the stock is very dynamic there is a good chance that, over the life of the option, it will make a major move; therefore, the option on that stock is more valuable. High volatility makes for higher option premiums.

Prevailing Interest Rate

The fourth factor influencing option premiums is the prevailing interest rate. Buying an option is similar to placing a down payment on the underlying stock. The higher the rate the more valuable this deferred financing feature becomes; therefore, the higher the interest rate the higher the option premium.

Stock Dividend

The fifth and final factor influencing option premiums is the stock dividend. High dividend stocks have options with low premiums. The

OPTION FUNDAMENTALS

shareholders are entitled to dividends which the option holder cannot receive. Thus, when high dividends are paid the stock becomes increasingly attractive *vis a vis* the option. Therefore, the higher the stock dividend the lower the option premium.

TIME VALUE

As stated earlier, time is an important element in option pricing. To clarify this relationship, options of different durations have been plotted on the option diagram in Exhibit S-4. If the option has nine months until expiration, it has a high premium and travels along a trajectory or track high in the option diagram. As the expiration date approaches, the option becomes less and less valuable and its track is correspondingly lower.

The erosion in time value is shown in different perspective in Exhibit S-5. Plotted is the time value of the option—the time value premium—as a function of the time in months remaining until expiration. The time value premium decay is not linear as one might expect. For a long-life option the premium declines rather slowly as time passes. As the option approaches expiration there is an acceleration in the rate at which premium decays.

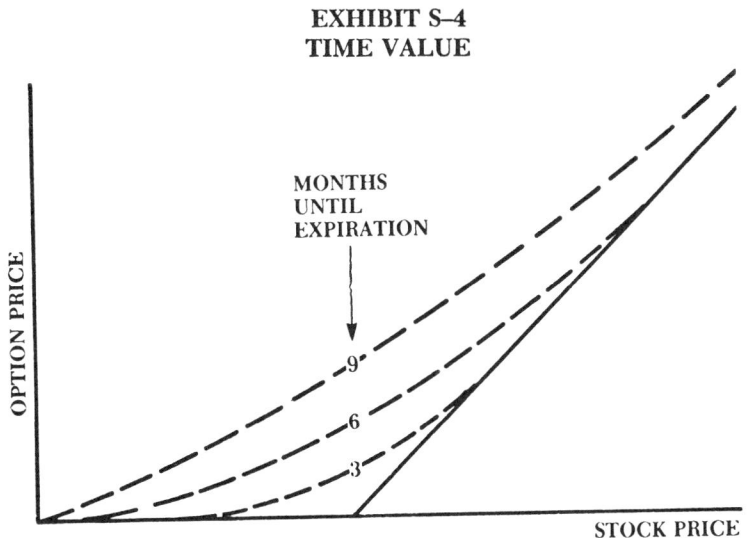

**EXHIBIT S-4
TIME VALUE**

STOCK INDEX OPTIONS

**EXHIBIT S-5
TIME VALUE PREMIUM DECAY**

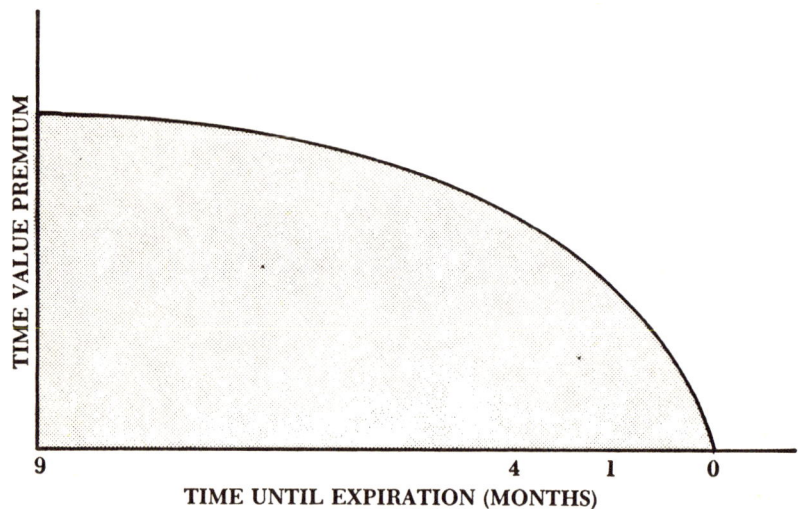

PUT OPTIONS

A put is an option to sell. It is a privilege, but not an obligation, to sell at a particular price for a specified period of time. While it is a common belief that puts are the opposite of calls, such a comparison is overly simplistic.

Put Buyers

The purchaser of a put option has contracted to sell stock at the exercise price. The forecast is lower stock prices and the objective is to buy cheap at some future point in time and to exercise the option contract enabling sale of the stock at the much higher exercise price.

Figure 1 of Exhibit S-6 shows graphically the outcome for a put option purchase. It is a plot of profit expressed in dollars as a function of the price of the underlying stock. In this example it was assumed that the stock price was at the exercise price when the transaction was entered.

As with calls, purchase of puts requires a cash outlay. At expiration, if the stock is unchanged or higher, the option will not be exercised. (This would entail buying stock in the market and selling it—putting

OPTION FUNDAMENTALS

EXHIBIT S-6
PROFIT PROFILES FOR PUT OPTION TRANSACTIONS

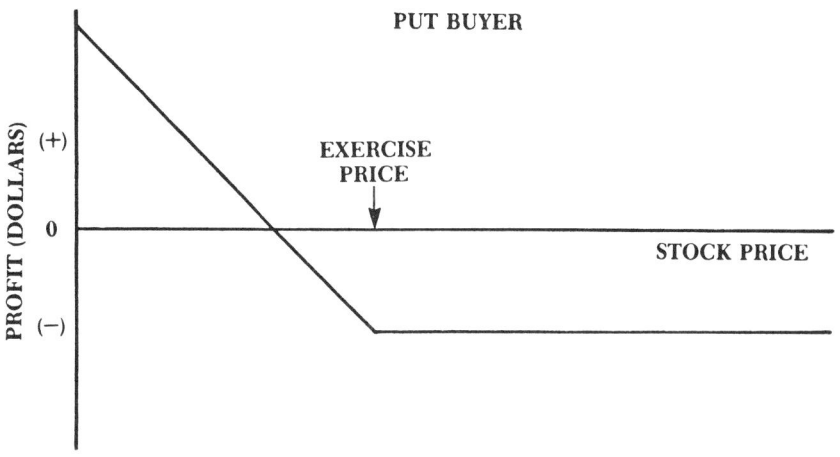

Figure 1

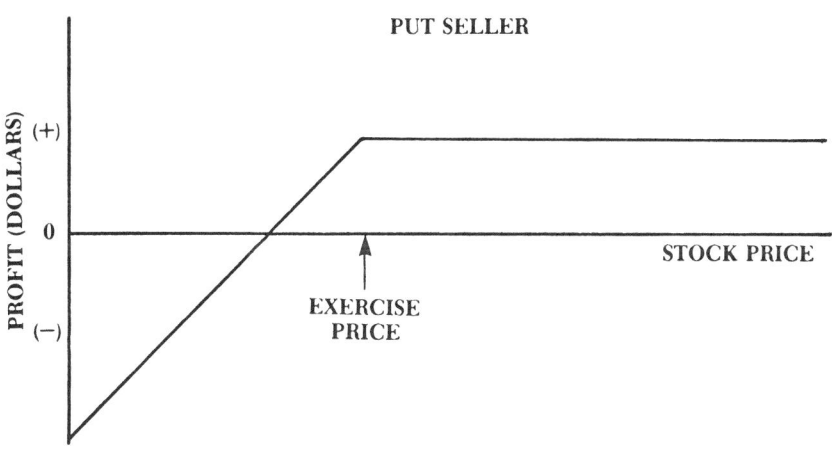

Figure 2

it—to the writer at a lower price). The original cost of the put will be the loss in the position.

If the stock declines the option privilege permits purchase of the stock in the marketplace with the opportunity to sell at the higher exercise price.

STOCK INDEX OPTIONS

The actual price of the put reflects this increase in value. Profits can be realized by closing the option position without initiating the exercise procedure.

Put Writers

The put option writer is obligated to buy stock at the exercise price no matter how low the stock might plunge. The writer's profit profile is shown in Figure 2 of Exhibit S–6.

If the stock price is unchanged when the option expires, the writer retains the proceeds from the sale of the options. Similarly if the stock advances, the buyer will not exercise the option and the writer retains the proceeds. If the stock declines, the option will be exercised. The writer must purchase stock at the exercise price which would be sold in the marketplace only at a loss.

The writer's loss position will be reflected in the option price but it is not necessary to wait for exercise to establish the loss. The option writer can buy back (cover) the position and terminate the obligation. Since the assignment procedure involves two stock commissions (purchase of the stock and subsequent resale), transaction costs are less when the option position is covered through an offsetting buy transaction.

**EXHIBIT S–7
OPTION DIAGRAM FOR PUTS**

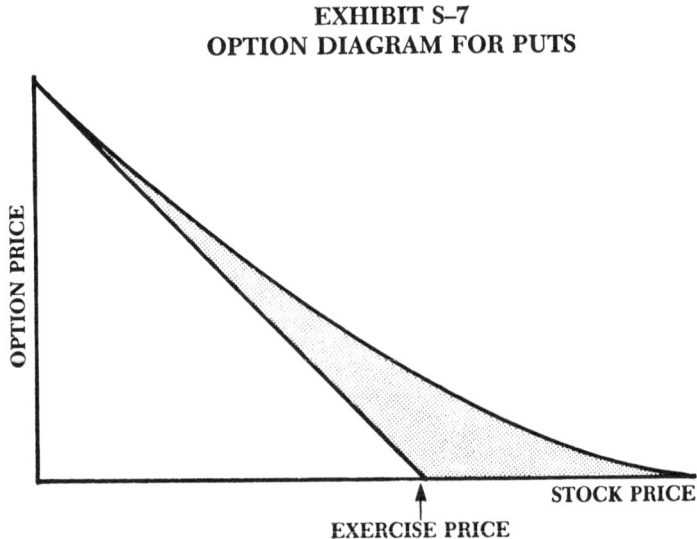

OPTION FUNDAMENTALS

Option Diagram for Puts

Exhibit S-7 is the option diagram for puts. It is the flip-flop of the call option diagram shown in Exhibit S-2. It is the put option price curve for various stock prices. Basically it shows that for declining stock prices puts acquire value and for advancing stock prices, puts become less and less valuable. Puts are purchased in anticipation of a stock price decline. Puts are sold in anticipation of a stock price advance.

STOCK OPTION TRADING

Stock options are traded on four exchanges: the American Stock Exchange, the Chicago Board Options Exchange, the Pacific Stock Exchange, and the Philadelphia Stock Exchange. Additionally, option contracts can be negotiated in the over-the-counter market. Using OTC options is cumbersome by comparison, and except in very special situations investors should be able to find options meeting their objectives within the listed sector. Options on more than 300 stocks are available on the four exchanges. A complete list of all optionable stocks is given in Appendix E.

When new options are introduced they are assigned arbitrarily to one of three expiration cycles as shown in Exhibit S-8. Each cycle has four expirations spaced three months apart. At any given time options are available for three of the four expiration months. Thus, the maximum life of any contract is nine months. When an expiration month is reached and the options expire, only two contracts remain having a life of three months and six months. At that time a new contract having a life of nine months is introduced.

EXHIBIT S-8
OPTION CYCLES

Cycle*	Expiration Months			
1	JAN	APR	JUL	OCT
2	FEB	MAY	AUG	NOV
3	MAR	JUN	SEP	DEC

* Cycles are not usually labeled 1, 2, or 3. Numbering is assigned here for pedagogical purposes only.

EXHIBIT S–9

Listed Options Quotations

Friday, June 22, 1984

Closing prices of all options. Sales unit usually is 100 shares. Security description includes exercise price. Stock close is New York or American exchange final price.

Chicago Board

Option & NY Close	Strike Price	Calls—Last Jul	Calls—Last Oct	Calls—Last Jan	Puts—Last Jul	Puts—Last Oct	Puts—Last Jan
Alcoa	30	2¾	4	4⅛	¼	¾	1¼
32⅛	35	5-16	1¼	2⅞	2½	3½	r
32⅛	40	1-16	½	r	r	r	r
32⅛	45	1-16	r	s	r	r	s
AT&T o	55	7¾	s	s	r	s	s
62⅞	60	2⅞	s	s	¼	s	s
62⅞	65	3-16	s	s	3⅝	s	s
AT&T	10	7	r	6½	r	1-16	r
17	15	2 1-16	2¼	2½	1-16	¼	½
17	20	1-16	3-16	7-16	r	r	3⅜
Atl R	40	4⅝	5⅛	r	r	⅝	r
44½	45	1⅛	2½	3⅛	1¼	r	2¾
44½	50	⅛	13-16	1¼	r	6⅛	r
44½	55	r	3-16	½	r	r	r
Avon	15	r	r	6¾	r	r	r
21¾	20	2 3-16	2 15-16	3½	⅛	¾	15-16
21¾	25	3-16	⅝	1 3-16	3¼	3¾	r
21¾	30	r	⅛	s	r	r	s
BankAm	15	¾	1 3-16	1½	¾	1⅝	1¼
14½	20	1-16	⅛	⅜	5¼	4⅝	4⅞
14½	25	1-16	r	r	r	r	r
Beth S	20	9-16	1 11-16	2½	15-16	1½	r
19⅝	25	r	r	11-16	5¼	r	r
Burl N	35	r	r	r	3-16	¾	r
39½	40	1 5-16	2¾	r	1⅝	2¼	3
39½	42½	¼	r	s	3½	r	s
39½	45	¼	1¼	r	5¾	5⅝	r
39½	47½	⅛	r	s	r	r	s
39½	50	1-16	r	s	r	r	s
ChiNw	20	r	5¼	r	⅛	r	r
23½	25	⅝	2	r	1¼	2¼	r
23½	30	r	1	r	r	r	r
CIGNA	30	r	r	r	3-16	1	1
32¾	35	¼	1	r	2¾	3	r
32¾	40	1-16	r	r	r	r	r
Citicp	25	6⅜	6½	r	⅛	9-16	¾
31¼	30	1⅜	2⅞	3½	⅝	1⅞	2⅝
31¼	35	1-16	⅞	1½	4¾	4¾	5
31¼	40	r	3-16	s	8¾	8⅞	s
Cullin	30	r	r	r	⅛	⅞	r
36¼	35	3	5⅛	r	1 1-16	1¾	r
36¼	40	⅝	2⅜	r	r	4	r
Delta	25	7½	r	r	1-16	r	r
31⅞	30	2⅛	3⅝	r	¼	1¼	1½
31⅞	35	7-16	1½	3	3¼	3½	4
31⅞	40	r	⅝	⅞	r	r	r
31⅞	45	1-16	⅛	s	r	r	s
Dig Eq	85	r	8¼	r	r	r	r
Eas Kd	60	11¼	12	13	1-16	⅜	¾
71	65	6¼	8	8⅞	⅛	⅞	1 9-16
71	70	2 5-16	4½	5⅝	1	2 1-16	3
71	75	½	2¼	3¼	r	4¾	3¼
71	80	1-16	13-16	s	r	r	s
Eckerd	25	5-16	⅞	r	r	r	r
23½	30	1-16	r	s	r	r	s
Engelh	30	¼	1	r	r	r	r
27	35	r	r	r	7½	r	r
Exxon	35	5⅝	5¾	6	1-16	¼	½
40¼	40	1⅛	2 1-16	2⅝	9-16	1¼	1⅞
40¼	45	⅛	7-16	11-16	4⅜	r	r
FedExp	25	r	r	r	1-16	¼	½
35⅜	30	5¾	6½	7⅜	3-16	¾	r
35⅜	35	1½	3⅝	4½	1⅜	2⅜	r
35⅜	40	¼	1⅞	2¾	4½	r	r
35⅜	45	r	11-16	s	r	r	s
FstChi	20	r	2⅞	r	⅜	r	r
21⅜	25	r	⅜	r	r	r	r
Fluor	15	3⅛	r	3⅞	r	r	½
17¾	20	⅛	13-16	1¼	2¼	2⅜	2¾
17¾	25	1-16	¼	7-16	r	r	r
Gt Wst	15	r	r	r	⅛	r	r

Option & NY Close	Strike Price	Calls—Last Aug	Calls—Last Nov	Calls—Last Feb	Puts—Last Aug	Puts—Last Nov	Puts—Last Feb
23⅛	25	⅛	⅜	9-16	r	r	r
CtIIII	10	¼	9-16	¾	4½	4⅝	4¾
5½	15	1-16	¼	⅜	9½	9⅜	9¼
5½	20	r	1-16	s	r	r	s
CData	25	7½	r	r	1-16	r	⅝
32¼	30	3⅜	4½	r	⅝	1⅛	r
32¼	35	⅞	2⅛	r	3¼	r	r
32¼	40	¼	⅞	s	r	r	s
CornGl	65	2¼	r	r	r	r	r
63¼	75	3-16	s	s	r	s	s
Datapt	20	2½	3¼	r	15-16	r	r
21⅛	25	⅝	r	2⅛	r	r	r
21⅛	30	⅛	r	s	r	r	s
Diebld	75	7⅝	r	r	r	r	r
81	80	3⅞	r	r	r	r	r
81	85	1⅞	r	r	r	r	r
Edwrds	15	r	r	7¼	r	r	r
22¾	20	3⅜	4	4	5-16	¾	r
22¾	25	11-16	1½	2¼	r	r	r
22¾	30	⅛	s	s	r	s	s
FptMc	15	3⅝	4	r	⅜	½	¾
17⅝	20	⅝	1½	2	2⅞	3¼	r
17⅝	25	3-16	9-16	⅞	7	r	r
Gn Dyn	40	r	r	r	r	⅜	r
50⅝	45	6½	r	r	7-16	1⅛	r
50⅝	50	2½	4¼	5	1⅝	2¾	r
50⅝	55	11-16	1¾	r	r	r	r
50⅝	60	1-16	s	s	r	s	s
Gen Fd	45	r	r	r	1-16	r	r
54⅝	50	5½	6¼	r	r	r	r
54⅝	55	1¾	2¾	3¾	r	r	r
Harris	25	2⅛	3½	r	⅞	1½	1½
25¾	30	⅜	1 5-16	r	r	r	r
Hewlet	30	r	8¼	9¼	3-16	r	r
36¼	35	3	4½	r	1	1¾	2⅛
36¼	40	13-16	2⅛	3⅛	4	4⅜	r
36¼	45	3-16	s	s	r	s	s
H Inns	45	1⅞	3½	4⅜	r	r	r
44⅛	50	½	1⅜	s	r	r	s
44⅛	55	⅛	s	s	r	s	s
Honwll	45	r	r	r	5-16	¾	r
52¾	50	5	6⅝	r	1 3-16	2	r
52¾	55	1 13-16	3¾	4⅞	3¼	3⅞	r
52¾	60	½	2	2⅝	7½	r	8¾
52¾	65	3-16	s	s	r	s	s
Humana	20	r	7⅜	r	r	r	r
27	25	3	4	r	11-16	1 5-16	1¾
27	30	9-16	1¾	2⅛	3½	r	r
In Flv	25	r	r	3⅜	r	r	r
Limitd	15	4	r	r	r	r	r
19⅜	20	⅞	2	r	r	r	r
19⅜	25	r	½	s	[illegible]	r	s
Medtrn	25	5	r	r	⅝	r	r
28⅜	30	r	r	r	2¼	r	r
28⅜	35	r	1½	r	r	r	r
Mobil	25	2¼	2⅞	3¼	¼	r	¾
27	30	¼	11-16	1⅛	2¾	3¼	r
27	35	1-16	3-16	r	r	r	r
N B I	20	r	4¼	5	15-16	1⅜	1⅞
22½	25	11-16	1 13-16	r	r	r	r
N Semi	18⅜	⅛	s	s	r	s	s
12¾	10	3¼	3¾	4⅛	⅛	7-16	⅝
12¾	15	9-16	1¼	1 11-16	2½	2⅞	3
12¾	20	1-16	⅜	¾	r	r	r
Nthrop	85	10¼	r	r	13-16	r	r
92½	90	6	8	r	2	3¼	r
92½	95	4	6⅛	r	r	r	r
92½	100	2	4⅜	5½	r	9½	r
Occi	25	4⅞	r	r	⅛	7-16	r
29⅜	30	1⅜	2 3-16	3	1½	1⅞	2½
29⅜	35	7-16	1⅛	1¾	5½	5⅝	5¾
29⅜	40	⅛	9-16	13-16	r	r	r
Ow Ill	30	2¾	3¼	r	r	⅝	r
31½	35	⅝	1	2¼	3¾	r	r

Source: *The Wall Street Journal*, June 25, 1984. Copyright 1984 by Dow Jones & Company, Inc. Reprinted by permission. All rights reserved.

OPTION FUNDAMENTALS

Exhibit S-9 illustrates option quotations as they appear daily in *The Wall Street Journal.* In the body of the listings the first options to be quoted are for Alcoa. The closing price for the stock (Friday, June 22, 1984) was 32⅛. The next column gives the various strike prices for which options are available (30, 35, 40, and 45). Listed across from the 30 dollar strike price are quotations for options at the various expiration months. The calls are: Jul 30 @ 2¾, Oct 30 @ 4, and Jan 30 @ 4⅛. The puts are: Jul 30 @ ¼, Oct 30 @ ¾, and Jan 30 @ 1¼.

An "r" entry in the listings indicates that the particular option did not trade that day while an "s" entry indicates that the option is not offered. It is not unusual for options to be inactively traded especially in the distant months and at strike prices away from the current stock price. It would be unreasonable to expect an interest in options to buy or sell Alcoa at $10 or $100. For this reason strikes are introduced near the current stock price and additional strikes are added as the stock moves above or below that level.

A code has been devised to quickly specify or identify a particular option. The code is shown in Exhibit S-10. The expiration month code contains information as to whether the option is a put or a call. The letters A through L are reserved for calls expiring January through December. The letters M through X are reserved for puts expiring January through December. Price codes are uniform for puts and calls; however, a single letter can represent more than one price. Symbols are assigned as follows:

$$\begin{matrix} \text{complete} \\ \text{option} \\ \text{specifier} \end{matrix} = \begin{matrix} \text{stock} \\ \text{symbol} \end{matrix} + \begin{matrix} \text{expiration} \\ \text{month} \\ \text{symbol} \end{matrix} + \begin{matrix} \text{exercise} \\ \text{price} \\ \text{symbol} \end{matrix}$$

As an example, the International Business Machines October call with a strike price of 110 would be identified as:

IBM JB

The October 110 put would be identified as:

IBM VB

A more detailed outline of option codes is given in Appendex I.

STOCK INDEX OPTIONS

EXHIBIT S–10
OPTION CODES

Call Code	Month	Put Code	Price Code		Price	
A	Jan	M	A	5	105	205
B	Feb	N	B	10	110	210
C	Mar	O	C	15	115	215
D	Apr	P	D	20	120	220
E	May	Q	E	25	125	225
F	Jun	R	F	30	130	230
G	Jul	S	G	35	135	235
H	Aug	T	H	40	140	240
I	Sep	U	I	45	145	245
J	Oct	V	J	50	150	250
K	Nov	W	K	55	155	255
L	Dec	X	L	60	160	260
			M	65	165	265
			N	70	170	270
			O	75	175	275
			P	80	180	280
			Q	85	185	285
			R	90	190	290
			S	95	195	295
			T	100	200	300

OPTION HEDGING

Naked options are volatile and therefore risky, speculative securities; however, when they are coupled with other securities the risk/reward characteristics can be tailored over a broad range. For purposes of this discussion an option used in conjunction with another security is called a hedge.

Depending upon which securities are grouped together, these combinations have special names. For example, a spread is a combination of two or more call options having different exercise prices or different expiration dates. Spreads can also be constructed with puts. Covered option writing is a combination of a long position in common stock coupled with the sale of a call option on the same stock. Protective puts are puts purchased in conjunction with a long position in the common stock. Straddles are combinations of puts and calls.

OPTION FUNDAMENTALS

Covered Writing

Ownership of stock combined with the sale of options on that stock on a one-for-one basis is known as covered writing. While the purpose of this strategy is often advertised as a means of augmenting portfolio income, that description is less than precise. Covered writing alters the risk/reward characteristics of stock ownership trading off upside potential for a decrease in downside exposure to loss.

Exhibit S-11 shows diagrammatically the mechanics of covered writing. Figure 1 is the profit profile for outright ownership of common stock. The only information conveyed by the diagram is that when the stock price advances a profit accrues and when the stock price declines a loss results. Figure 2 of Exhibit S-11 shows the profit profile resulting from the sale of a call option. Proceeds of the option sale are retained by the writer if the underlying stock is unchanged or declines. A loss results if the underlying stock advances. Figure 3 of Exhibit S-11 shows the outcome at expiration for the two positions combined. If the underlying stock price is unchanged the premium received is the only profit component. If the stock advances, the resulting gain is offset by the loss on the option. The profit profile is flat on the upside no matter how far the stock advances. On the downside the loss on the stock is cushioned by the option premium received. If the stock drops by an amount greater than this premium a net loss results.

Protective Puts

One of the most useful applications of put options is to insure long positions. The strategy is diagrammed in Exhibit S-12. At-the-money or slightly out-of-the-money puts are purchased in conjunction with a long position in the underlying stock. The puts "kick in" as the stock declines and thus offset the loss. Unfortunately puts are not cheap insurance and this is the major shortcoming of the strategy. Unless the investor is fairly accurate in timing put purchases, repetitive premium costs may be more detrimental than the loss which the insurance is intended to prevent.

Figure 1 of Exhibit S-12 is, once again, the profit profile for outright ownership of common stock. It shows that when the stock price advances, a profit accrues and when the stock price declines a loss results. Figure 2 of Exhibit S-12 is the profit profile for the purchase of a put option. If the stock price is unchanged or higher the total premium paid is forgone and is a loss. If the stock declines a profit accrues.

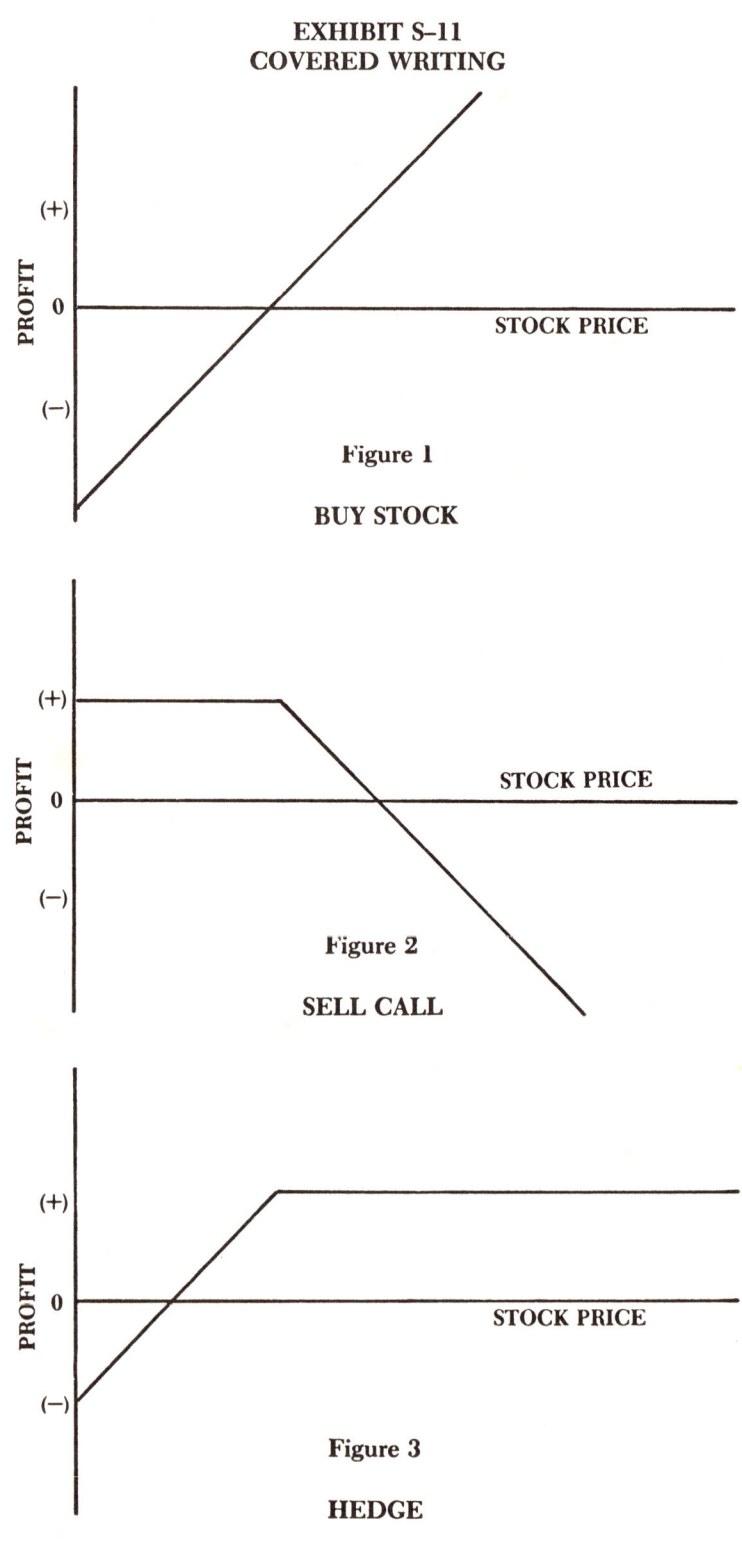

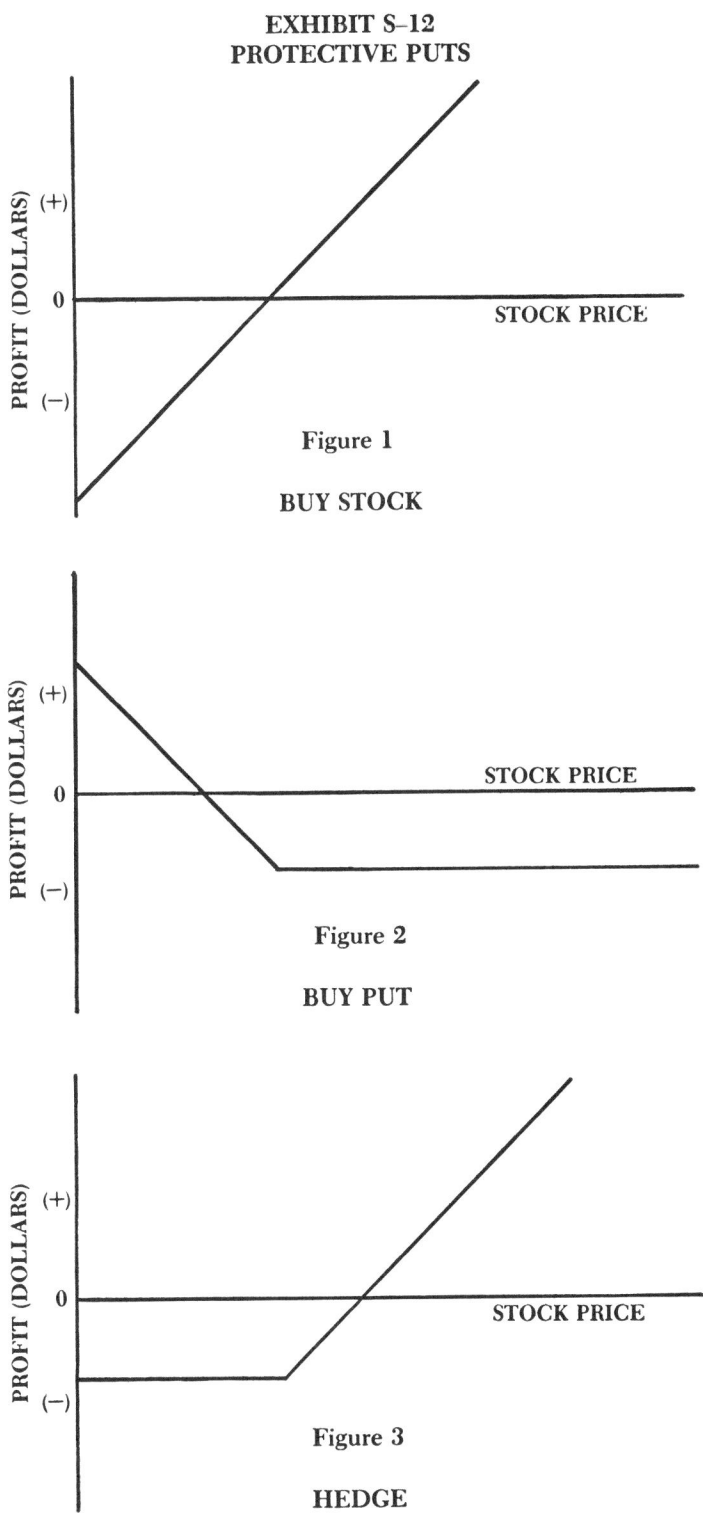

STOCK INDEX OPTIONS

Figure 3 of Exhibit S-12 shows the outcome at expiration for the two positions combined. If the underlying stock price is unchanged, the premium paid for the put is the only loss component. The same is also true if the stock is at any lower price. On the upside, however, the potential of the stock is not limited. The profit is merely reduced by the amount paid for the puts initially.

Straddles

A straddle is a combination of a put and a call. Straddles can be purchased which consists of buying a put and a call and straddles can be sold which consists of writing a put and a call.

Straddle Purchase

To purchase a straddle an investor buys equal quantities of both puts and calls on the same stock at the same exercise price. The purchase of a straddle is undertaken when the investor is on the fence; that is, a major move in the stock is anticipated but the direction of the move is uncertain. A more accurate justification for purchasing straddles is a perceived increase in the volatility of the underlying stock.

The mechanics of straddle purchases are shown in Exhibit S-13. Figure 1 is the profit profile for the purchase of a call. Figure 2 is the profit profile for the purchase of a put. Figure 3 of Exhibit S-13 is the outcome for the two positions combined. If a major move materializes, the investment is outstanding, especially in view of the limited initial investment. If the market is unchanged, the loss is 100 percent of the dollars invested.

Straddles are purchased when an increase in the stock's volatility is anticipated. Such a prediction, however, must be correct time and again; if not, and the strategy is repeated often enough, the frequent losses will just balance the occasional windfalls.

Straddle Sale

To write a straddle an investor sells equal quantities of both puts and calls on the same stock at the same exercise price. The sale of a straddle is undertaken when the investor anticipates the stock to be trendless and in a narrow trading range. A more accurate justification for selling straddles is a perceived decrease in the volatility of the underlying stock.

The mechanics of straddle sales are shown in Exhibit S-14. Figure

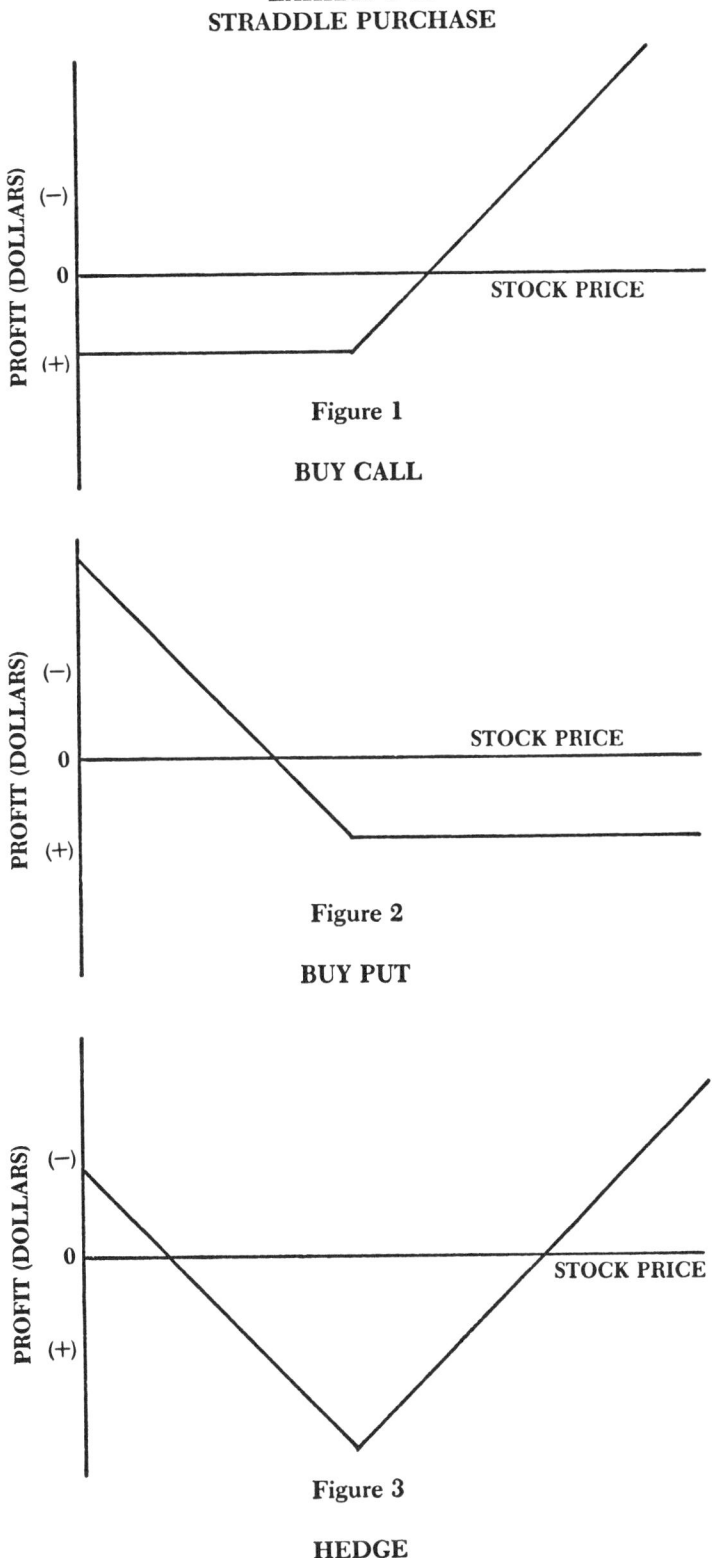

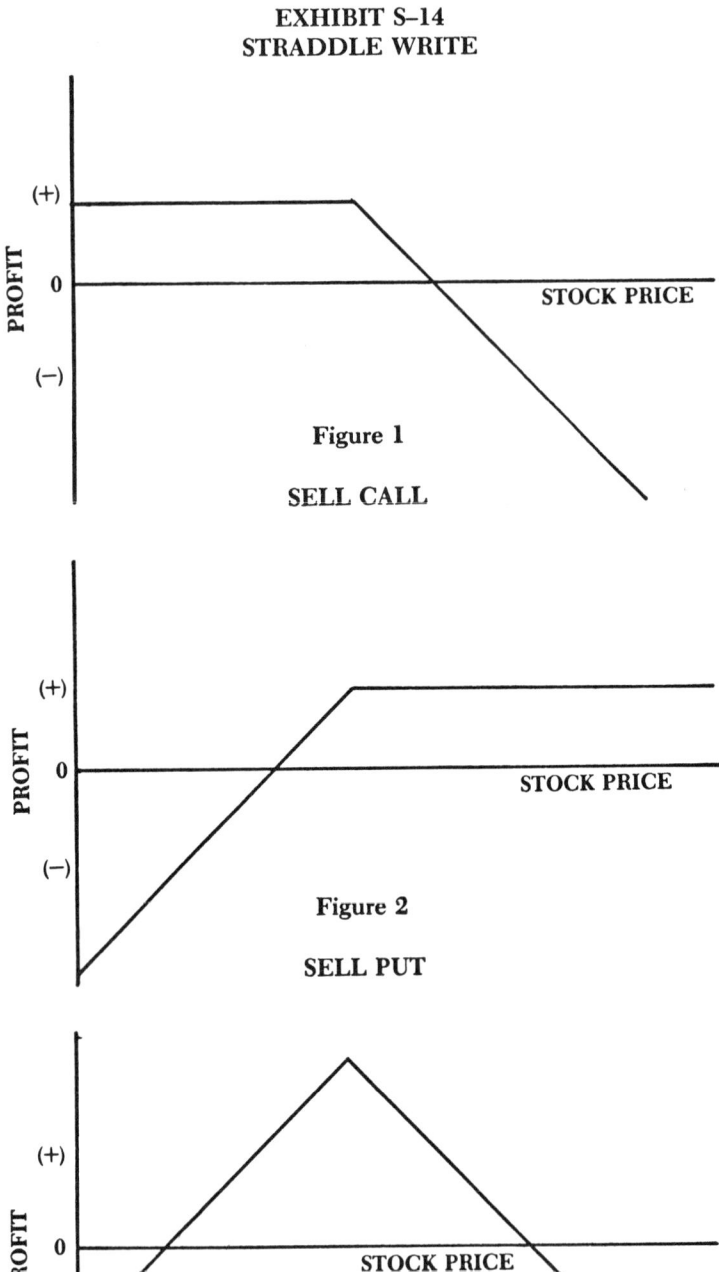

OPTION FUNDAMENTALS

1 is the profit profile for the purchase of a call. Figure 2 is the profit profile for the purchase of a put. Figure 3 of Exhibit S–14 is the outcome for the two positions combined. If the stock is unchanged at expiration, the investment is outstanding; however, a major move in the stock in either direction will result in substantial losses.

Straddles are sold when a decrease in the stock's volatility is anticipated; however, the market's best judgment of present and future volatility is already programmed into the current option price. The tent shaped profit profiles are, of course, highest and widest when option premiums are high. But option premiums are proportional to the volatility of the underlying stock so risk of an adverse move also increases. If the investor is correct about future volatility then this strategy will produce profits regularly. However, if future volatility does not drop, gains from those cases when the market is relatively unchanged will be offset by losses when the market moves significantly.

Writing straddles can be tricky business. Whipsaws have caused more than one investor to be burned in both sides of the hedge. If the stock makes a major move in one direction, the temptation is to close out the losing position and retain the remaining option with the intent of capturing all of its time value premium. The stock then makes a major reversal driving the other leg into a loss position as well.

APPENDIXES

APPENDIX A

OPTIONABLE INDEXES

AMEX COMPUTER TECHNOLOGY INDEX

The Amex Computer Technology Index is a narrow-based capitalization-weighted index that measures computer industry performance through changes in the aggregate market value of 30 leading U.S. corporations involved in various phases of the computer industry.

The Computer Technology Index is market-value weighted. The impact of a component issue's price change is proportional to the issue's overall market value (share price × number of shares outstanding).

The Computer Technology Index was introduced with a benchmark value of 100 as of July 29, 1983.

AMEX COMPUTER TECHNOLOGY INDEX—COMPONENT STOCKS

Advanced Micro Devices	Mohawk Data Sciences
Amdahl	Motorola
Automatic Data Processing	National Semiconductor
Burroughs	NBI, Inc.
Commodore International	NCR Corporation
Computer Sciences	Paradyne
Control Data	Prime Computer
Cray Research	Sperry Corporation
Data General	Storage Technology
Datapoint	Tandy
Digital Equipment	Telex
Electronic Data Systems	Texas Instruments
Hewlett-Packard	Tymshare
Honeywell	Wang Laboratories, Cl. B.
International Business Machines	Xerox

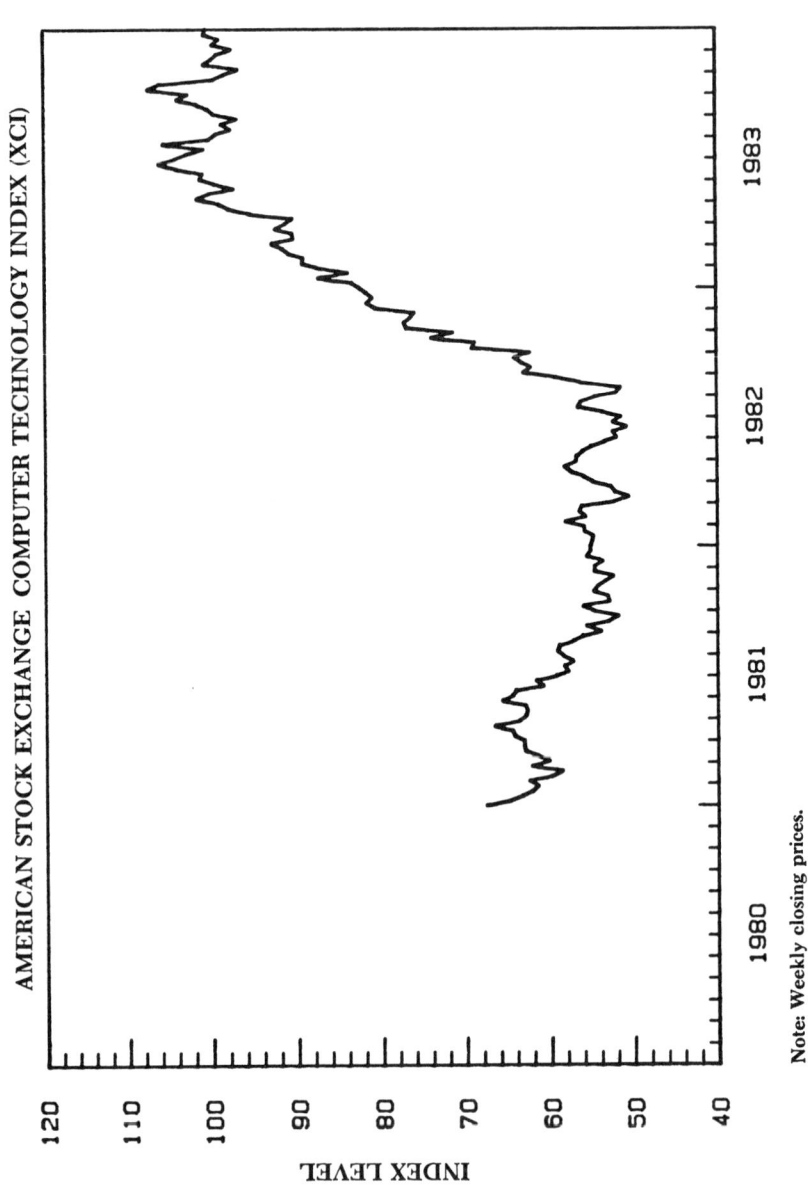

OPTIONABLE INDEXES

AMEX MAJOR MARKET INDEX

The Amex Major Market Index is a broad-based price-weighted average of 20 well-known blue chip stocks. It is designed to measure the market performance of major U.S. industrial corporations.

The Major Market Index is price-weighted. Changes in the index correspond to percentage changes in the sum of the prices of the component stocks.

AMEX MAJOR MARKET INDEX—COMPONENT STOCKS

* American Express	* International Paper
* American Telephone & Telegraph	Johnson and Johnson
Coca Cola	* Merck
Dow Chemical	* Minnesota Mining & Manufacturing
* duPont	Mobil
* Eastman Kodak	Philip Morris
* Exxon	* Procter and Gamble
* General Electric	* Sears, Roebuck
* General Motors	* Standard Oil of California
* International Business Machines	* United States Steel

* Included in the Dow Jones Industrial Average

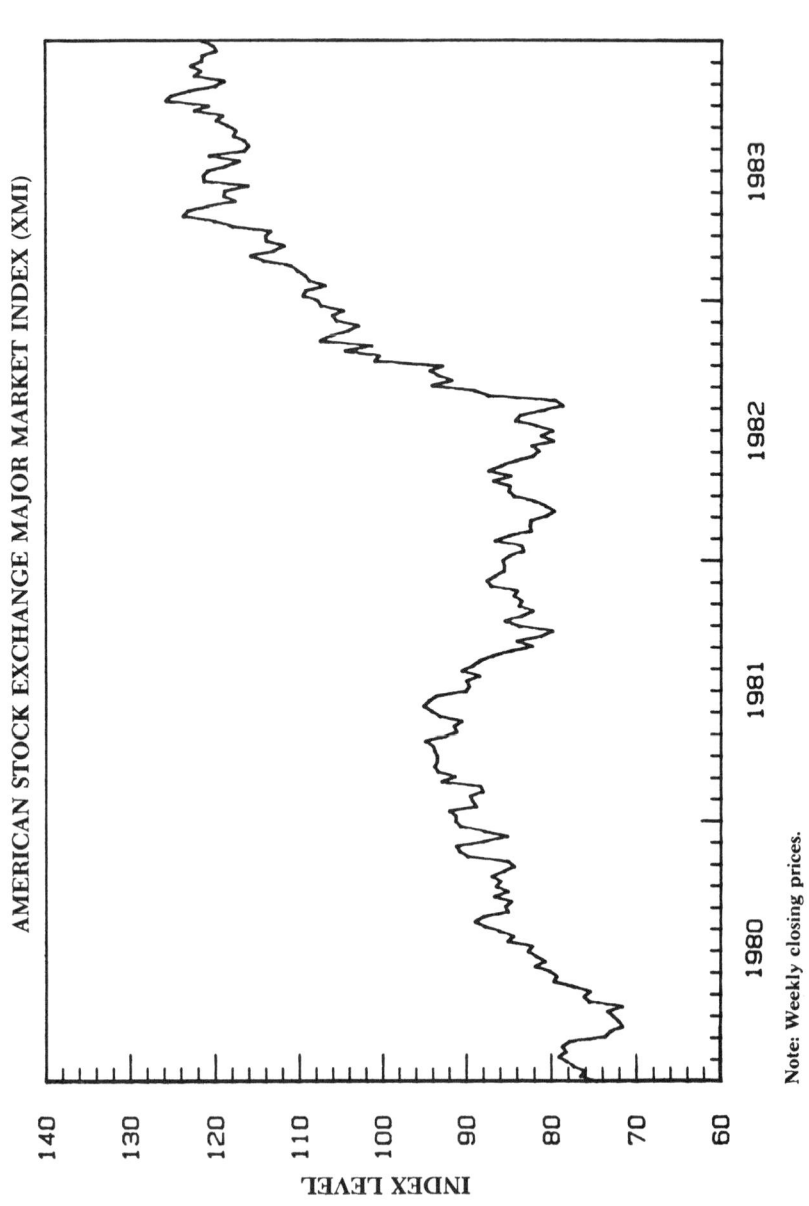

OPTIONABLE INDEXES

AMEX MARKET VALUE INDEX

The Amex Market Value Index is a broad-based capitalization-weighted index that measures the changes in the aggregate market value of the 800-plus common stocks, ADRs and warrants listed on the American Stock Exchange.

The index is market-value weighted. The impact of a component issue's price change is proportional to the issue's overall market value (share price × number of shares outstanding).

The index was introduced at a base level of 100 in September 1973 and was adjusted to one half of its previous level in July 1983. As a result, changes in the index are now measured against an adjusted base level of 50.

One unique aspect of the index design is that cash dividends paid by a component stocks are reflected in the index; that is, they are treated as if "reinvested." The index therefore reflects the total return of its components.

AMEX MARKET VALUE INDEX— COMPONENT ISSUE INDUSTRY GROUPS

Issue	Percent of Total Index Value*
Natural Resources	36.17
High Technology	15.47
Service	11.80
Consumer Goods	10.18
Capital Goods	6.55
Financial	5.03
Housing, Construction, Land	4.66
Retail	3.42
Unclassified	6.72
	100.00

* As of 2/29/84

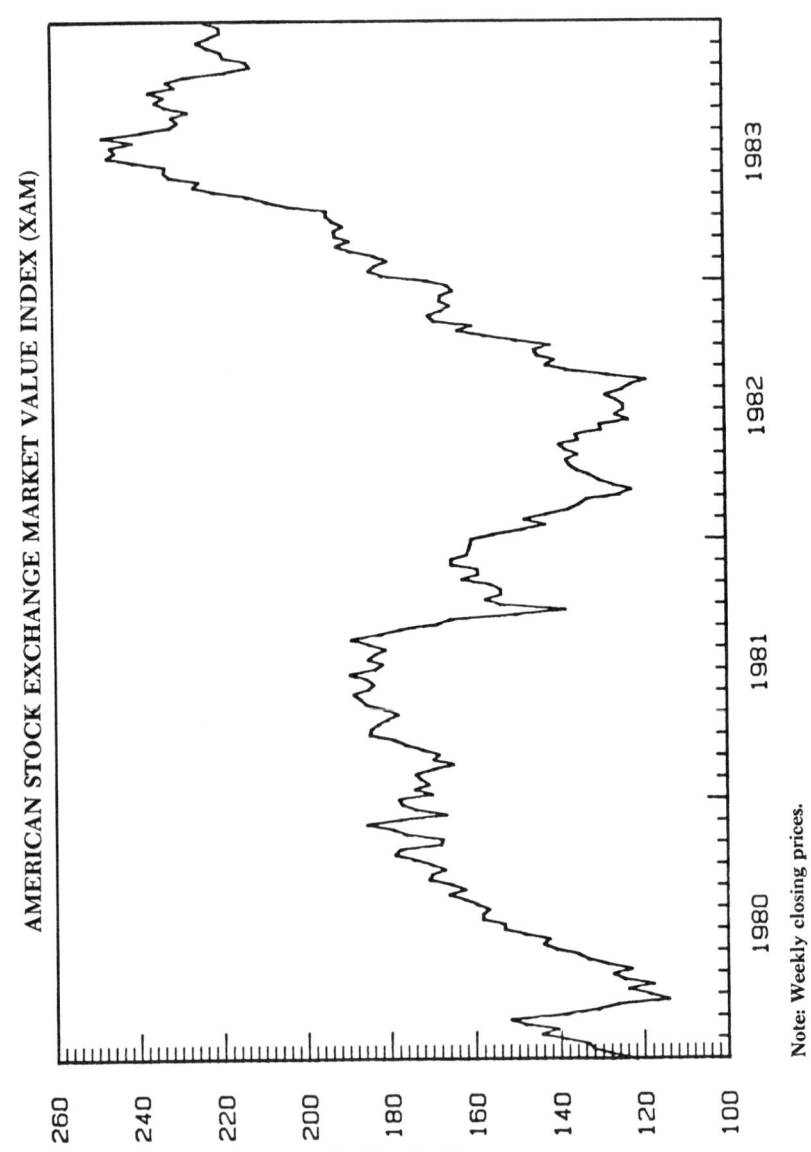

OPTIONABLE INDEXES

AMEX OIL AND GAS INDEX

The Amex Oil and Gas Index is a narrow-based capitalization-weighted index that measures oil and gas performance through changes in the aggregate market value of 30 leading U.S. corporations involved in various phases of the oil and gas industry.

The Oil and Gas Index is market-value weighted. The impact of a component issue's price change is proportional to the issue's overall market value (share price × number of shares outstanding).

The Oil and Gas Index was introduced with a benchmark value of 100 as of July 29, 1983.

AMEX OIL AND GAS INDEX—COMPONENT STOCKS

Amerada Hess	Pennzoil
Apache Corporation	Phillips Petroleum
Atlantic Richfield	Pogo Producing
Diamond Shamrock	Royal Dutch Petroleum
Exxon Corporation	Sabine Corporation
Gulf Oil	Shell Oil
Imperial Oil	Standard Oil of California
Inexco Oil	Standard Oil of Indiana
Kerr McGee	Standard Oil of Ohio
Louisiana Land	Sun Company
Mesa Petroleum	Superior Oil
Mitchell Energy	Texaco
Mobil Corporation	Texas Oil and Gas
Noble Affiliates	Tosco Corporation
Occidental Petroleum	Unocal Corporation

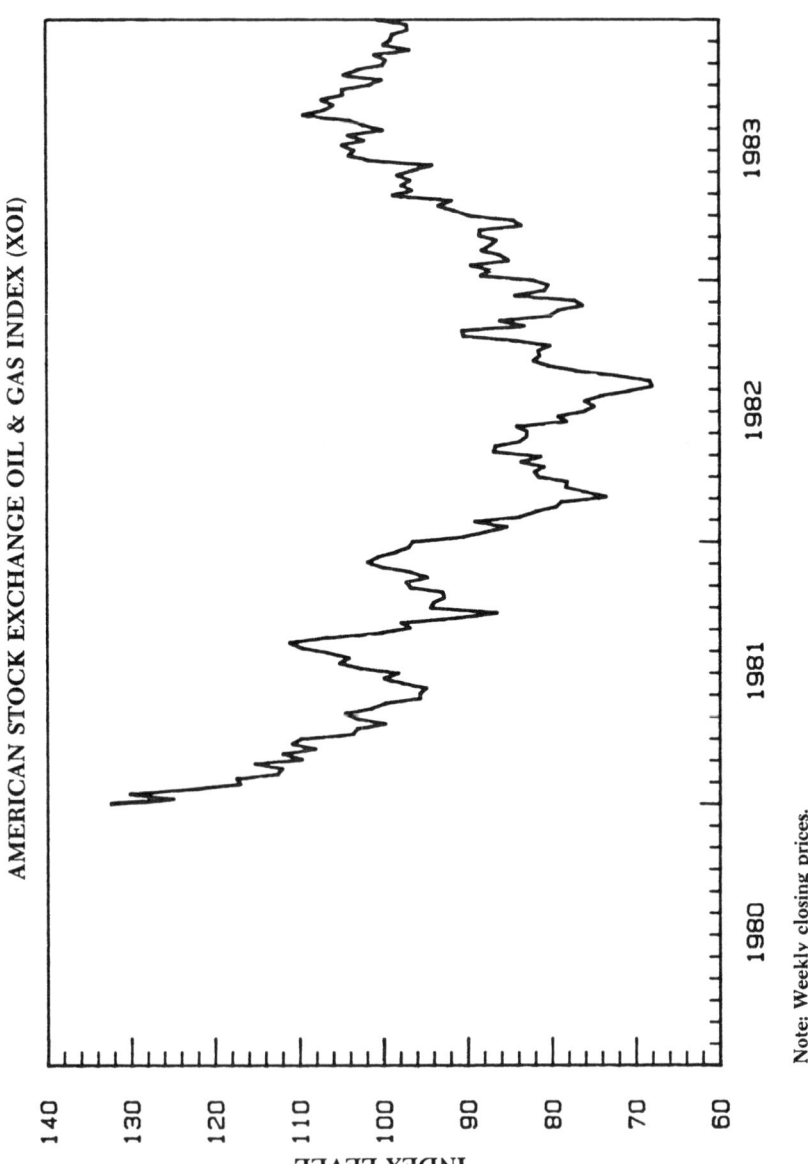

OPTIONABLE INDEXES

AMEX TRANSPORTATION INDEX

The Amex Transportation Index is a narrow-based price-weighted index that measures the performance of the transportation industry through changes in the sum of the prices of 20 widely-held and actively traded corporations involved in a number of diversified transportation systems.

The Transportation Index was introduced with a benchmark value of 150 as of December 30, 1983.

AMEX TRANSPORTATION INDEX—COMPONENT STOCKS

* AMR Corp.
* Burlington Northern
* CSX Corp.
* Canadian Pacific
* Carolina Freight
  Chicago & Northwestern Transportation
* Consolidated Freightways
* Delta Air Lines
* Federal Express
* Norfolk Southern Corp.
* Northwest Airlines
* Overnite Transportation Co.
  RLC Corp.
* Santa Fe Southern Pacific
* Transway International Corp.
* Trans World Corp.
* UAL, Inc.
* US Air Group
* Union Pacific Corp.
  Western Air Lines

* A Component of the Dow Jones Transportation Average

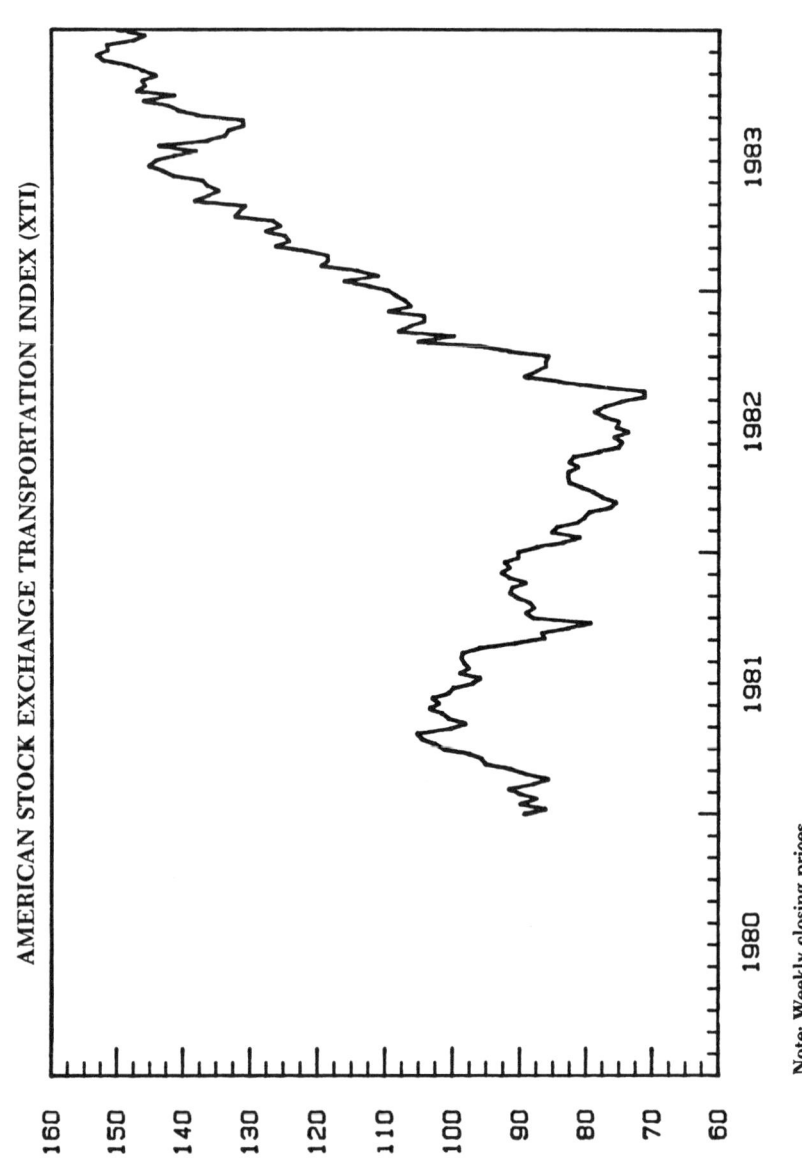

OPTIONABLE INDEXES

NEW YORK STOCK EXCHANGE COMPOSITE INDEX

The New York Stock Exchange Composite Index is a broad-based capitalization-weighted index that measures the changes in the aggregate market value of the 1500-plus common stocks listed on the New York Stock Exchange.

The NYSE Index is market-value weighted. The impact of a component issue's price change is proportional to the issue's overall market value (share price × number of shares outstanding).

The NYSE Index was introduced with a benchmark value of 50 as of December 31, 1965.

NYSE COMPOSITE INDEX
TEN LARGEST COMPONENTS*

Issue	Percent of market value of all NYSE listed common stocks
International Business Machines	4.70%
Exxon Corp.	2.37
General Electric Co.	1.69
General Motors Corp.	1.39
Shell Oil	1.16
Standard Oil of Indiana	1.14
Schlumberger, Ltd.	1.08
American Telephone & Telegraph	1.01
Mobil Corp.	0.88
Standard Oil of California	0.87

* As of 3/30/84

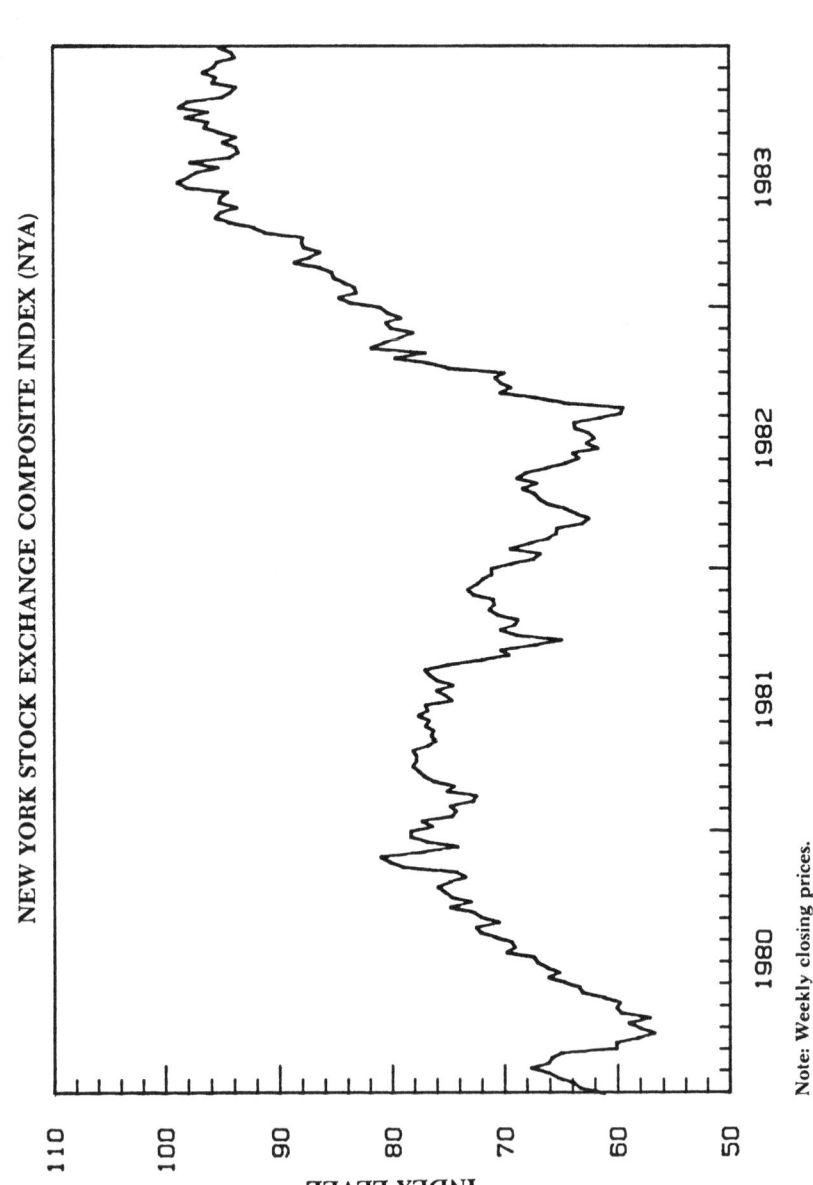

Note: Weekly closing prices.

OPTIONABLE INDEXES

NEW YORK STOCK EXCHANGE TELEPHONE INDEX

The NYSE Telephone Index is a narrow-based capitalization-weighted index of the common stocks of the companies which comprised the "old" AT&T.

The NYSE Telephone Index was introduced with a benchmark value of 100 as of December 30, 1983, the last trading day before the AT&T divestiture.

NEW YORK STOCK EXCHANGE TELEPHONE INDEX—COMPONENT STOCKS

American Telephone & Telegraph
American Information Technologies
Bell Atlantic
Bell South
NYNEX Corp.
Pacific Telesis
Southwestern Bell
U S West Inc.

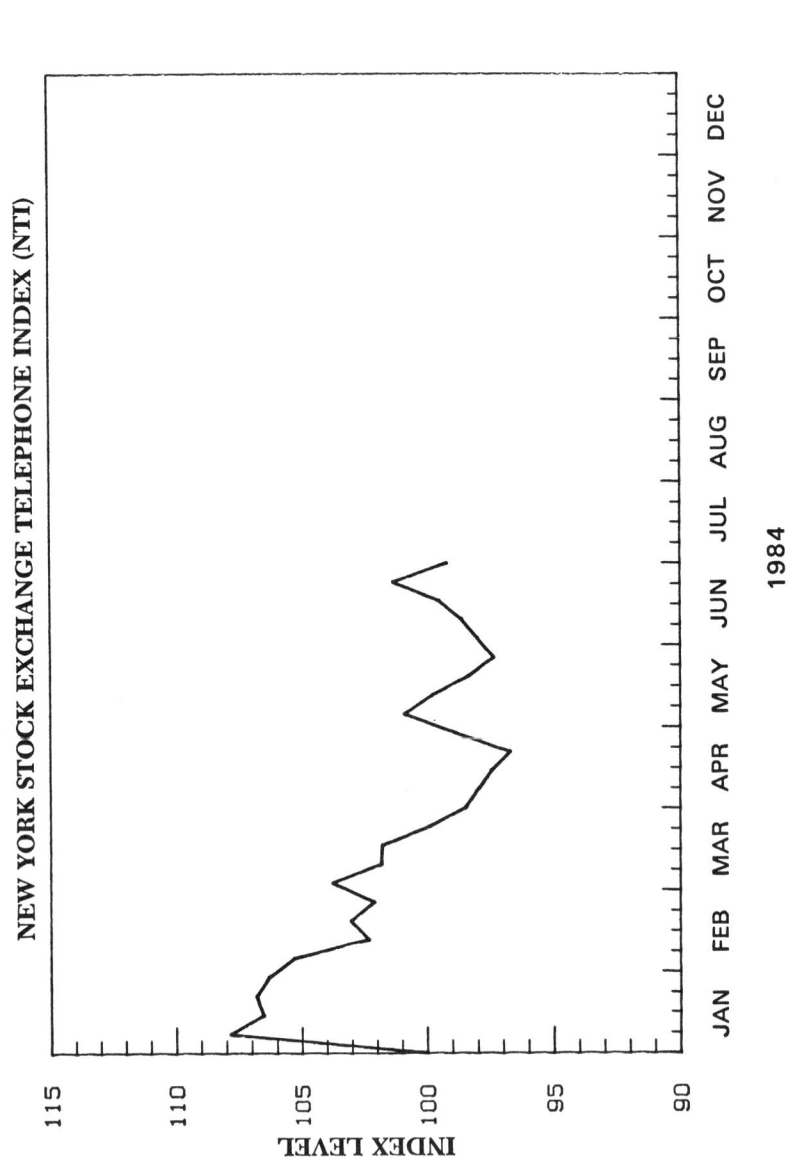

OPTIONABLE INDEXES

PACIFIC STOCK EXCHANGE TECHNOLOGY INDEX

The Pacific Stock Exchange Technology Index is a broad-based price-weighted average of 100 securities representing a broad spectrum of companies principally engaged in manufacturing or service-related products within advanced technology fields.

The index value is derived by summing the prices per share of each of the underlying securities included in the index, and dividing by a divisor. The divisor is adjusted only in order to maintain the continuity of the index.

PACIFIC STOCK EXCHANGE TECHNOLOGY INDEX—
COMPONENT STOCKS

ADAC Laboratories
Advanced Micro Devices, Inc.
Altos Computer Systems
Amdahl Corporation
Analog Devices, Inc.
Apollo Computer, Inc.
Apple Computer, Inc.
Applied Magnetics Corporation
Applied Materials, Inc.
ASK Computer Systems, Inc.
Avantek, Inc.
AVX Corporation
BMC Industries, Inc.
Burroughs Corporation
Centronics Data Computer Corp.
Cetus Corporation
Cipher Data Products, Inc.
Cobe Laboratories, Inc.
Commodore International Limited
Communications Industries, Inc.
Communications Satellite Corp.
Computer & Communications Technology
Computervision Corporation
Conrac Corporation
Control Data Corporation
Control Laser Corporation
Convergent Technologies, Inc.
Corvus Systems, Inc.
CPT Corporation
Cray Research, Inc.
Data I/O Corporation
Data General Corporation
Datapoint Corporation
Datum, Inc.
Digital Equipment Corporation
Dysan Corporation
Electro-Biology, Inc.
Electronic Associates, Inc.
Electronic Memories & Magnetics Corp.
Evans & Sutherland Computer Corp.
Finnigan Corporation
Floating Point Systems, Inc.
Flow General, Inc.
Fluke (John) Manufacturing Co., Inc.
Fortune Systems Corporation
GCA Corporation
Genentech, Inc.
General DataComm Industries, Inc.
GenRad, Inc.
Gould, Inc.
Granger Associates
Harris Corporation
Healthdyne, Inc.
Hewlett-Packard Company
Honeywell, Inc.
Hybritech, Inc.
Information Displays, Inc.
Intel Corporation
Intergraph Corporation
Intermedics, Inc.
International Business Machines
Lexidata Corporation
Medtronic, Inc.
Micom Systems, Inc.
Millipore Corporation
Modular Computer Systems, Inc.
Monolithic Memories, Inc.
Motorola, Inc.
National Micronetics, Inc.
National Semiconductor Corporation
NBI, Inc.
NCR Corporation
Network Systems Corporation
Nicolet Instrument Corporation
Novo Industri A/S
ONYX + IMI Incorporated
Paradyne Corporation
Perkin-Elmer Corporation
Prime Computer, Inc.
Quantum Corporation
Rogers Corporation
Scientific-Atlanta, Inc.
Seagate Technology
Silicon Systems, Inc.
Spectra-Physics, Inc.
Sperry Corporation
Standard Microsystems Corporation
Storage Technology
Tandem Computers Incorporated
Tandon Corporation
Tektronix, Inc.
TeleVideo Systems, Inc.
Telex Corporation
Teradyne, Inc.
Texas Instruments
Timeplex Communications, Inc.
Varian Associates, Inc.
Vector Graphic, Inc.
Verbatim Corporation
Wang Laboratories, Inc.

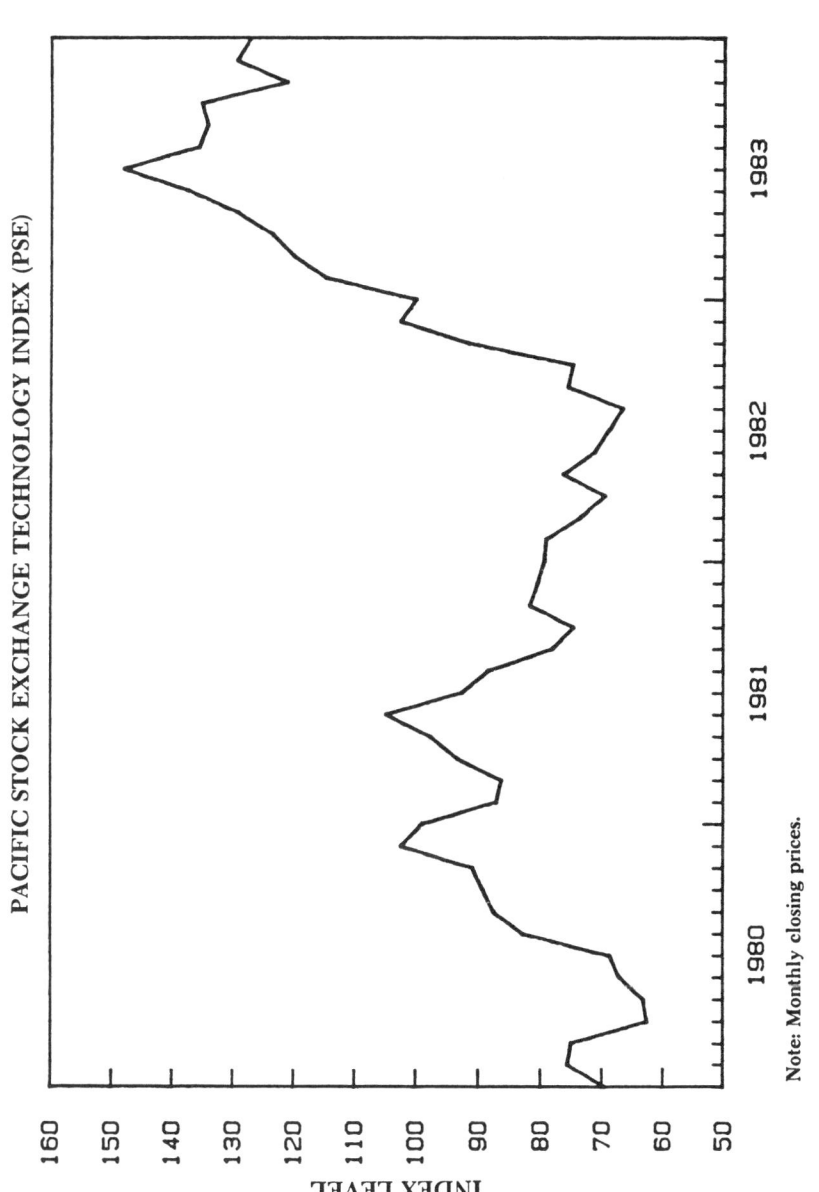

STOCK INDEX OPTIONS

PHILADELPHIA STOCK EXCHANGE GAMING/HOTEL INDEX

The Philadelphia Stock Exchange Gaming/Hotel Index is a narrow-based capitalization-weighted index of nine stocks designed to represent a cross section of widely-held U.S. corporations involved in various phases of the gaming and hotel industries.

PHILADELPHIA STOCK EXCHANGE GAMING/HOTEL INDEX—COMPONENT STOCKS

Showboat
Resorts International
Bally
Caesar's World
Golden Nugget
Hilton Hotels
Holiday Inns
MGM Grand Hotels
Ramada Inns

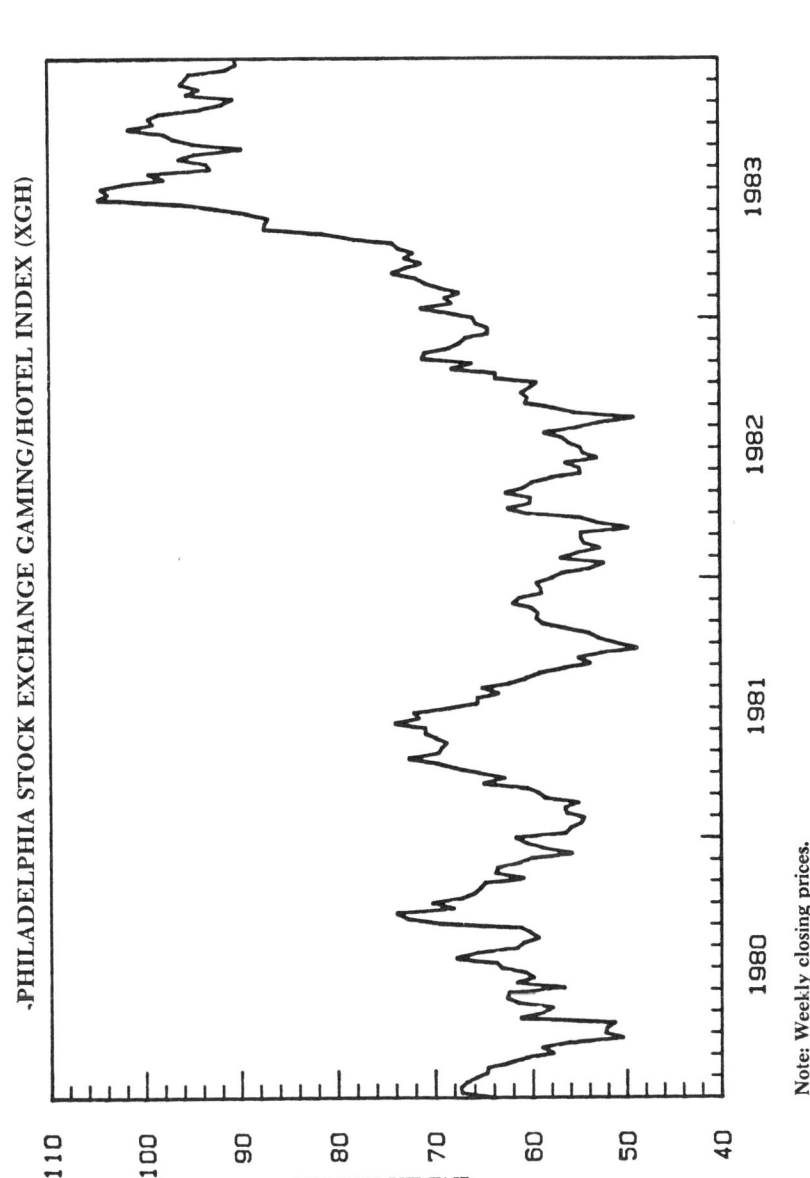

STOCK INDEX OPTIONS

PHILADELPHIA STOCK EXCHANGE GOLD/SILVER INDEX

The Philadelphia Stock Exchange Gold/Silver Index is a narrow-based capitalization-weighted index of seven stocks designed to represent a cross section of widely-held U.S. corporations involved primarily in the mining of gold/silver.

PHILADELPHIA STOCK EXCHANGE GOLD/SILVER INDEX—COMPONENT STOCKS

ASA Ltd.
Callahan Mining
Campbell Red Lake
Dome Mines
Hecla Mining
Homestake Mining
Sunshine Mining

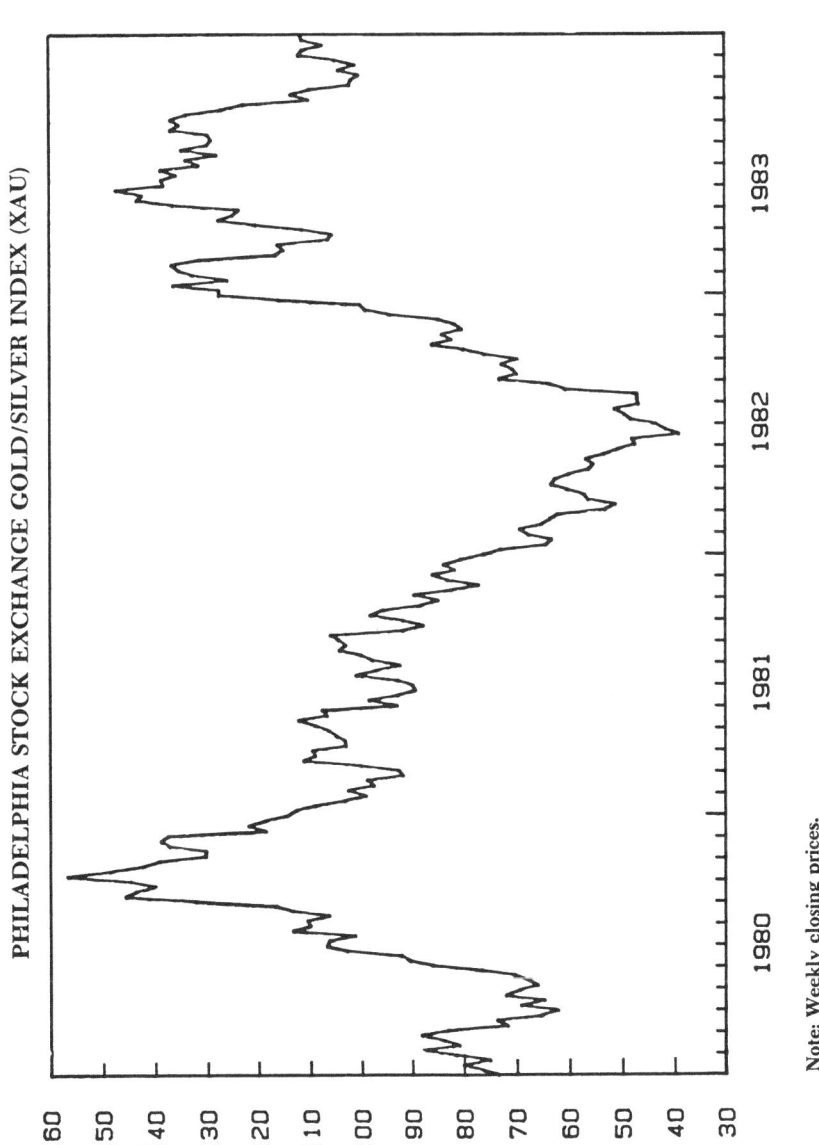
Note: Weekly closing prices.

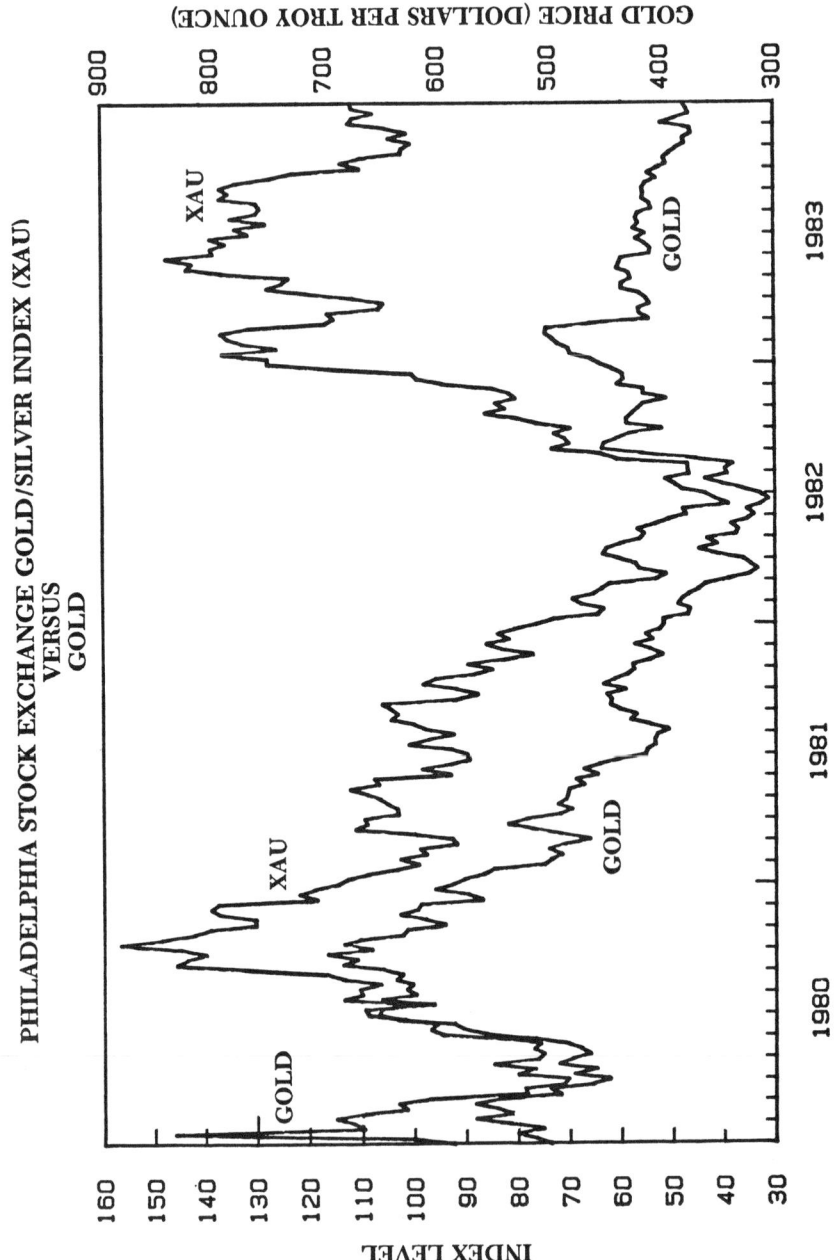

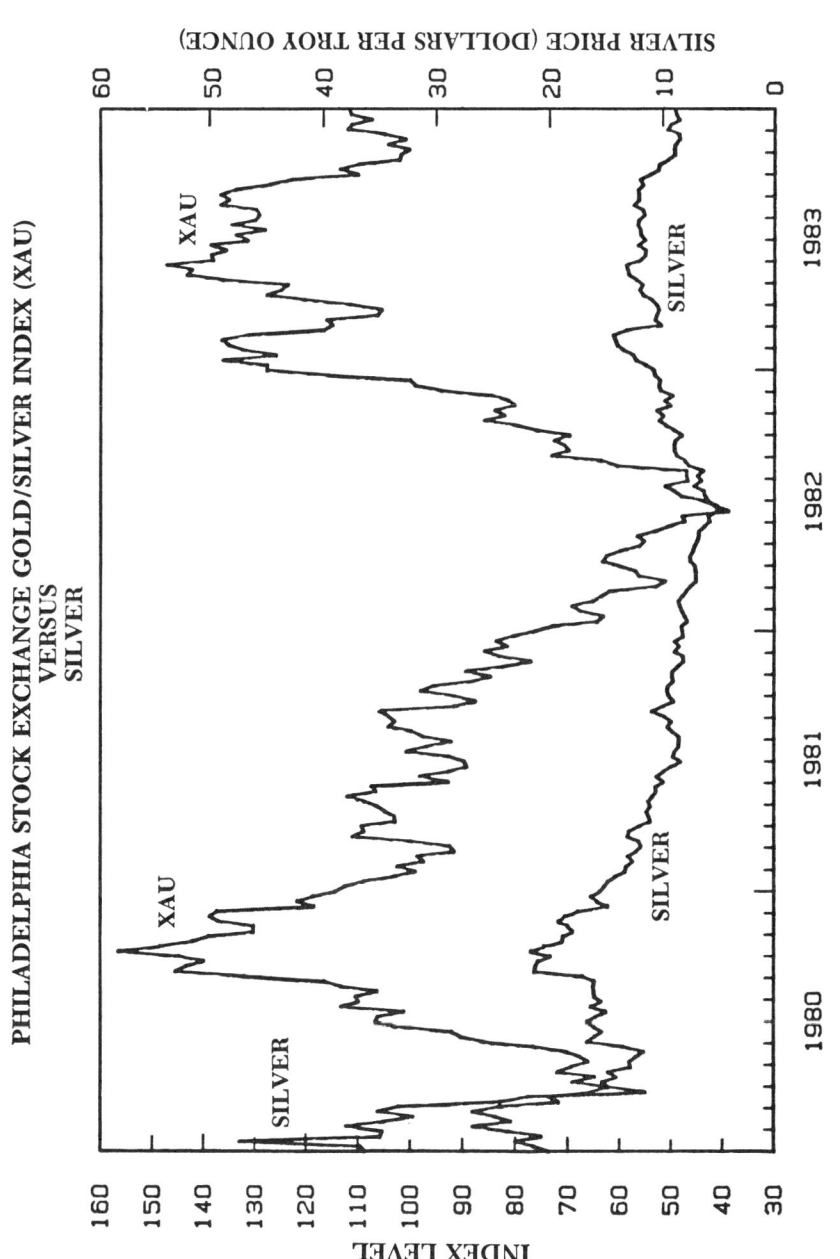

STOCK INDEX OPTIONS

S&P 100 INDEX

The S&P 100 Index is a broad-based capitalization-weighted index that measures changes in the market value of 100 stocks on which options are currently listed on the CBOE. It is intended to be a broad, highly representative index of the market as a whole.

In computing the S&P 100, the current market price of each of the stocks in the index is multiplied by its number of outstanding shares. The resulting market values are then added to determine the aggregate market value of the stocks comprising the index. To determine the current value of the S&P 100 Index, the aggregate market value is divided by the base value and multiplied by 100. The S&P 100 base value initially was based on the aggregate market value of the 100 stocks as of January 2, 1976.

S&P 100 STOCK INDEX—COMPONENT STOCKS

Aluminum Co. of America
American Electric Power
American Express
American Hospital Supply
American Telephone & Telegraph
AMP
Atlantic Richfield
Avon Products
BankAmerica
Baxter Travenol Labs
Bethlehem Steel
Black & Decker
Boeing
Boise Cascade
Bristol-Myers
Brunswick
Burlington Northern
Burroughs
Champion International
CIGNA
Citicorp
Coca Cola
Colgate-Palmolive
Commonwealth Edison
Computer Sciences
Control Data
Datapoint
Delta Airlines
Digital Equipment
Disney Productions
Dow Chemical
duPont
Eastman Kodak
Esmark
Exxon
Fluor
Ford Motor
General Dynamics
General Electric
General Foods
General Motors
Great Western Financial
Gulf + Western
Halliburton
Harris
Hewlett-Packard
Holiday Inns
Homestake Mining
Honeywell
Hughes Tool
Humana
International Business Machines
International Flavors & Fragrances
International Minerals & Chemicals
International Paper
International Telephone & Telegraph
Johnson & Johnson
K mart
Litton Industries
McDonald's
Merck
Merrill Lynch
Minnesota Mining & Manufacturing
Mobil
Monsanto
National Semiconductor
NCR
Norfolk Southern
Northern Telecom Ltd.
Northwest Airlines
Northwest Industries
Owens-Illinois
PepsiCo
Polaroid
Ralston Purina
Raytheon
RCA
Revlon
R. J. Reynolds
Rockwell International
Safeway Stores
Schlumberger
Sears, Roebuck
Skyline
Sperry
Squibb
Standard Oil of Indiana
Storage Technology
Superior Oil
Tandy
Tektronix
Teledyne
Texas Instruments
UAL
Upjohn
United Technologies
Warner Communications
Weyerhaeuser
Williams Companies
Xerox

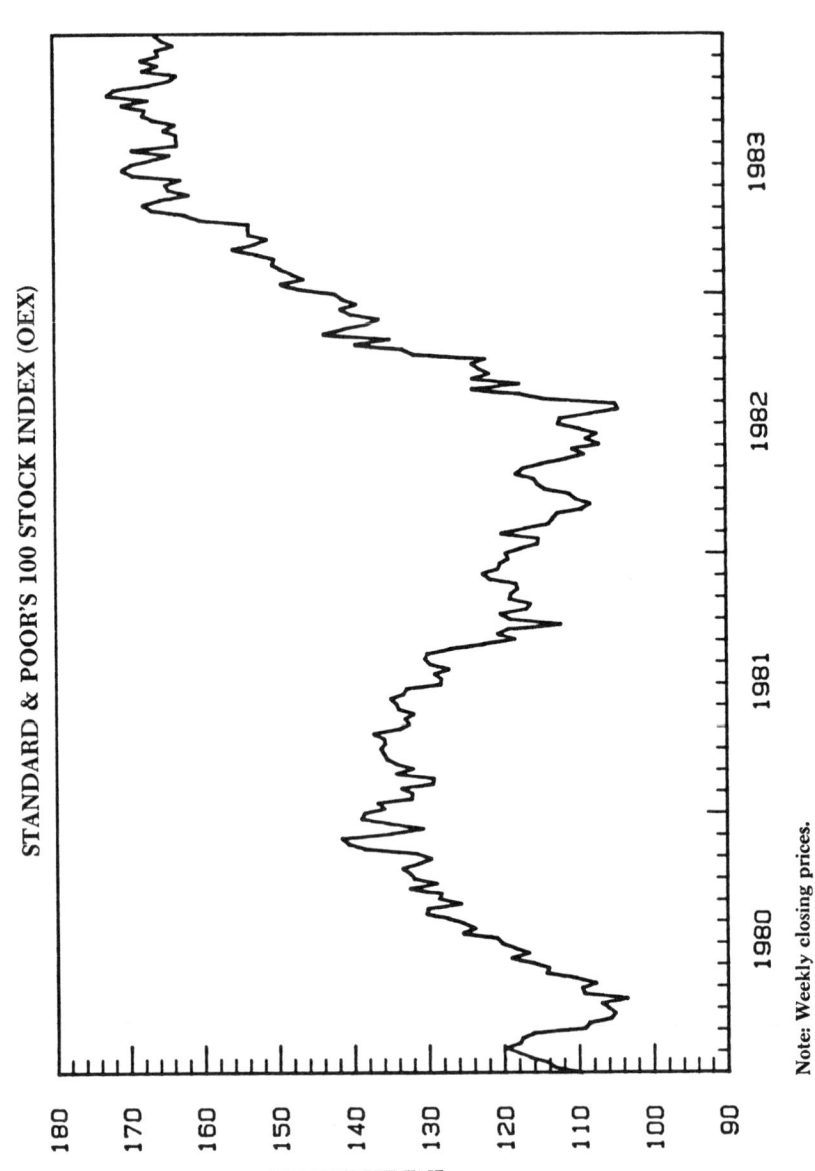

OPTIONABLE INDEXES

S&P 500 INDEX

The S&P 500 Index is a broad-based capitalization-weighted index that measures the changes in the aggregate market value of 500 stocks representing all major industries in approximately the same proportion to their representation on the New York Stock Exchange.

In computing the S&P 500, the current market price of each of the stocks in the index is multiplied by the number of outstanding shares. The resulting market values are then added to determine the aggregate market value of the stocks comprising the index.

To determine the current value of the S&P 500 Index, the ratio of the aggregate market value of the 500 stocks to the base value is multiplied by ten. The S&P 500 base value is based on average weekly aggregate market values of the stocks for the period 1941–1943.

S&P 500 INDEX—TEN LARGEST COMPONENTS

Issue	Percent of Market Value*
International Business Machines	5.80
Exxon Corp.	2.86
General Electric	2.04
General Motors	1.88
Shell Oil	1.54
American Telephone & Telegraph	1.42
Standard Oil of Indiana	1.37
Schlumberger, Ltd.	1.21
Royal Dutch	1.20
Mobil Corp.	1.10

* As of 2/29/84

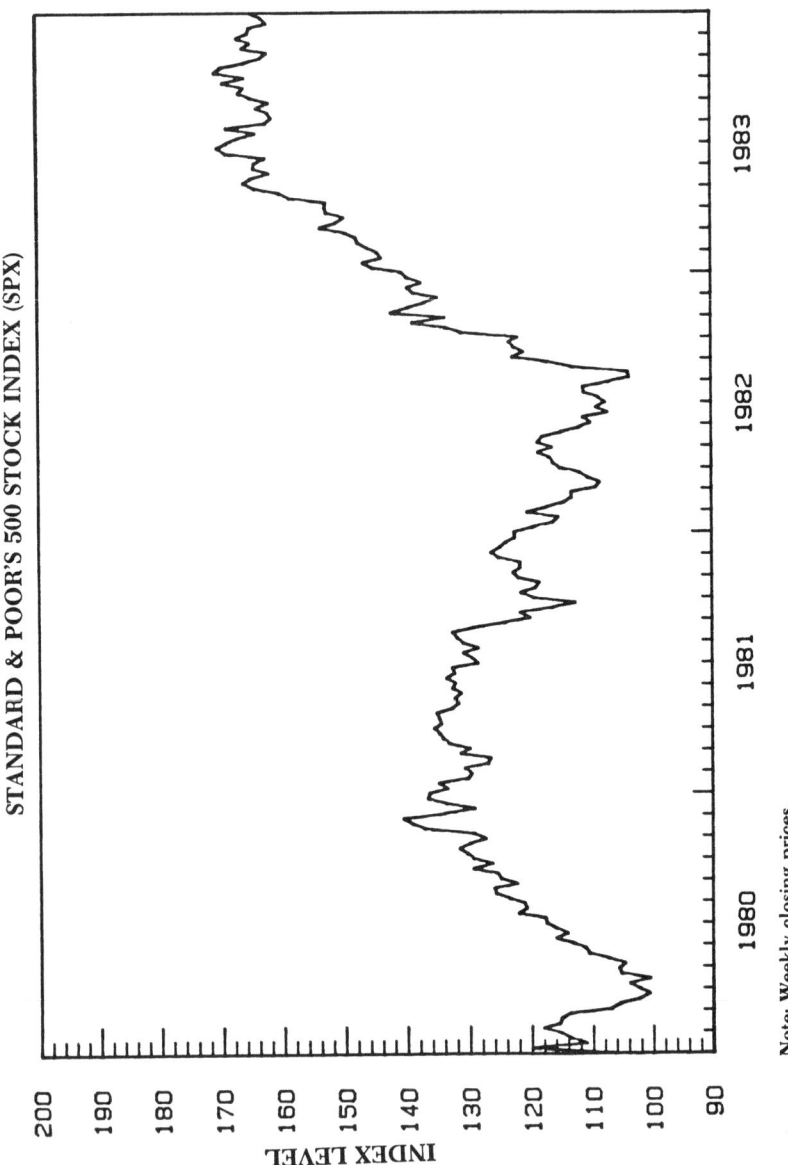

OPTIONABLE INDEXES

S&P TRANSPORTATION INDEX

The S&P Transportation Index is a narrow-based capitalization-weighted index of 20 stocks in companies which are a major factor in the U.S. transportation industry. The index is similar to the Dow Jones Transportation Average in that 13 issues are common to both indexes.

The S&P Transportation Index was introduced with a benchmark value of 100 as of February 1, 1984.

S&P TRANSPORTATION INDEX—
COMPONENT STOCKS

* AMR Corp.	* Northwest Airlines
* Burlington Northern	* Overnite Transportation Co.
* CSX Corp	* Pan American World Airway
Chicago & Northwestern Transportation	Roadway Services
* Consolidated Freightways	Ryder System
* Delta Air Lines	* Santa Fe Southern Pacific
Emery Air Freight	Tiger International
* Federal Express	* UAL, Inc.
Leaseway Transport	* Union Pacific Corp.
* Norfolk Southern Corp.	Yellow Freight System

* A Component of the Dow Jones Transportation Average

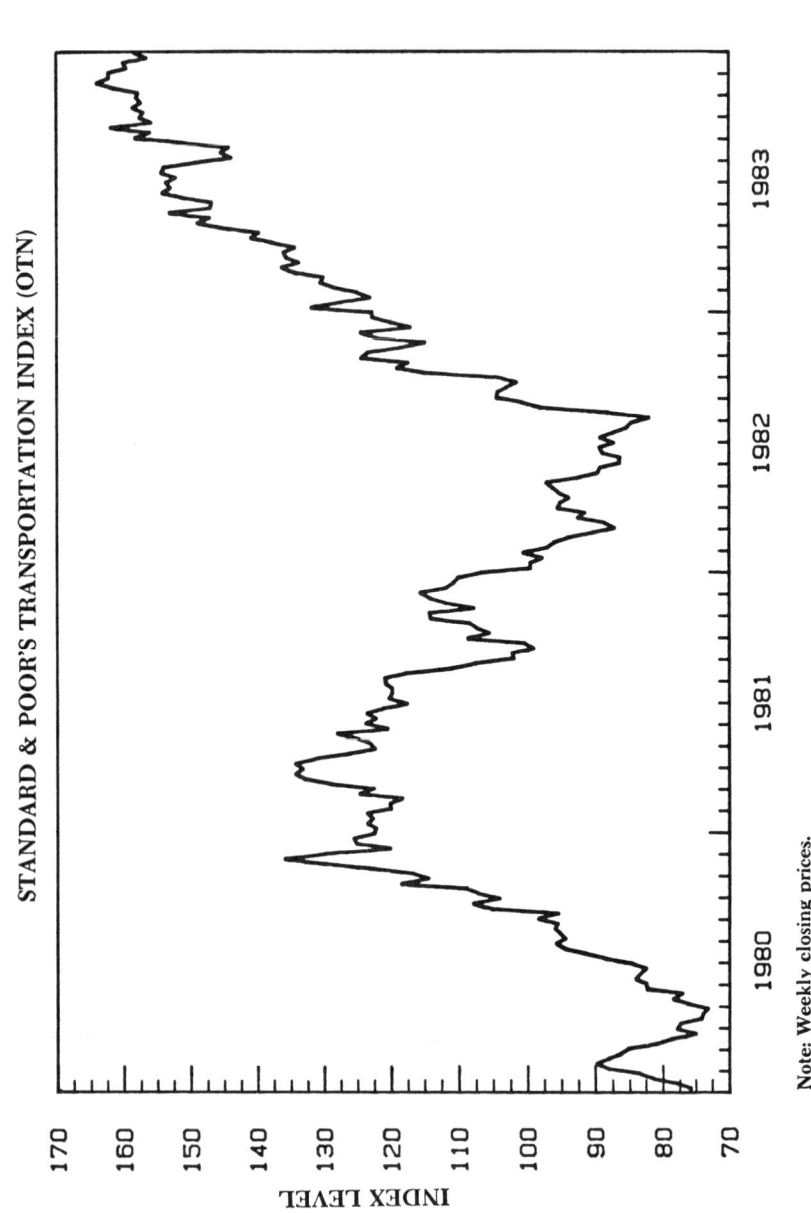

APPENDIX B

NONOPTIONABLE INDEXES

DOW JONES INDUSTRIAL AVERAGE

The Dow Jones Industrial Average is a broad-based price-weighted average of 30 high quality blue chip stocks compiled and published by *The Wall Street Journal* and its sister publication *Barron's National Business and Financial Weekly*. The component stocks are chosen as representative of the broad market and American industry. The companies are major factors in their industries and their stocks are widely held by individuals and institutional investors. Except for American Telephone and Telegraph, a utility, and American Express, a financial issue, all the stocks included in the Dow are industrials and all are listed on the New York Stock Exchange.

DOW JONES INDUSTRIAL AVERAGE—COMPONENT STOCKS

Allied Corp.	International Business Machines
Aluminum Co. of America	International Harvester
American Brands	International Paper
American Can	Merck
American Express	Minnesota Mining & Manufacturing
American Telephone & Telegraph	Owens-Illinois
Bethlehem Steel	Procter & Gamble
duPont	Sears, Roebuck
Eastman Kodak	Standard Oil of California
Exxon	Texaco
General Electric	Union Carbide
General Foods	United Technologies
General Motors	United States Steel
Goodyear	Westinghouse Electric
Inco	Woolworth

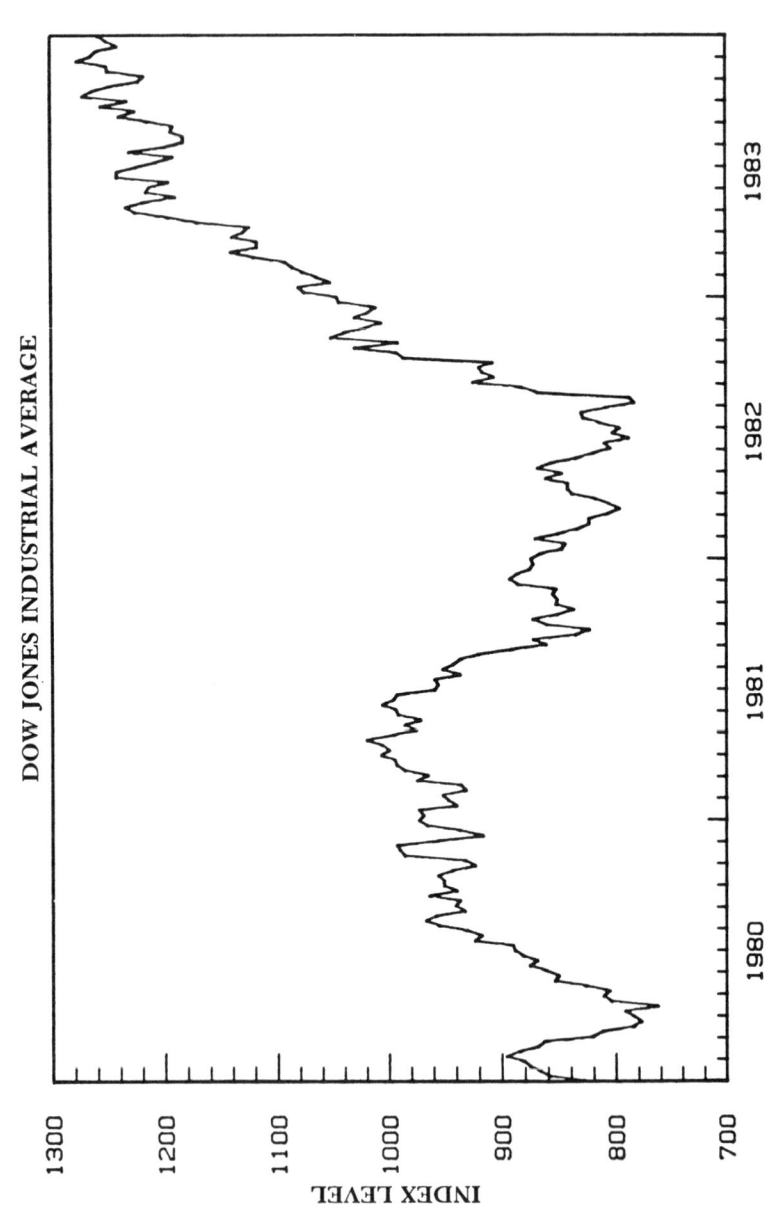

NONOPTIONABLE INDEXES

NASDAQ-OTC COMPOSITE INDEX

The NASDAQ (National Association of Securities Dealers Automated Quotations) OTC Composite Index is a capitalization-weighted index which measures performance of issues traded over-the-counter. The index is comprised of approximately 3,500 issues—all domestic OTC common stocks which are included in the NASDAQ system with the exception of those traded on an exchange and those with only one market maker.

The NASDAQ-OTC Index is maintained by the National Association of Securities Dealers, Inc. The index was introduced with a benchmark value of 100 as of February 5, 1971.

NASDAQ-OTC COMPOSITE INDEX—
TEN LARGEST COMPONENTS

Issue	Market Value*
Intel Corporation	$4,663,517,000
American International Group, Inc.	4,650,950,000
MCI Communications Corporation	3,373,827,000
Berkshire Hathaway, Inc.	1,502,570,000
Apple Computer, Inc.	1,440,693,000
Farmers Group, Inc.	1,413,252,000
Tandem Computers, Incorporated	1,401,698,000
Roadway Services, Inc.	1,380,138,000
The St. Paul Companies, Inc.	1,207,289,000
PACCAR, Inc.	1,048,047,000

* As of 12/31/83

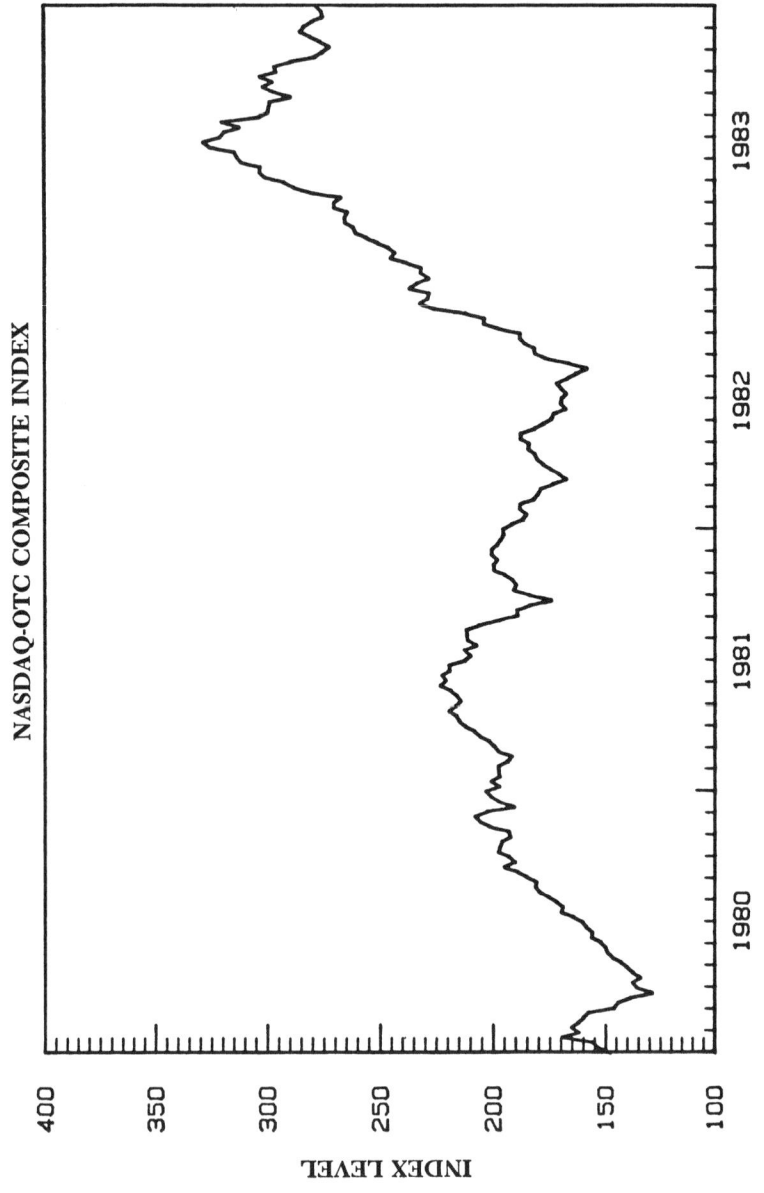

NONOPTIONABLE INDEXES

VALUE LINE COMPOSITE AVERAGE

The Value Line Composite Average is a *geometric* average (reported as an index) of approximately 1,700 stocks—those issues reviewed on a regular basis in The Value Line Investment Survey.

The geometric average is computed by taking the nth root of the product of the price changes of the n stocks (in this case 1,700) in the sample. The objective of the index is to reflect price change of the typical stock.

The Value Line Composite Average is maintained by Arnold Bernhard & Co., publishers of The Value Line Investment Survey. The Value Line Composite Average was introduced with a benchmark value of 100 as of June 30, 1961.

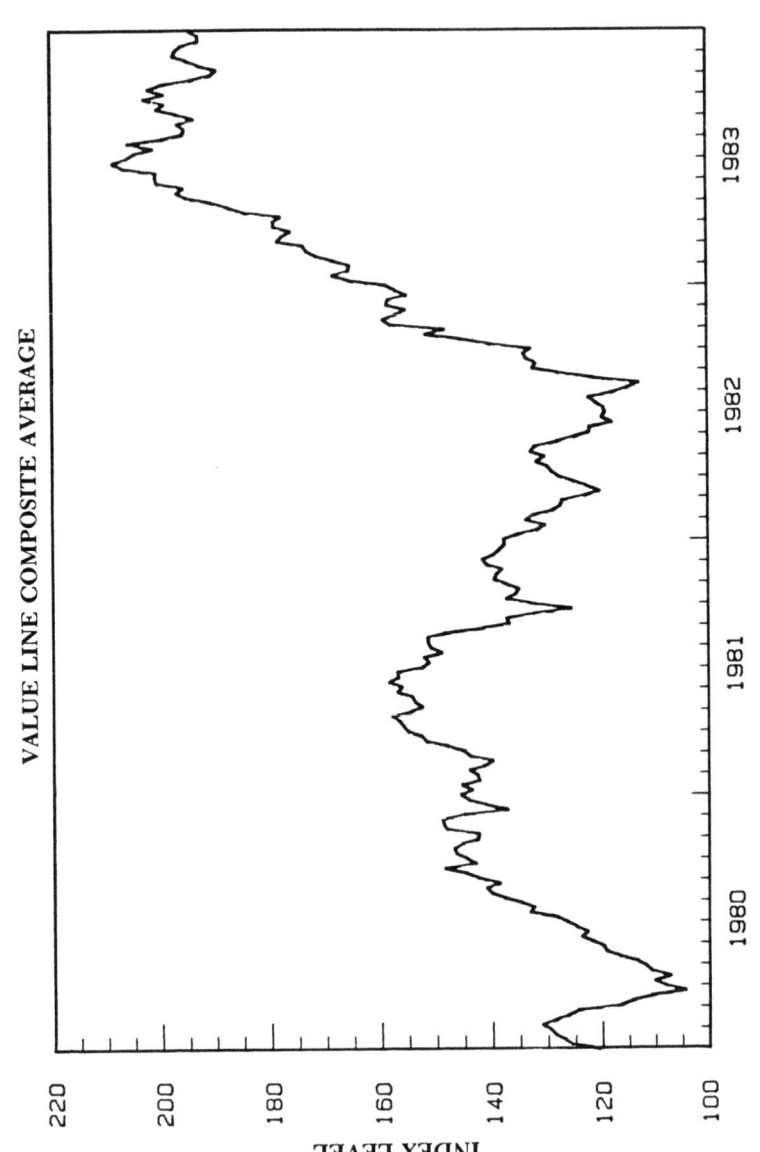

NONOPTIONABLE INDEXES

WILSHIRE 5000 EQUITY INDEX

The Wilshire 5000 Equity Index is a capitalization-weighted index of all (approximately 5,000) actively traded common stocks in the U.S.; that is, equity securities for which daily pricing is available. It is designed to measure the value and change in value of the United States Equity marketplace. The computation is similar to that for the S&P 500 and the NYSE Composite Index.

The Wilshire 5000 Equity Index is maintained by Wilshire Associates, Santa Monica, California. The index was introduced with a benchmark value of 1,404.596 as of December 31, 1980.

WILSHIRE 5000 EQUITY INDEX—COMPONENT WEIGHTING

Market	Percent of Total Index Value*
New York Stock Exchange	87
American Stock Exchange	5
Over-the-Counter	7

* As of 12/31/83

WILSHIRE 5000 EQUITY INDEX—TEN LARGEST COMPONENTS

Issue	Percent of Index*
International Business Machines	4.06
Exxon Corp.	1.91
General Electric	1.39
General Motors	1.20
Shell Oil	1.05
Standard Oil of Indiana	.92
American Telephone & Telegraph	.90
Schlumberger Ltd.	.86
Gulf Corp.	.74
Mobil Corp.	.73

* As of 3/22/84

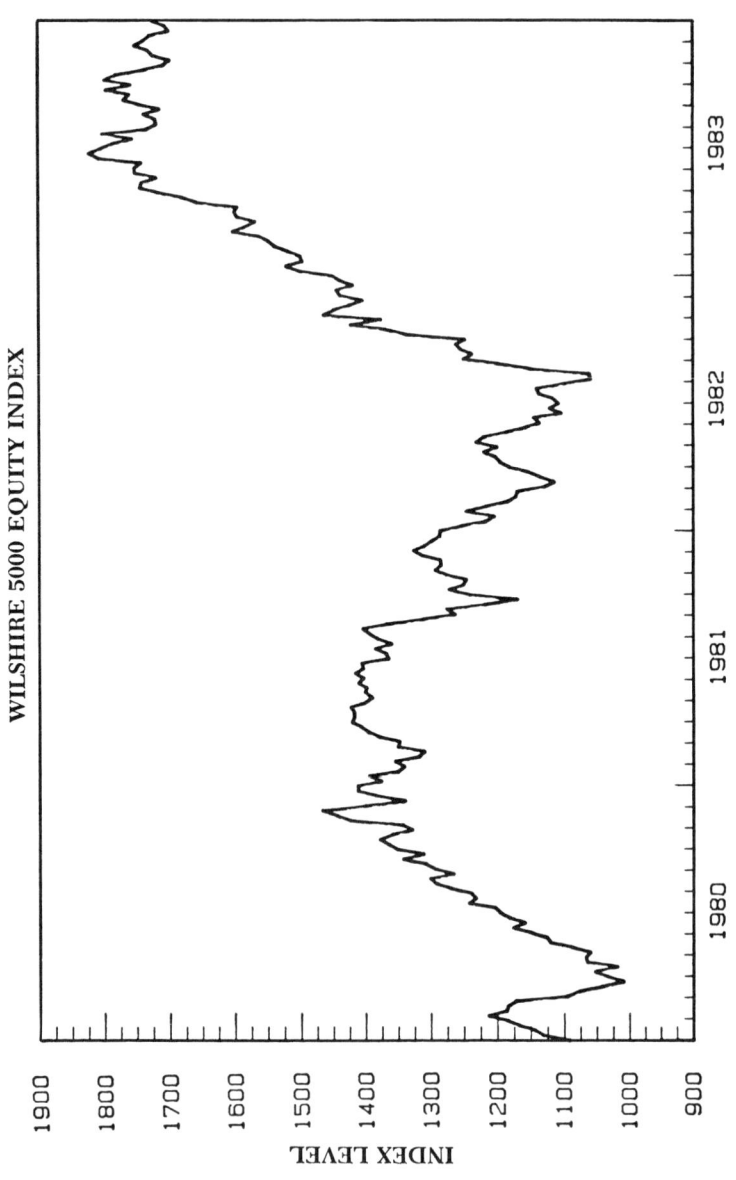

APPENDIX C
INDEX OPTIONS
(Contract Specifications)

AMEX COMPUTER TECHNOLOGY INDEX OPTIONS

EXCHANGE	Amex
SYMBOL	XCI
UNDERLYING INDEX	The AMEX Computer Technology Index, a group of 30 stocks representing a cross section of widely-held U.S. corporations involved in various phases of the computer industry.
TRADING UNIT	Each index option contract represents $100 (the index multiplier) times the current value of the index.
EXPIRATION CYCLE	Monthly including the current month and the next two consecutive months.
EXPIRATION DATE	The Saturday following the third Friday of the expiration month.
EXERCISE PRICES	Set at 5 point intervals to bracket the current value of the index. New exercise prices added when the current value of the index touches an existing strike.
PREMIUM QUOTATION	Premiums are expressed in terms of points and fractions of a point. Each point (1.0) of premium has a value of $100.
MINIMUM TICK	⅛ point for premiums of 3 points or more, ¹⁄₁₆ point for premiums of less than 3 points.
MARGIN REQUIREMENTS	As with stock options, 30% of the current index value (index number × $100) plus or minus the amount by which the option is in- or out-of-the-money, with a minimum of $250 per contract.
EXERCISE SETTLEMENT	Cash payment based on the dollar difference between the index number and the exercise price of the contract multiplied by 100. The index number is determined following the close of trading on the day the exercise notice is submitted.

STOCK INDEX OPTIONS

EXERCISE PROCEDURE   Instructions to exercise must be given no later than 4:10 P.M. (N.Y. time)

POSITION AND EXERCISE LIMITS   4,000 contracts on the same side of the market.

TRADING HOURS   10:00 A.M. to 4:10 P.M. (N.Y. time).

TRADING SYSTEM   Specialist/Registered Option Trader.

INDEX OPTIONS

AMEX MAJOR MARKET INDEX OPTIONS

EXCHANGE	Amex
SYMBOL	XMI
UNDERLYING INDEX	The Amex Major Market Index, a group of 20 stocks from leading blue chip corporations 15 of which are included in the Dow Jones Industrial Average. The objective is to mirror the Dow without actually duplicating it.
TRADING UNIT	Each index option contract represents $100 (the index multiplier) times the current value of the index.
EXPIRATION CYCLE	Monthly including the current month and the next two consecutive months.
EXPIRATION DATE	The Saturday following the third Friday of the expiration month.
EXERCISE PRICES	Set at 5 point intervals to bracket the current value of the index. New exercise prices added as the index moves.
PREMIUM QUOTATION	Premiums are expressed in terms of points and fractions of a point. Each point (1.0) of premium has a value of $100.
MINIMUM TICK	⅛ point for premiums of 3 points or more, ¹⁄₁₆ point for premiums of less than 3 points.
MARGIN REQUIREMENTS	The current premium plus 10% of the current index value (index number × $100). If the option is out-of-the-money, the out-of-the-money amount can be deducted provided the result does not come to less than the current premium plus 2% of the index value.
EXERCISE SETTLEMENT	Cash payment based on the dollar difference between the index number and the exercise price of the contract multiplied by 100. The index number is determined following the close of trading on the day the exercise notice is submitted.
EXERCISE PROCEDURE	Instructions to exercise must be given no later than 4:10 P.M. (N.Y. time).
POSITION AND EXERCISE LIMITS	15,000 contracts on the same side of the market.
TRADING HOURS	10:00 A.M. to 4.10 P.M. (N.Y. time).
TRADING SYSTEM	Specialist/Registered Option Trader.

STOCK INDEX OPTIONS

AMEX MARKET VALUE INDEX OPTIONS

EXCHANGE	Amex
SYMBOL	XAM
UNDERLYING INDEX	The Amex Market Value Index which measures changes in the aggregate market value of 800+ common stocks, ADRs and warrants listed in the American Stock Exchange.
TRADING UNIT	Each index option contract represents $100 (the index multiplier) times the current value of the index.
EXPIRATION CYCLE	Monthly including the current month and the next two consecutive months.
EXPIRATION DATE	The Saturday following the third Friday of the expiration month.
EXERCISE PRICES	Set at 5 point intervals to bracket the current value of the index. New exercise prices added as the index moves.
PREMIUM QUOTATION	Premiums are expressed in terms of points and fractions of a point. Each point (1.0) of premium has a value of $100.
MINIMUM TICK	$\frac{1}{8}$ point for premiums of 3 points or more, $\frac{1}{16}$ point for premiums of less than 3 points.
MARGIN REQUIREMENTS	The current premium plus 10% of the current index value (index number $\times$ $100). If the option is out-of-the-money, the out-of-the-money amount can be deducted provided the result does not come to less than the current premium plus 2% of the index value.
EXERCISE SETTLEMENT	Cash payment based on the dollar difference between the index number and the exercise price of the contract multiplied by 100. The index number is determined following the close of trading on the day the exercise notice is submitted.
EXERCISE PROCEDURE	Instructions to exercise must be given no later than 4:10 P.M. (N.Y. time).
POSITION AND EXERCISE LIMITS	10,000 contracts on the same side of the market.
TRADING HOURS	10:00 A.M. to 4:10 P.M. (N.Y. time).
TRADING SYSTEM	Specialist/Registered Option Trader

INDEX OPTIONS

AMEX OIL AND GAS INDEX OPTIONS

EXCHANGE	Amex
SYMBOL	XOI
UNDERLYING INDEX	The Amex Oil and Gas Index, a group of 30 stocks representing a cross section of widely-held U.S. corporations involved in various phases of the oil and gas industry.
TRADING UNIT	Each index option contract represents $100 (the index multiplier) times the current value of the index.
EXPIRATION CYCLE	Monthly including the current month and the next two consecutive months.
EXPIRATION DATE	The Saturday following the third Friday of the expiration month.
EXERCISE PRICES	Set at 5 point intervals to bracket the current value of the index. New exercise prices added when the current value of the index touches an existing strike.
PREMIUM QUOTATION	Premiums are expressed in terms of points and fractions of a point. Each point (1.0) of premium has a value of $100.
MINIMUM TICK	$\frac{1}{8}$ point for premiums of 3 points or more, $\frac{1}{16}$ point for premiums of less than 3 points.
MARGIN REQUIREMENTS	As with stock options, 30% of the current index value (index number × $100) plus or minus the amount by which the option is in- or out-of-the-money, with a minimum of $250 per contract.
EXERCISE SETTLEMENT	Cash payment based on the dollar difference between the index number and the exercise price of the contract multiplied by 100. The index number is determined following the close of trading on the day the exercise notice is submitted.
EXERCISE PROCEDURE	Instructions to exercise must be given no later than 4:10 P.M. (N.Y. time).
POSITION AND EXERCISE LIMITS	8,000 contracts on the same side of the market.
TRADING HOURS	10:00 A.M. to 4:10 P.M. (N.Y. time).
TRADING SYSTEM	Specialist/Registered Option Trader.

STOCK INDEX OPTIONS

AMEX TRANSPORTATION INDEX OPTIONS

EXCHANGE	Amex
SYMBOL	XTI
UNDERLYING INDEX	The Amex Transportation Index, a group of 20 stocks representing a cross section of widely-held and actively traded corporations involved in various transportation systems.
TRADING UNIT	Each index option contract represents $100 (the index multiplier) times the current value of the index.
EXPIRATION CYCLE	Monthly including the current month and the next two consecutive months.
EXPIRATION DATE	The Saturday following the third Friday of the expiration month.
EXERCISE PRICES	Set at 5 point intervals to bracket the current value of the index. New exercise prices added when the current value of the index touches an existing strike.
PREMIUM QUOTATION	Premiums are expressed in terms of points and fractions of a point. Each point (1.0) of premium has a value of $100.
MINIMUM TICK	$\frac{1}{8}$ point for premiums of 3 points or more, $\frac{1}{16}$ point for premiums of less than 3 points.
MARGIN REQUIREMENTS	As with stock options, 30% of the current index value (index number × $100) plus or minus the amount by which the option is in- or out-of-the-money, with a minimum of $250 per contract.
EXERCISE SETTLEMENT	Cash payment based on the dollar difference between the index number and the exercise price of the contract multiplied by 100. The index number is determined following the close of trading on the day the exercise notice is submitted.
EXERCISE PROCEDURE	Instructions to exercise must be given no later than 4:10 P.M. (N.Y. time).
POSITION AND EXERCISE LIMITS	8,000 contracts on the same side of the market.
TRADING HOURS	10:00 A.M. to 4:10 P.M. (N.Y. time).
TRADING SYSTEM	Specialist/Registered Option Trader.

INDEX OPTIONS

NYSE COMPOSITE INDEX OPTIONS

EXCHANGE	NYSE
SYMBOL	NYA
UNDERLYING INDEX	The NYSE Composite Index which is the computed value of the 1500+ stocks listed on the NYSE.
TRADING UNIT	Each index option contract represents $100 (the index multiplier) times the current value of the NYSE index.
EXPIRATION CYCLE	The next three months superimposed on the March, June, September, December cycle.
EXPIRATION DATE	The Saturday following the third Friday of the expiration month.
EXERCISE PRICES	Set at 5 point intervals to bracket the current value of the index.
PREMIUM QUOTATIONS	Premiums are expressed in terms of points and fractions of a point. Each point (1.0) of premium has a value of $100.
MINIMUM TICK	⅛ point for premiums of 3 points or more, ¹⁄₁₆ point for premiums of less than 3 points.
MARGIN REQUIREMENTS	The current premium plus 10% of the current index value (index number × $100). If the option is out-of-the-money, the out-of-the-money amount can be deducted provided the result does not come to less than the current premium plus 2% of the index value.
EXERCISE SETTLEMENT	Cash payment based on the dollar difference between the index number and the exercise price of the contract multiplied by 100. The index number is determined following the close of trading on the day the exercise notice is submitted.
EXERCISE PROCEDURE	Instructions to exercise must be given no later than 4:10 P.M. (N.Y. time).
POSITION LIMIT	A value of $300 million in contracts of either long or short calls, or long or short puts, or an aggregate of a value of $300 million in contracts of long calls and short puts, or short calls and long puts.
EXERCISE LIMIT	No more than 25,000 contracts within a five business day period.
TRADING HOURS	10:00 A.M. to 4:10 P.M. (N.Y. time).
TRADING SYSTEM	Modified Specialist/Competitive Option Trader.

STOCK INDEX OPTIONS

NYSE TELEPHONE INDEX OPTIONS

EXCHANGE	NYSE
SYMBOL	NTI
UNDERLYING INDEX	The NYSE Telephone Index, a group of nine stocks resulting from the divestiture of the "old" American Telephone & Telegraph.
TRADING UNIT	Each index option contract represents $100 (the index multiplier) times the current value of the index.
EXPIRATION CYCLE	The next three months superimposed on the January, April, July, October cycle.
EXPIRATION DATE	The Saturday following the third Friday of the expiration month.
EXERCISE PRICES	Set at 5 point intervals to bracket the current value of the index. New exercise prices added as the index moves.
PREMIUM QUOTATION	Premiums are expressed in terms of points and fractions of a point. Each point (1.0) of premium has a value of $100.
MINIMUM TICK	$\frac{1}{8}$ point for premiums of 3 points or more, $\frac{1}{16}$ point for premiums of less than 3 points.
MARGIN REQUIREMENTS	As with stock options, 30% of the current index value (index number × $100) plus or minus the amount by which the option is in- or out-of-the-money, with a minimum of $250 per contract.
EXERCISE SETTLEMENT	Cash payment based on the dollar difference between the index number and the exercise price of the contract multiplied by 100. The index number is determined following the close of trading on the day the exercise notice is submitted.
EXERCISE PROCEDURE	Instructions to exercise must be given no later than 4:10 P.M. (N.Y. time).
POSITION LIMIT	6,000 contracts on the same side of the market.
EXERCISE LIMIT	No more than 6,000 contracts within a five business day period.
TRADING HOURS	10:00 A.M. to 4:10 P.M. (N.Y. time).
TRADING SYSTEM	Modified Specialist/Competitive Option Trader.

INDEX OPTIONS

PACIFIC STOCK EXCHANGE TECHNOLOGY INDEX OPTIONS

EXCHANGE	Pacific Stock Exchange
SYMBOL	PSE
UNDERLYING INDEX	The Pacific Stock Exchange Technology Index, a group of 100 stocks representing a broad spectrum of companies principally engaged in manufacturing or service-related products within advanced technology fields.
TRADING UNIT	Each index option contract represents $100 (the index multiplier) times the current value of the index.
EXPIRATION CYCLE	Monthly including the current month and the next three consecutive months.
EXPIRATION DATE	The Saturday following the third Friday of the expiration month.
EXERCISE PRICES	Set at 5 point intervals to bracket the current value of the index. New exercise prices added when the current value of the index touches an existing strike.
PREMIUM QUOTATION	Premiums are expressed in terms of points and fractions of a point. Each point (1.0) of premium has a value of $100.
MINIMUM TICK	$1/8$ point for premiums of 3 points or more, $1/16$ point for premiums of less than 3 points.
MARGIN REQUIREMENTS	The current premium plus 10% of the current index value (index number × $100). If the option is out-of-the-money, the out-of-the-money amount can be deducted provided the result does not come to less than the current premium plus 2% of the index value.
EXERCISE SETTLEMENT	Cash payment based on the dollar difference between the index number and the exercise price of the contract multiplied by 100. The index number is determined following the close of trading on the day the exercise notice is submitted.
EXERCISE PROCEDURE	Instructions to exercise must be given no later than 4:10 P.M. (N.Y. time).
POSITION AND EXERCISE LIMITS	4,000 contracts on the same side of the market.
TRADING HOURS	10:00 A.M. to 4:10 P.M. (N.Y. time).
TRADING SYSTEM	Specialist/Registered Option Trader.

PHILADELPHIA STOCK EXCHANGE GAMING/HOTEL INDEX OPTIONS

EXCHANGE	Philadelphia Stock Exchange
SYMBOL	XGH
UNDERLYING INDEX	The Philadelphia Stock Exchange Gaming/Hotel Index, a group of 9 stocks representing a cross section of widely-held U.S. corporations involved in various phases of the gaming and hotel industries.
TRADING UNIT	Each index option contract represents $100 (the index multiplier) times the current value of the index.
EXPIRATION CYCLE	The March, June, September and December quarterly cycle with additional options introduced to give monthly expirations in the three months following the current expiration month.
EXPIRATION DATE	The Saturday following the third Friday of the expiration month.
EXERCISE PRICES	Set at 5 point intervals to bracket the current value of the index. New exercise prices added when the current value of the index touches an existing strike.
PREMIUM QUOTATION	Premiums are expressed in terms of points and fractions of a point. Each point (1.0) of premium has a value of $100.
MINIMUM TICK	⅛ point for premiums of 3 points or more, ¹⁄₁₆ point for premiums of less than 3 points.
MARGIN REQUIREMENTS	As with stock options, 30% of the current index value (index number × $100) plus or minus the amount by which the option is in- or out-of-the-money, with a minimum of $250 per contract.
EXERCISE SETTLEMENT	Cash payment based on the dollar difference between the index number and the exercise price of the contract multiplied by 100. The index number is determined following the close of trading on the day the exercise notice is submitted.
EXERCISE PROCEDURE	Instructions to exercise must be given no later than 4:10 P.M. (N.Y. time).
POSITION AND EXERCISE LIMITS	4,000 contracts on the same side of the market.
TRADING HOURS	10:00 A.M. to 4:10 P.M. (N.Y. time).
TRADING SYSTEM	Specialist/Registered Option Trader.

PHILADELPHIA STOCK EXCHANGE GOLD/SILVER INDEX OPTIONS

EXCHANGE	Philadelphia Stock Exchange
SYMBOL	XAU
UNDERLYING INDEX	The Philadelphia Stock Exchange Gold/Silver Index, a group of 7 stocks representing a cross section of widely-held U.S. corporations involved primarily in the mining of gold/silver.
TRADING UNIT	Each index option contract represents $100 (the index multiplier) times the current value of the index.
EXPIRATION CYCLE	The March, June, September, and December quarterly cycle with additional options introduced to give monthly expirations in the three months following the current expiration month.
EXPIRATION DATE	The Saturday following the third Friday of the expiration month.
EXERCISE PRICES	Set at 5 point intervals to bracket the current value of the index. New exercise prices added when the current value of the index touches an existing strike.
PREMIUM QUOTATION	Premiums are expressed in terms of points and fractions of a point. Each point (1.0) of premium has a value of $100.
MINIMUM TICK	$\frac{1}{8}$ point for premiums of 3 points or more, $\frac{1}{16}$ point for premiums of less than 3 points.
MARGIN REQUIREMENTS	As with stock options, 30% of the current index value (index number $\times$ $100) plus or minus the amount by which the option is in- or out-of-the-money, with a minimum of $250 per contract.
EXERCISE SETTLEMENT	Cash payment based on the dollar difference between the index number and the exercise price of the contract multiplied by 100. The index number is determined following the close of trading on the day the exercise notice is submitted.
EXERCISE PROCEDURE	Instructions to exercise must be given no later than 4:10 P.M. (N.Y. time).
POSITION AND EXERCISE LIMITS	4,000 contracts on the same side of the market.
TRADING HOURS	10:00 A.M. to 4:10 P.M. (N.Y. time).
TRADING SYSTEM	Specialist/Registered Option Trader.

STOCK INDEX OPTIONS

S&P 100 INDEX OPTIONS

EXCHANGE	CBOE
SYMBOL	OEX
UNDERLYING INDEX	The S&P 100 Index, a group of 100 stocks for which options are currently trading on the CBOE. It is intended to be a broad, highly representative index of the market as a whole.
TRADING UNIT	Each index option contract represents $100 (the index multiplier) times the current value of the index.
EXPIRATION CYCLE	Monthly including the current month and the next three consecutive months.
EXPIRATION DATE	The Saturday following the third Friday of the expiration month.
EXERCISE PRICES	Set at 5 point intervals to bracket the current value of the index. New exercise prices are added when the current value of the index approaches the limits of the existing strikes.
PREMIUM QUOTATION	Premiums are expressed in terms of points and fractions of a point. Each point (1.0) of premium has a value of $100.
MINIMUM TICK	$\frac{1}{8}$ point for premiums of 3 points or more, $\frac{1}{16}$ point for premiums of less than 3 points.
MARGIN REQUIREMENTS	The current premium plus 10% of the current index value (index number × $100). If the option is out-of-the-money, the out-of-the-money amount can be deducted provided the result does not come to less than the current premium plus 2% of the index value.
EXERCISE SETTLEMENT	Cash payment based on the dollar difference between the index number and the exercise price of the contract multiplied by 100. The index number is determined following the close of trading on the day the exercise notice is submitted.
EXERCISE PROCEDURE	Instructions to exercise must be given no later than 4:10 P.M. (N.Y. time).
POSITION AND EXERCISE LIMITS	15,000 contracts on the same side of the market.
TRADING HOURS	10:00 A.M. to 4:10 P.M. (N.Y. time).
TRADING SYSTEM	Market-Makers, Floor Brokers, and a Public Limit Order Book.

INDEX OPTIONS

S&P 500 INDEX OPTIONS

EXCHANGE	CBOE
SYMBOL	SPX
UNDERLYING INDEX	The S&P 500 Index, a group of 500 stocks representing all major industries in approximately the same proportion to their representation on the New York Stock Exchange.
TRADING UNIT	Each index option contract represents $100 (the index multiplier) times the current value of the index.
EXPIRATION CYCLE	March/June/September/December.
EXPIRATION DATE	The Saturday following the third Friday of the expiration month.
EXERCISE PRICES	Set at 5 point intervals to bracket the current value of the index. New exercise prices are added when the current value of the index approaches the limits of the existing strikes.
PREMIUM QUOTATION	Premiums are expressed in terms of points and fractions of a point. Each point (1.0) of premium has a value of $100.
MINIMUM TICK	$\frac{1}{8}$ point for premiums of 3 points or more, $\frac{1}{16}$ point for premiums of less than 3 points.
MARGIN REQUIREMENTS	The current premium plus 10% of the current index value (index number × $100). If the option is out-of-the-money, the out-of-the-money amount can be deducted provided the result does not come to less than the current premium plus 2% of the index value.
EXERCISE SETTLEMENT	Cash payment based on the dollar difference between the index number and the exercise price of the contract multiplied by 100. The index number is determined following the close of trading on the day the exercise notice is submitted.
EXERCISE PROCEDURE	Instructions to exercise must be given no later than 4:10 P.M. (N.Y. time).
POSITION AND EXERCISE LIMITS	15,000 contracts on the same side of the market.
TRADING HOURS	10:00 A.M. to 4:10 P.M. (N.Y. time).
TRADING SYSTEM	Market-Makers, Floor Brokers, and a Public Limit Order Book.

STOCK INDEX OPTIONS

S&P TRANSPORTATION INDEX OPTIONS

EXCHANGE	CBOE
SYMBOL	OTN
UNDERLYING INDEX	The S&P Transportation Index, a group of 20 stocks representing a cross section of widely-held and actively traded corporations involved in various transportation systems.
TRADING UNIT	Each index option contract represents $100 (the index multiplier) times the current value of the index.
EXPIRATION CYCLE	Monthly including the current month and the next three consecutive months.
EXPIRATION DATE	The Saturday following the third Friday of the expiration month.
EXERCISE PRICES	Set at 5 point intervals to bracket the current value of the index. Additional exercise prices are added as the index value reaches the limits of existing exercise prices.
PREMIUM QUOTATION	Premiums are expressed in terms of points and fractions of a point. Each point (1.0) of premium has a value of $100.
MINIMUM TICK	$\frac{1}{8}$ point for premiums of 3 points or more, $\frac{1}{16}$ point for premiums of less than 3 points.
MARGIN REQUIREMENTS	As with stock options, 30% of the current index value (index number × $100) plus or minus the amount by which the option is in- or out-of-the-money, with a minimum of $250 per contract.
EXERCISE SETTLEMENT	Cash payment based on the dollar difference between the index number and the exercise price of the contract multiplied by 100. The index number is determined following the close of trading on the day the exercise notice is submitted.
EXERCISE PROCEDURE	Instructions to exercise must be given no later than 4:10 P.M. (N.Y. time).
POSITION AND EXERCISE LIMITS	6,000 contracts on the same side of the market.
TRADING HOURS	10:00 A.M. to 4:10 P.M. (N.Y. time).
TRADING SYSTEM	Market-makers, Floor Brokers, and a Public Limit Order Book.

APPENDIX D

VALUE LINE EVALUATIONS

Value Line Options

Published and Copyrighted 1984 by VALUE LINE, INC. 711 Third Avenue, New York, N.Y. 10017

VOL. 15 NO. 20   **PART B: OPTION EVALUATION SECTION**   **MAY 28, 1984**

May 28, 1984

```
                                                                COVERED
                                       -OPTION BUYER- -OPTION WRITER-
                                    Performance       Performance
       Description   Recent Est. Change Rank          Rank
       of Each       Market Normal Per  | Relative   Current           Leverage to
       Security      Price  Price  Point| Volatility Leverage  Rel.    Expiration
                                                     +10%-10%  Vol.+10% Unch.-10%
Amex Computer Tec Index ( 2.6% yield ) ASE
   XCI units    86.72                2      65%
      Jun  95  FS   .25    .17   15  1↑ 9000 +970% -95% 3    50 +10%  +0 -10%
           90  FR  1.25    .84   36  2  3800 +405   -95  2   50  +5   +1  -9
           85  FQ  3.63   3.02   60  3↓ 1750 +195   -90  1↑  50  +2   +2  -6
      Jul  95  GS   .88    .94   23  1↓ 3000 +360   -90  2   50 +11   +1  -9
           90  GR  2.56   2.18   41  2  1950 +195   -80  2   55  +7   +3  -7
           85  GQ  4.88   4.49   60 (3) 1250 +135   -75 (2)  50  +4   +4  -5
      Aug  95  HS  NEW    1.51   27  -  1950 +230   -80   -  55 +11   +2  -8
           90  HR  NEW    2.94   42  -  1600 +175   -80   -  50  +7   +4  -7
           85  HQ  NEW    5.28   60  -  1100 +125   -70   -  45  +4   +4  -4
   P  Jun  85  RJ   .81    .68   40  2  4900  -95  +760
   P       90  RR  3.50   3.61   68  2↑ 1050  -95  +240
   P       95  RS  8.38   8.31   88  3   500  -80  +100
   P  Jul  85  SQ  1.75   1.72   41  3↓ 2400  -85  +320
   P       90  SR  4.13   4.48   66  3↓ 1000  -85  +190
   P       95  SS  8.28   8.61   93 (3)  480  -90  +105
   P  Aug  85  TQ  NEW    2.23   41  -  1900  -75  +240
   P       90  TR  4.25   4.95   65 (3)  950  -85  +185
   P       95  TS  NEW    8.88   80  -   500  -65  +90

Amex Major Market Index ( 4.8% yield ) ASE
   XMI units   109.70                3      35%
      Jun 120  FD   .06    .05   11  -  9999 +990%-100% -    25  +9%  +0 -10%
          115  FC   .25    .30   27  1↓ 3100 +990  -100  5↑  25  +5   +0 -10
          110  F3  1.81   1.61   49  3  2300 +495  -100  2↑  30  +2   +2  -8
          105  FA  5.50   5.06   70  3↓  690 +185   -95   -  20  +1   +1  -5
      Jul 120  GD   .25    .51   15  2  5900 +990   -95   4  25 +10   +0 -10
          115  GC  1.06   1.31   31  2↑ 2600 +550   -95   3  25  +6   +1  -9
          110  GB  3.13   3.06   50  3  1500 +260   -90  2↑  30  +3   +3  -7
          105  GA  6.50   6.11   68 (3)  650 +145   -85 (3)  25  +2   +2  -4
      Aug 120  HD   .56    .85   19 (1) 3000 +630   -90  (4) 25 +10   +1 -10
          115  HC  1.75   1.85   34  2  1750 +340   -90   3  30  +7   +2  -9
          110  HB  3.88   3.72   51 (4) 1200 +205   -85 (2) 30   +4   +4  -7
   P  Jun 105  RA   .19    .18   29  1  9999 -100  +990
   P      110  RB  1.50   1.52   51  2  2000 -100  +650
   P      115  RC  5.30   5.43   74  2   440 -100  +205
   P      120  RD 10.30  10.31   93  2   260  -90  +105
   P  Jul 105  SA   .50    .86   30  2  4200  -95  +990
   P      110  SB  2.13   2.63   51  3  1550  -95  +430
   P      115  SC  5.38   6.02   74  2↑  440 -100  +205
   P      120  SD 10.50  10.49   86 (3)  270  -75  +105
   P  Aug 110  TB  2.50   3.23   51  3  1300  -90  +355
   P      115  TC  5.50   6.45   73 (2)  450  -95  +195
   P      120  TD 10.30  10.70   92 (3)  260  -90  +105

Amex Market Value Index ( no div'd being paid ) ASE
   XAM units   202.68                3      65%
      Jun 220  FD   .06    .13   12  -  9999 +990%-100% -    45  +9%  +0 -10%
          215  FC   .13    .35   21  -  9999 +990  -100   -  40  +6   +0 -10
          210  FB   .50    .94   32  2  9999 +990  -100  5↓  40  +4   +0 -10
          205  FA  2.00   2.30   45  2  4400 +805  -100   4  40  +2   +1  -9
          200  FT  4.63   4.84   57 (1) 2100 +395  -100 (5)  35  +1   +1  -8
      Jul 220  GD   .50   1.14   17 (1) 9600 +990   -95 (5)  45  +9   +0 -10
          215  GC   .75   1.92   24 (2) 7500 +990   -95 (5)  40  +6   +0 -10
          210  GB  2.25   3.16   35 (2) 3400 +540   -95 (4)  40  +5   +1  -9
          205  GA  3.88   4.99   46  1  2400 +385   -95   4  40  +3   +2  -8
          200  GT  6.75   7.52   57 (1) 1550 +250   -90 (5)  40  +2   +2  -7
      Aug 215  HC  NEW    2.83   30  -  2500 +345   -90   -  45  +8   +1  -9
          210  HB  NEW    4.24   39  -  2100 +280   -90   -  45  +6   +2  -8
          205  HA  NEW    6.18   43  -  1700 +225   -85   -  45  +4   +3  -7
          200  HT  8.25   8.70   57 (2) 1300 +195   -85 (4)  40  +3   +3  -6
   P  Jun 200  RT  1.31   1.19   43  2  5800 -100  +990
   P      205  RA  4.00   3.63   56  2  2200 -100  +465
   P      210  RB  8.13   7.65   67  2  1100  -95  +240
   P      215  RC 12.32  12.39   80 (1)  650 -100  +165
   P      220  RD 17.32  17.34   90 (2)  500  -95  +115
   P  Jul 200  ST  2.38   2.92   43 (2) 3400  -95  +645
   P      205  SA  4.63   5.38   55  2  1850  -95  +390
   P      210  SB  8.00   8.83   67 (2) 1000  -95  +245
   P      215  SC 12.32  13.02   80 (2)  650  -95  +165
   P      220  SD 17.32  17.63   90 (2)  500  -95  +115
   P  Aug 200  TT  3.00   3.63   43 (2) 2700  -95  +495
   P      205  TA  NEW    6.10   54  -  1500  -90  +275
   P      210  TB  NEW    9.42   65  -   950  -85  +195
   P      215  TC  NEW   13.43   75  -   660  -85  +145
```

Source: Value Line Options, May 28, 1984. Copyright 1984 by Value Line, Inc. Reprinted with permission. All rights reserved.

VALUE LINE EVALUATIONS

										— OPTION BUYER —			COVERED — OPTION WRITER —			
Description of Each Security			Recent Market Price	Est. Normal Price	Change Per Point	Performance Rank		Relative Volatility	Current Leverage +10% -10%		Performance Rank Rel. Vol.		Leverage to Expiration +10% Unch. -10%			

Amex Oil & Gas Index (5.1% yield) ASE
XOI units 119.23 3 70%

	Jun	125	FE	.44	67	28	2	9700	+990%	-100%	5	45	+5%	+0	-10%
		120	FD	2.00	2.14	47	2	3400	+465	-95	4	50	+2	+2	-8
		115	FC	5.25	5.20	67	(2)	1250	+210	-95	(4)	40	+1	+1	-6
		110	FB	10.50	9.49	80	(3)	750	+105	-75	(3)	35	+1	+1	-1
		105	FA	14.50	14.30	92	(2)	470	+80	-70	(-)	20	+0	+0	+0
	Jul	125	GE	1.00	2.01	31	(2)	4400	+635	-95	(4)	45	+6	+1	-9
		120	GD	3.00	3.84	48	(2)	2200	+295	-90	(3)	45	+3	+3	-8
		115	GC	6.63	6.68	65	(2)	1100	+150	-80	(3)	40	+2	+2	-5
		110	GB	10.50	10.41	79	(2)	650	+105	-75	(5)	30	+1	+1	-1
		105	GA	15.50	14.77	86	(2)	490	+70	-60	(5)	25	+1	+1	+1
	Aug	125	HE	1.25	2.86	32	(1)	3500	+515	-90	(4)	45	+6	+1	-9
		120	HD	3.38	4.81	49	(2)	1850	+255	-85	(4)	45	+4	+3	-7
		115	HC	NEW	7.58	65	-	960	+130	-75	-	40	+3	+3	-4
P	Jun	105	RA	.19	.01	7	(1)	9999	-85	+770					
P		110	RB	.13	.06	15	(-)	9999	-95	+990					
P		115	RC	.25	.42	32	(1)	9999	-100	+990					
P		120	RD	1.75	2.13	53	1↓	3000	-100	+625					
P		125	RE	5.77	6.00	74	(1)	890	-100	+205					
P	Jul	105	SA	NEW	.21	8	-	9999	-85	+805					
P		110	SB	.31	.57	17	(1)	9999	-90	+990					
P		115	SC	.81	1.51	33	(1)	5400	-95	+880					
P		120	SD	2.50	3.53	53	(2)	2200	-95	+410					
P		125	SE	6.25	6.87	72	(2)	890	-90	+185					
P	Aug	115	TC	NEW	2.17	35	-	2400	-80	+300					
P		120	TD	NEW	4.27	51	-	1550	-80	+205					
P		125	TE	6.50	7.46	71	(2)	870	-85	+175					

Amex Transportation Ind (2.8% yield) ASE
XTI units 116.96 3 50%

	Jun	135	FG	.13	.06	6	(-)	9999	+990%	-95%	(-)	40	+10%	+0	-10%
		130	FF	.19	.19	11	(2)	9999	+990	-95	(4)	40	+10	+0	-10
		125	FE	.38	.58	21	1↓	7500	+990	-95	4↓	35	+7	+0	-10
		120	FD	1.63	1.65	39	3	3400	+470	-95	2	40	+4	+1	-9
		115	FC	4.00	4.00	58	3	1650	+245	-95	2↓	40	+2	+2	-7
	Jul	135	GG	.25	.59	9	(2)	5500	+715	-90	(4)	40	+10	+0	-10
		130	GF	.50	1.13	15	(2)	4300	+630	-90	(3)	40	+10	+0	-10
		125	GE	1.38	2.08	28	(2)	2600	+385	-90	(3)	40	+8	+1	-9
		120	GD	3.13	3.67	43	(3)	1850	+235	-85	(2)	40	+5	+3	-8
		115	GC	5.63	6.08	58	(3)	1200	+160	-80	(2)	40	+3	+3	-5
	Aug	130	HF	NEW	1.86	25	-	1700	+230	-80	-	45	+12	+2	-9
		125	HE	1.75	3.03	30	(2)	2000	+315	-80	(4)	40	+8	+2	-9
		120	HD	NEW	4.78	46	-	1350	+150	-75	-	45	+7	+4	-6
		115	HC	NEW	7.20	59	-	1000	+120	-70	-	40	+5	+5	-4
P	Jun	115	RC	1.25	1.13	42	3↓	3800	-95	+685					
P		120	RD	3.88	3.85	62	2	1200	-95	+280					
P		125	RE	8.04	8.19	83	(2)	460	-95	+145					
P		130	RF	13.04	13.07	97	(2)	330	-85	+90					
P		135	RG	NEW	18.04	98	-	260	-65	+65					
P	Jul	115	SC	1.50	2.64	42	(2)	2700	-90	+560					
P		120	SD	4.38	5.27	61	3	1050	-90	+240					
P		125	SE	8.04	8.99	83	(2)	460	-95	+145					
P		130	SF	13.04	13.42	96	(3)	320	-85	+90					
P		135	SG	NEW	18.19	93	-	270	-55	+65					
P	Aug	115	TC	NEW	3.33	42	-	1600	-75	+220					
P		120	TD	NEW	5.94	58	-	930	-70	+155					
P		125	TE	NEW	9.49	72	-	520	-70	+110					
P		130	TF	NEW	13.72	83	-	350	-60	+80					

	Description of Each Security	Recent Market Price	Est. Normal Price	Change Per Point	Performance Rank Relative Volatility	—OPTION BUYER— Current Leverage +10% -10%		Performance Rank Rel. Vol.	COVERED —OPTION WRITER— Leverage to Expiration +10% Unch. -10%	

NYSE Composite Index (4.6% yield)NYS
NYA units 88.43   3   20%

Jun	105	FA	.06	.00	4 (-)	5900	+945% -95%(-)	20	+10%	+0	-10%
	100	FT	.06	.01	7	-	9400 +990 -100	-	15	+10	+0 -10
	95	FS	.06	.10	16	-	9999 +990 -100	-	15	+8	+0 -10
	90	FR	.81	.83	42	4	2800 +805 -100	2	20	+3	+1 -9
	85	FQ	4.13	3.81	68	4↓	600 +200 -95	-	15	+1	+1 -6
Jul	100	GT	.06	.20	7	-	8600 +990 -95	-	15	+10	+0 -10
	95	GS	.38	.66	21	1↓	3000 +905 -95	4↓	15	+8	+0 -10
	90	GR	1.69	1.97	43	4	1600 +365 -95	2↓	20	+4	+2 -8
	85	GQ	5.00	4.75	67 (4)	580	+150 -85	(2)	20	+2	+2 -5
Aug	100	HT	.13	.39	9 (-)	4600	+990 -90	(-)	15	+10	+0 -10
	95	HS	.63	1.03	24 (2)	2000	+575 -90	(4)	20	+8	+1 -9
	90	HR	2.19	2.50	45	4	1250 +275 -90	2	20	+4	+3 -8
	85	HQ	NEW	5.23	66	-	530 +145 -80	-	20	+2	+2 -4
Sep	105	IA	.06	.28	4	-	5100 +990 -85	-	20	+10	+0 -10
	100	IT	.31	.66	12	1↓	2300 +615 -90	4	20	+10	+0 -10
	95	IS	1.13	1.47	27	3	1300 +345 -85	3	20	+9	+1 -9
	90	IR	3.00	3.08	47	4	830 +195 -80	2	20	+5	+4 -7
	85	IQ	6.25	5.77	66 (4)	480	+115 -70	(2)	20	+3	+3 -3
Dec	100	LT	1.00	1.30	20	1↓	830 +270 -80	4	20	+11	+1 -9
	95	LS	2.38	2.38	34	3	630 +180 -75	3	20	+10	+3 -8
	90	LR	4.38	4.16	50	4	470 +130 -70	3↓	20	+7	+5 -5
	85	LQ	7.75	6.80	65 (4)	370	+85 -65	(2)	20	+5	+5 -1
P Jun	85	RQ	.13	.16	31	-	8300 -100 +990				
P	90	RR	1.94	2.05	59	3↓	770 -100 +435				
P	95	RS	6.63	6.59	84	3	210 -90 +135				
P	100	RT	11.75	11.57	91 (4)	155	-65 +75				
P	105	RA	16.57	16.57	100 (4)	105	-55 +55				
P Jul	85	SQ	.44	.74	31	3↓	3000 -95 +990				
P	90	SR	2.38	2.85	58	4↓	760 -95 +340				
P	95	SS	6.75	6.83	81	3	220 -85 +130				
P	100	ST	NEW	11.62	94	-	130 -65 +75				
P Aug	85	TQ	.63	1.11	32 (4)	2200	-95 +810				
P	90	TR	2.69	3.27	58	4	720 -90 +290				
P	95	TS	NEW	7.05	78	-	240 -75 +120				
P	100	TT	NEW	11.69	92	-	135 -65 +75				
P Sep	85	UQ	.88	1.50	33	3	1550 -90 +570				
P	90	UR	3.00	3.71	57	4	580 -85 +250				
P	95	US	6.75	7.32	81	4	200 -85 +130				
P	100	UT	11.57	11.81	98 (5)	130	-75 +75				
P	105	UA	16.57	16.64	100 (5)	100	-55 +55				
P Dec	85	XQ	1.44	2.27	34	2	610 -80 +335				
P	90	XR	3.38	4.53	56	2	390 -80 +215				
P	95	XS	6.75	7.92	81	2	260 -85 +130				
P	100	XT	11.57	12.14	98 (4)	145	-75 +75				

NYSE Telephone Index (9.0% yield)NYS
NTI units 97.34   -   45%

Jun	110	FB	.06	.06	7 (-)	9999	+990%-100%(-)	35	+10%	+0	-10%
	105	FA	.13	.27	16 (-)	9999	+990 -100 (-)	30	+8	+0 -10
	100	FT	.63	1.10	37 (-)	4800	+990 -100 (-)	30	+3	+1 -9
	95	FS	3.00	3.50	62 (-)	1150	+305 -100 (-)	25	+1	+1 -7
Jul	110	GB	.13	.56	9 (-)	9500	+990 -90 (-)	35	+10	+0 -10
	105	GA	.38	1.21	20 (-)	5100	+950 -90 (-)	30	+8	+0 -10
	100	GT	.75	2.54	37 (-)	3600	+880 -90 (-)	30	+4	+1 -9
	95	GS	3.25	4.91	61 (-)	1000	+275 -90 (-)	25	+1	+1 -7
Aug	110	HB	NEW	.99	19	-	1900 +290 -85	-	40	+11	+1 -9
	105	HA	NEW	1.84	30	-	1650 +235 -80	-	35	+10	+2 -8
	100	HT	NEW	3.33	45	-	1400 +180 -80	-	40	+6	+4 -7
	95	HS	NEW	5.69	61	-	900 +135 -75	-	35	+4	+4 -4
Oct	110	JB	.38	1.89	13 (-)	3500	+610 -70 (-)	35	+10	+0 -10
	105	JA	NEW	3.00	35	-	980 +155 -75	-	35	+11	+3 -7
	100	JT	1.88	4.68	40 (-)	1350	+340 -80 (-)	25	+5	+2 -8
	95	JS	4.25	7.03	60 (-)	690	+195 -80 (-)	25	+2	+2 -6
Jan	105	AA	1.63	4.21	29 (-)	1700	+275 -70 (-)	35	+10	+2 -8
	100	AT	3.13	5.97	43 (-)	1050	+200 -70 (-)	30	+6	+3 -7
	95	AS	NEW	8.31	62	-	420 +85 -60	-	25	+7	+7 -2
P Jun	95	RS	.13	1.25	38 (-)	9999	-95 +990				
P	100	RT	2.66	3.78	63 (-)	960	-100 +365				
P	105	RA	NEW	7.91	82	-	430 -80 +120				
P	110	RB	NEW	12.71	94	-	270 -70 +75				
P Jul	95	SS	.75	2.80	39 (-)	3600	-90 +920				
P	100	ST	3.63	5.27	62 (-)	930	-90 +245				
P	105	SA	NEW	8.81	74	-	470 -65 +100				
P	110	SB	NEW	13.12	86	-	290 -55 +70				
P Aug	95	TS	NEW	3.61	39	-	1350 -65 +150				
P	100	TT	NEW	6.06	55	-	860 -60 +115				
P	105	TA	NEW	9.43	70	-	460 -55 +90				
P	110	TB	NEW	13.51	82	-	300 -50 +65				
P Oct	95	VS	1.75	4.98	40 (-)	1600	-80 +370				
P	100	VT	NEW	7.42	52	-	550 -50 +85				
P	105	VA	NEW	10.58	65	-	400 -50 +70				
P	110	VB	14.00	14.37	78 (-)	280	-45 +60				
P Jan	95	MS	2.50	6.35	41 (-)	1550	-70 +250				
P	100	MT	NEW	8.75	49	-	380 -40 +70				
P	105	MA	NEW	11.75	61	-	310 -40 +60				

	Description of Each Security	Recent Market Price	Est. Normal Price	Change Per Point	OPTION BUYER Performance Rank Relative Volatility	Current Leverage	COVERED OPTION WRITER Performance Rank Rel. Vol.	Leverage to Expiration +10% Unch. -10%
PSE Technology Index (1.5% yield) PAC
PSE units	102.88			3	40%			
Jun 115 FC	.13	.17	9 (−)	9999	+990% −95%(−)	30	+10% +0 −10%
110 FB	.63	.58	24	24 4400	+685 −95 3↓	30	+8 +1 −9
105 FA	1.88	1.78	42	4 2800	+370 −95 2	40	+4 +2 −8
100 FT	5.00	4.40	63	(5) 1250	+170 −85 (1)	35	+2 +2 −5
95 FS	NEW	8.37	82	− 440	+120 −85 −	20	+1 +1 −2
Jul 110 GB	1.75	2.00	31	(3) 1950	+275 −85 (3)	35	+9 +2 −8
105 GA	3.50	3.68	46	(4) 1600	+190 −80 (2)	40	+6 +4 −7
100 GT	6.63	6.25	62	(4) 950	+120 −75 (1)	35	+4 +4 −4
95 GS	NEW	9.69	76	− 490	+95 −70 −	25	+2 +2 −1
Aug 110 HP	NEW	2.89	36	− 1350	+175 −75 −	40	+10 +3 −7
105 HA	NEW	4.71	49	− 1250	+140 −75 −	40	+7 +5 −6
100 HT	NEW	7.27	62	− 830	+110 −70 −	35	+5 +5 −3
Sep 115 IC	NFW	2.46	28	− 1150	+165 −75 −	40	+13 +2 −8
110 IB	NEW	3.81	39	− 1000	+140 −70 −	35	+11 +4 −7
105 IA	NEW	5.72	50	− 820	+115 −65 −	35	+8 +6 −5
100 IT	NEW	8.27	62	− 610	+90 −60 −	30	+6 +6 −2
P Jun 95 RS	.19	.13	16	(2) 9700	−95 +990
P 100 RT	1.00	.75	36	4↓ 3700	−95 +655
P 105 RA	3.00	3.08	60	3↓ 1250	−95 +315
P 110 RB	7.12	7.29	83	2↓ 380	−95 +145
P 115 RC	12.12	12.15	98	(3) 260	−80 +85
P Jul 95 SS	NEW	.77	20	− 3000	−80 +450
P 100 ST	1.75	1.98	37	(4) 2100	−85 +355
P 105 SA	4.25	4.38	57	(4) 1050	−80 +195
P 110 SB	7.50	8.01	78	(3) 410	−80 +130
P Aug 100 TT	2.00	2.64	38	(4) 1750	−80 +305
P 105 TA	4.25	5.05	57	(4) 930	−80 +195
P 110 TB	NEW	8.51	71	− 450	−65 +105
P Sep 100 UT	NEW	3.30	38	− 1100	−65 +170
P 105 UA	NEW	5.72	54	− 720	−65 +130
P 110 UB	NFW	9.06	69	− 440	−60 +95
P 115 UC	NFW	13.10	80	− 290	−55 +70
PHL Gaming−Hotel Index (1.8% yield) PHL
XGH units	79.10			3	65%
Jun 100 FT	.13	.03	4	(−) 2100	+415% −90%(−)	65	+10% +0 −10%
95 FS	.13	.09	5	(−) 5800	+585 −90 (−)	60	+10 +0 −10
90 FR	.13	.28	9	(−) 9999	+990 −90 (−)	50	+10 +0 −10
85 FQ	.38	.87	22	(2) 6600	+820 −90 (4)	45	+8 +0 −10
80 FP	1.75	2.42	46	(3) 3000	+325 −90 (2)	50	+3 +2 −8
Jul 85 GQ	NEW	2.52	36	− 1700	+155 −75 −	55	+11 +3 −7
80 GP	3.00	4.43	49	(3) 1700	+180 −75 (2)	50	+5 +4 −6
75 GO	NFW	7.21	68	− 850	+85 −60 −	45	+4 +4 −1
Aug 85 HQ	NFW	3.48	40	− 1250	+120 −65 −	60	+12 +5 −6
80 HP	NEW	5.49	54	− 1150	+95 −60 −	60	+9 +7 −3
75 HO	NEW	8.22	68	− 750	+75 −55 −	45	+6 +6 +0
Sep 100 IT	.25	1.23	7	(1) 2400	+360 −55 (3)	60	+10 +0 −10
95 IS	NEW	1.92	24	− 1050	+130 −65 −	60	+13 +2 −8
90 IR	1.00	2.96	20	(1) 1650	+255 −65 (4)	50	+11 +1 −9
85 IQ	2.13	4.47	34	(1) 1150	+185 −65 (4)	45	+10 +3 −8
80 IP	NEW	6.55	56	− 760	+80 −55 −	50	+10 +9 −2
Dec 90 LR	NEW	4.65	40	− 640	+80 −55 −	50	+17 +6 −4
85 LQ	4.00	6.35	41	(1) 640	+110 −55 (5)	40	+13 +5 −5
80 LP	NEW	8.53	59	− 480	+60 −45 −	40	+13 +12 +1
75 LO	NEW	11.20	69	− 410	+55 −45 −	30	+10 +10 +5
P Jun 80 RP	2.19	2.39	55	(3) 2100	−90 +305
P 85 RQ	5.90	6.21	85	(2) 560	−95 +135
P 90 RR	10.90	10.95	99	(3) 360	−70 +75
P 95 RS	NEW	15.91	99	− 290	−50 +50
P 100 RT	NEW	20.90	100	− 240	−40 +40
P Jul 75 SO	NEW	1.70	30	− 2200	−70 +210
P 80 SP	NEW	3.79	51	− 1400	−65 +145
P 85 SQ	NEW	7.13	71	− 630	−60 +95
P Aug 75 TO	NEW	2.37	31	− 1600	−60 +150
P 80 TP	NEW	4.53	50	− 1150	−60 +115
P 85 TQ	NEW	7.73	67	− 600	−55 +85
P Sep 80 UP	NEW	5.26	48	− 830	−50 +95
P 85 UQ	NEW	8.36	64	− 550	−50 +75
P 90 UR	NEW	12.21	77	− 380	−45 +55
P 95 US	NEW	16.57	86	− 290	−40 +45
P 100 UT	NEW	21.24	92	− 240	−35 +35
P Dec 75 XO	NFW	4.35	32	− 660	−40 +75
P 80 XP	NEW	6.61	46	− 530	−40 +70
P 85 XQ	7.13	9.58	71	(1) 550	−60 +100
P 90 XR	12.00	13.18	79	(3) 310	−45 +60

STOCK INDEX OPTIONS

May 28, 1984

						—OPTION BUYER—		COVERED —OPTION WRITER—	
Description of Each Security		Recent Market Price	Est. Normal Price	Change Per Point	Performance Rank Relative Volatility	Current Leverage +10%-10%		Performance Rank Rel. Vol. +10% Unch. -10%	

PHL Gold-Silver Index (1.8% yield) PHL
XAU units 113.29   3   85%

Jun	140	FH	.13	.07	4 (-)	4500	+570%	-90%(-)	80	+10% +0	-10%
	135	FG	.25	.15	7 (2)	6200	+520	-90 (3)	75	+10 +0	-10
	130	FF	.25	.34	9 2	9600	+725	-90 3	70	+10 +0	-10
	125	FE	.50	.75	16 2	7300	+650	-90 3	65	+10 +0	-10
	120	FD	1.13	1.63	29 2	5000	+485	-90 3	60	+7 +1	-9
	115	FC	3.00	3.28	46 3	3100	+260	-90 2	65	+4 +3	-8
	110	FB	5.63	5.94	63 (3)	1650	+170	-85 (3)	55	+2 +2	-5
	105	FA	9.13	9.57	79 (2)	840	+115	-80 (5)	35	+1 +1	-2
	100	FT	14.50	13.88	86 (3)	630	+75	-60 (4)	30	+1 +1	+1
Jul	125	GE	1.44	2.74	24 (2)	2900	+290	-80 (3)	65	+11 +1	-9
	120	GD	2.88	4.16	36 (2)	2200	+205	-75 (3)	65	+9 +3	-8
	115	GC	4.63	6.15	48 3	1850	+165	-75 2	60	+6 +4	-6
	110	GB	7.63	8.75	62 (3)	1200	+115	-70 (2)	55	+4 +4	-4
	105	GA	NEW	11.95	73 -	790	+80	-60 -	45	+4 +4	+1
Aug	115	HC	NEW	7.66	53 -	1250	+95	-60 -	65	+9 +7	-3
	110	HB	NEW	10.25	63 -	970	+80	-60 -	55	+7 +7	-1
Sep	140	IH	1.25	2.16	14 (2)	1500	+195	-65 (2)	75	+11 +1	-9
	135	IG	1.88	2.94	20 (2)	1450	+170	-65 (2)	75	+12 +2	-8
	130	IF	2.38	3.98	25 (2)	1410	+170	-65 (3)	70	+12 +2	-8
	125	IE	4.00	5.33	34 (2)	1200	+130	-65 (3)	65	+14 +4	-7
	120	ID	5.63	7.05	43 (2)	1050	+115	-60 (3)	60	+11 +5	-5
	115	IC	7.75	9.19	53 (3)	890	+95	-60 (3)	55	+9 +7	-3
	110	IB	10.50	11.76	62 (3)	740	+80	-55 (3)	45	+7 +7	-1
	105	IA	13.00	14.77	71 (2)	610	+70	-50 (4)	35	+5 +5	+2
	100	IT	NEW	18.18	78 -	520	+55	-45 -	35	+5 +5	+5
Dec	135	LG	NEW	5.04	33 -	800	+90	-55 -	65	+15 +5	-6
	130	LF	5.25	6.34	35 (2)	770	+85	-55 (3)	60	+15 +5	-6
	125	LE	6.75	7.91	42 (2)	700	+90	-55 (3)	55	+17 +6	-4
	120	LD	8.75	9.79	50 (2)	630	+75	-50 (4)	50	+15 +8	-2
	115	LC	10.75	12.01	57 (2)	560	+70	-50 (4)	45	+12 +10	-1
	110	LB	NEW	14.58	65 -	510	+55	-45 -	40	+11 +11	+3
	105	LA	NEW	17.49	72 -	460	+50	-40 -	35	+10 +10	+6
P Jun	100	RT	.25	.14	9 (1)	9999	-80	+695			
P	105	RA	.38	.46	18 (2)	9999	-90	+990			
P	110	RB	1.63	1.42	36 2	4300	-90	+420			
P	115	RC	3.63	3.68	56 3	2200	-90	+260			
P	120	RD	7.00	7.37	76 (2)	910	-90	+160			
P	125	RE	12.25	11.91	84 (3)	630	-65	+90			
P	130	RF	16.71	16.77	99 (3)	450	-65	+70			
P	135	RG	21.71	21.73	100 (3)	390	-50	+50			
P	140	RH	NEW	26.71	99 -	340	-40	+40			
P Jul	105	SA	1.13	1.80	23 (2)	3900	-75	+380			
P	110	SB	2.75	3.31	38 (3)	2400	-75	+235			
P	115	SC	5.38	5.66	53 (3)	1500	-70	+155			
P	120	SD	8.00	8.90	71 (3)	880	-70	+125			
P	125	SE	11.75	12.85	91 (3)	570	-80	+95			
P Aug	110	TB	NEW	4.34	38 -	1650	-60	+135			
P	115	TC	NEW	6.72	51 -	1250	-60	+115			
P Sep	100	UT	1.63	2.34	17 (2)	2100	-55	+180			
P	105	UA	2.75	3.59	26 (2)	1650	-60	+160			
P	110	UB	4.25	5.37	38 (3)	1300	-60	+145			
P	115	UC	6.75	7.76	51 (3)	970	-55	+115			
P	120	UD	NEW	10.78	60 -	720	-50	+80			
P	125	UE	12.50	14.37	81 (3)	550	-60	+85			
P	130	UF	NEW	18.40	79 -	450	-45	+55			
P	135	UG	NEW	22.77	85 -	380	-40	+45			
P	140	UH	NEW	27.37	90 -	330	-35	+40			
P Dec	105	XA	NEW	5.35	28 -	820	-40	+80			
P	110	XB	5.13	7.28	39 (2)	820	-50	+120			
P	115	XC	7.00	9.69	51 2	750	-55	+110			
P	120	XD	10.00	12.59	63 (2)	600	-55	+90			
P	125	XE	13.50	15.96	75 (2)	500	-50	+75			
P	130	XF	18.25	19.74	80 (3)	380	-45	+55			
P	135	XG	NEW	23.84	79 -	340	-35	+40			

VALUE LINE EVALUATIONS

	Description of Each Security	Recent Market Price	Est. Normal Price	Change Per Point	Performance Rank Relative Volatility	—OPTION BUYER— Current Leverage +10% -10%	Performance Rank Rel. Vol.	COVERED —OPTION WRITER— Leverage to Expiration +10% Unch. -10%
S&P 100 Index (4.7% yield) CBO								
OEX units		152.35			3	50%		
Jun 175	FO	.06	.01	4	(-)	9999 +990%-100%(-)	40 +10%	+0 -10%
170	FN	.06	.05	7	-	9999 +990 -100	-	40 +10 +0 -10
165	FM	.06	.16	13	-	9999 +990 -100	-	35 +8 +0 -10
160	FL	.44	.53	27	2	8900 +990 -100	4	35 +5 +0 -10
155	FK	1.56	1.61	42	2	3900 +720 -100	4	35 +3 +1 -9
150	FJ	4.00	4.05	58	2	1650 +340 -100	4+	30 +1 +1 -8
145	FI	8.25	7.89	73	2	770 +175 -95	4	25 +1 +1 -5
140	FH	13.00	12.50	84	(2)	490 +115 -85	(-)	20 +0 +0 -2
Jul 175	GO	.06	.27	5	-	9999 +990 -95	-	40 +10 +0 -10
170	GN	.13	.53	9	-	9999 +990 -95	-	40 +10 +0 -10
165	GM	.56	1.04	19	2	5700 +925 -95	4	35 +9 +0 -10
160	GL	1.38	1.97	30	2	3300 +580 -95	4+	35 +6 +1 -9
155	GK	3.13	3.57	44	(3)	2100 +335 -90	(3)	35 +4 +2 -8
150	GJ	5.88	6.03	58	(2)	1250 +210 -90	(3)	35 +2 +2 -6
145	GI	9.50	9.36	70	(2)	720 +140 -85	(4)	30 +2 +2 -4
Aug 175	HO	.19	.60	7	1	9200 +990 -90	4	40 +10 +0 -10
170	HN	.38	1.02	12	1	6400 +910 -90	4	40 +10 +0 -10
165	HM	.94	1.73	21	2	3600 +600 -90	4	35 +9 +1 -9
160	HL	2.19	2.87	33	2	2200 +370 -90	4+	35 +7 +1 -9
155	HK	4.13	4.61	45	2	1650 +250 -85	3	35 +5 +3 -7
150	HJ	6.88	7.05	58	2	1100 +175 -85	3+	35 +3 +3 -6
145	HI	10.50	10.23	69	(2)	680 +125 -75	(4)	30 +2 +2 -3
P Jun 140	RH	.06	.04	12	-	9999 -100 +990		
P 145	RI	.13	.22	26	-	9999 -100 +990		
P 150	RJ	.94	1.05	42	2	5200 -100 +990		
P 155	RK	3.50	3.61	59	2	1500 -100 +410		
P 160	RL	7.65	7.84	75	1+	610 -100 +200		
P 165	RM	12.65	12.68	89	2	410 -95 +120		
P 170	RN	17.65	17.66	97	(3)	320 -80 +85		
P 175	RO	23.00	22.65	91	(3)	300 -55 +65		
P Jul 145	SI	.56	1.16	27	2	6600 -95 +990		
P 150	SJ	1.88	2.58	42	2	2800 -95 +595		
P 155	SK	4.25	5.10	58	2	1300 -95 +320		
P 160	SL	7.88	8.72	74	2+	620 -95 +190		
P 165	SM	13.00	13.08	83	2	430 -80 +115		
P 170	SN	17.75	17.82	92	(3)	330 -70 +85		
P 175	SO	NEW	22.71	96	-	280 -60 +65		
P Aug 145	TI	.94	1.91	28	1	4100 -90 +825		
P 150	TJ	2.50	3.53	43	2	2200 -90 +430		
P 155	TK	4.88	6.04	57	3	1200 -90 +270		
P 160	TL	8.13	9.45	73	2+	620 -90 +180		
P 165	TM	13.00	13.54	83	2	420 -80 +115		
P 170	TN	NEW	18.08	87	-	330 -65 +80		
P 175	TO	NEW	22.85	93	-	280 -60 +65		
S&P 500 Index (4.6% yield) CBO								
SPX units		153.89			3	45%		
Jun 170	FN	.13	.05	10	(-)	9999 +990%-100%(-)	30 +10%	+0 -10%
165	FM	.38	.19	20	(2)	8300 +990 -100	(4)	30 +7 +0 -10
160	FL	.88	.66	32	2	5100 +990 -100	4	30 +5 +1 -9
155	FK	2.25	2.05	47	(3)	2900 +540 -100	(3)	35 +2 +1 -9
145	FI	10.00	9.20	76	(3)	630 +145 -90	(4)	25 +1 +1 -4
Sep 165	IM	NEW	2.64	30	-	1600 +270 -85	-	35 +9 +2 -8
160	IL	4.00	4.07	40	(2)	1300 +220 -85	(3)	35 +7 +3 -8
155	IK	NEW	6.09	50	-	980 +175 -80	-	30 +5 +4 -6
150	IJ	NEW	8.75	61	-	710 +140 -75	-	30 +3 +3 -5
P Jun 145	RI	.13	.10	22	(-)	9999 -100 +990		
P 155	RK	2.25	2.48	54	(2)	2000 -100 +635		
P 160	RL	6.11	6.38	70	(1)	650 -100 +250		
P 165	RM	11.11	11.15	85	(2)	390 -95 +140		
P 170	RN	NEW	16.12	94	-	300 -85 +95		
P Sep 150	UJ	2.25	3.30	38	(2)	1850 -85 +435		
P 155	UK	3.13	5.55	53	(2)	1200 -95 +430		
P 160	UL	6.11	8.65	69	(1)	700 -95 +255		
P 165	UM	11.11	12.48	84	(2)	400 -95 +140		

STOCK INDEX OPTIONS

Description of Each Security	Recent Market Price	Est. Normal Price	Change Per Point	OPTION BUYER Performance Rank / Relative Volatility	Current Leverage +10%	-10%	COVERED OPTION WRITER Performance Rank / Rel. Vol.	Leverage to Expiration +10%	Unch.	-10%
S&P Transportation Ind (3.4% yield) CBO										
OTN units 128.48				3	45%					
Jun 150 FJ	.13	.04	5	(-) 9600	+970%	-95%	(-) 40	+10%	+0	-10%
145 FI	.19	.12	9	(2) 9400	+990	-95	(3) 35	+10	+0	-10
140 FH	.31	.36	16	2 7800	+990	-95	4↓ 35	+9	+0	-10
135 FG	.81	.98	29	2↑ 4700	+810	-95	3↓ 35	+6	+1	-9
130 FF	2.63	2.46	46	4↓ 2700	+355	-95	2 40	+3	+2	-8
Jul 150 GJ	NEW	.52	11	- 2900	+430	-90	- 40	+10	+0	-10
145 GI	NEW	.94	17	- 2600	+370	-85	- 40	+11	+1	-9
140 GH	1.63	1.67	25	(3) 2200	+310	-85	(3) 35	+10	+1	-9
135 GG	2.75	2.89	36	(3) 1900	+250	-85	(2) 40	+7	+2	-8
Aug 140 HH	NEW	2.60	29	- 1550	+210	-80	- 40	+11	+2	-8
135 HG	NEW	4.01	39	- 1400	+175	-75	- 40	+8	+3	-7
130 HF	NEW	5.99	50	- 1250	+140	-75	- 40	+6	+5	-6
P Jun 130 RF	2.63	3.00	56	(2) 1700	-100	+450				
P 135 RG	6.52	6.88	75	(2) 540	-100	+195				
P 140 RH	11.52	11.59	91	(2) 340	-90	+110				
P 145 RI	16.52	16.53	99	(3) 270	-75	+80				
P 150 RJ	NEW	21.52	99	- 220	-60	+60				
P Jul 135 SG	7.25	8.05	72	(3) 590	-85	+170				
P 140 SH	11.52	12.20	91	(2) 340	-90	+110				
P 145 SI	16.52	16.81	98	(3) 270	-75	+80				
P 150 SJ	NEW	21.64	95	- 230	-55	+60				
P Aug 130 TF	NEW	5.49	52	- 1100	-75	+170				
P 135 TG	NEW	8.70	66	- 610	-70	+125				
P 140 TH	NEW	12.65	78	- 380	-65	+95				

APPENDIX E

COMMON STOCKS HAVING LISTED OPTIONS

**COMMON STOCKS
HAVING LISTED OPTIONS**

AMF, Inc.
AMR Corp.
ASA Ltd.
Abbott Labs
Advanced Micro Devices
Aetna Life & Casualty
Air Products & Chemicals
Alexander & Alexander
Allied Corp.
Allis-Chalmers
Aluminum Co. of America
AMAX, Inc.
Amdahl Corp.
Amerada Hess Corp.
American Brands
American Broadcasting Co.
American Can
American Cyanamid
American Electric Power
American Express
American Home Products
American Hospital Supply
American Medical International
American Telephone & Telegraph
AMP, Inc.

Anacomp
Anheuser-Busch
Apache Corp.
Archer Daniels Midland
Arkla, Inc.
Armco, Inc.
ASARCO, Inc.
Ashland Oil
Atlantic Richfield
Automatic Data Processing
Avco Corp.
Avnet, Inc.
Avon Products

Baker International Corp.
Bally Manufacturing Corp.
BankAmerica Corp.
Bard (C.R.), Inc.
Bausch & Lomb
Baxter Travenol Labs.
Beatrice Foods
Becton Dickinson & Co.
Bethlehem Steel
Beverly Enterprises
Black & Decker

STOCK INDEX OPTIONS

Blue Bell, Inc.
Boeing
Boise Cascade Corp.
Bristol-Myers
Browning Ferris Ind.
Brunswick Corp.
Bucyrus-Erie
Burlington Northern
Burroughs Corp.

CBS, Inc.
CIGNA Corp.
CSX Corp.
Campbell Red Lake
Capital Cities Communications
Caterpillar Tractor
Celanese Corp.
Cessna Aircraft
Champion International Corp.
Charter Co.
Chase Manhattan Corp.
Chicago & Northwestern
  Transportation
Church's Fried Chicken
Cincinnati Milacron
Citicorp
City Investing Co.
Clorox Co.
Coastal Corp.
Coca-Cola
Coleco Industries, Inc.
Colgate-Palmolive
Colt Industries, Inc.
Combustion Engineering
Comdisco, Inc.
Commodore International
Commonwealth Edison
Communications Satellite
Community Psychiatric Centers
Computer Sciences
Computervision Corp.
Consolidated Edison
Continental Illinois Corp.
Continental Telecom, Inc.
Control Data
Cooper Industries

Corning Glass Works
Cray Research
Crown Zellerbach
Cullinet Software

Dart & Kraft, Inc.
Data General Corp.
Datapoint Corp.
Dataproducts Corp.
Dayton Hudson Corp.
Deere & Co.
Delta Air Lines
Denny's Inc.
Diamond Shamrock
Diebold, Inc.
Digital Equipment
Disney (Walt) Productions
Dome Mines
Dominion Resources
Donaldson, Lufkin & Jenrette
Dow Chemical
Dresser Industries
Duke Power
duPont

EG&G, Inc.
E-Systems
Eastern Gas & Fuel
Eastman Kodak
Eckerd (Jack) Corp.
Edwards (A. G.) Inc.
Electronic Data Systems
Emerson Electric
Emery Air Freight
Engelhard Corp.
ENSERCH Corp.
Esmark, Inc.
Exxon Corp.

Federal Express
Financial Corp. of America
Firestone Tire
First Boston Inc.
First Chicago Corp.
First Mississippi
Fleetwood Enterprises

COMMON STOCKS

Flow General
Fluor Corp.
Ford Motor
Foster Wheeler
Freeport-McMoRan

GAF Corp
GCA Corp
GTE Corp
General Dynamics
General Electric
General Foods
General Instrument
General Motors
Genuine Parts Co.
GEO International
Georgia Pacific
Getty Oil
Gillette
Global Marine
Golden Nugget
Goodyear Tire
Gould, Inc.
Grace (W. R.)
Great Western Financial
Greyhound Corp.
Gulf Canada Ltd.
Gulf Corp.
Gulf + Western Ind.

Hall (Frank B) & Co.
Halliburton Co.
Harris Corp.
Hecla Mining
Hercules, Inc.
Hewlett-Packard
Hilton Hotels
Hitachi Ltd. (ADR)
Holiday Inns, Inc.
Homestake Mining
Honeywell, Inc.
Hospital Corp. of America
Household International
Houston Natural Gas
Hughes Tool

Humana Inc.
Hutton (E. F.) Group

ITT Corp.
Inexco Oil
International Business Machines
International Flavors &
   Fragrances
International Minerals &
   Chemicals
International Paper

Johnson & Johnson
Joy Manufacturing

K mart Corp.
Kaneb Services
Kerr-McGee Corp.
Key Pharmaceutical

LTV Corp.
Lear Siegler, Inc.
Lehman Corp.
Levi Strauss & Co.
Lilly, Eli
Limited, Inc.
Litton Industries
Lockheed Corp.
Loral Corp.
Louisiana Land & Exploration
Louisiana-Pacific

M/A-Com. Inc.
MCA, Inc.
MGM/UA Entertainment
MAPCO, Inc.
Marriott Corp.
Martin Marietta
Mary Kay Cosmetics
Masonite Corp.
Mattel, Inc.
McDermott International
McDonald's Corp.
McDonnell Douglas
Medtronic, Inc.
Merck & Co.

STOCK INDEX OPTIONS

Merrill Lynch & Co.
Mesa Petroleum
Metromedia, Inc.
Middle South Utilities
Minnesota Mining & Manufacturing
Mitchell Energy & Development
Mitel Corp.
Mobil Corp.
Mohawk Data Sciences
Monsanto
Morgan (J. P.) & Co.
Motorola, Inc.
Murphy Oil Corp.

NBI, Inc.
NCR Corp.
NL Industries, Inc.
National Distillers & Chemical
National Medical Care
National Medical Enterprises
National Patent Development
National Semiconductor
Newmont Mining
Noble Affiliates
Norfolk Southern Corp.
Northern Telecom Ltd.
Northrop Corp.
Northwest Airlines
Northwest Industries
Novo Industry A/S (ADR)

Oak Industries, Inc.
Occidental Petroleum
Ocean Drilling & Exploration
Owens-Corning Fiberglas
Owens-Illinois, Inc.

PPG Industries
Paine Webber, Inc.
Paradyne Corp.
Parker Drilling
Penn Central Corp.
Penney (J. C.)
Pennzoil Company

PepsiCo, Inc.
Perkin-Elmer Corp.
Petrolane, Inc.
Pfizer, Inc.
Phelps Dodge
Phibro-Salomon
Philip Morris
Phillips Petroleum
Pitney-Bowes
Pittston Co
Pogo Producing Co.
Polaroid Corp.
Prime Computer
Procter & Gamble

RCA Corp.
Ralston Purina
Raychem Corp.
Raytheon Co.
Reading & Bates
Resorts International "A"
Revlon, Inc.
Reynolds Industries
Reynolds Metals
Rockwell International Corp.
ROLM Corp.
Rowan Cos.
Royal Dutch Petroleum
Ryder System

Sabine Corp.
Safeway Stores
Santa Fe Southern Pacific
Schering-Plough
Schlumberger Ltd.
Scientific Atlantic
Scott Paper
Seagram Co.
Searle (G. D.)
Sears, Roebuck
Sedco, Inc.
Shaklee Corp.
Shell Oil
Signal Cos.
Singer Co.

COMMON STOCKS

Skyline Corp.
Smith International, Inc.
Smithkline Beckman
Sony Corp. (ADR)
Southern Co.
Southland Royalty
Southwest Airlines
Sperry Corp.
Squibb Corp.
Standard Oil of California
Standard Oil of Indiana
Standard Oil of Ohio
Sterling Drug
Storage Technology
Storer Communications
Sun Company
Superior Oil Co.
Sybron Corp.
Syntex

TIE/communications
TRW, Inc.
Tandy Corp.
Tektronix, Inc.
Teledyne, Inc.
Telex Corp.
Tenneco, Inc.
Tesoro Petroleum
Texaco, Inc.
Texas Instruments
Texas Oil & Gas
Textron, Inc.
Thrifty Corp.
Tidewater, Inc.
Time, Inc.
Tosco Corp.
Toys "R" Us
Transamerica
Trans World Corp.

Travelers Corp.
Tri-Continental

UAL, Inc.
Union Carbide
Union Pacific Corp.
USAir Group, Inc.
U.S. Home Corp.
United States Steel
United Technologies
Unocal Corp.
Upjohn Co.

Valero Energy
Varian Associates
Veco Instruments
Verbatim Corp.
Viacom International

Wal-Mart Stores
Walter (Jim) Corp.
Wang Labs "B"
Warner Communications
Warner-Lambert
Waste Management, Inc.
Wendy's International, Inc.
Western Co. of North America
Western Union Corp.
Westinghouse Electric
Weyerhaeuser Co.
Whittaker Corp.
Williams Companies
Williams Electronics
Winnebago Industries
Woolworth (F. W.)

Xerox Corp.

Zapata Corp.
Zenith Electronics

APPENDIX F
COMPUTER DATA BASES

COMPUTER DATA BASES

Bridge Data
10050 Manchester Road
St. Louis, MO 63122

Chronometrics
327 S. LaSalle Street
Chicago, IL 60604

Commodity Information Service Company
327 S. LaSalle Street
Chicago, IL 60604

Monchik-Weber
11 Broadway
New York, NY 10004

National Computer Network of Chicago
1929 N. Harlem Avenue
Chicago, IL 60635

Network Utilities
327 S. LaSalle Street
Chicago, IL 60604

On-Line Response, Inc.
327 S. LaSalle Street
Chicago, IL 60604

The Options Group
50 Broadway
New York, NY 10004

Track Data Corp.
327 S. LaSalle Street
Chicago, IL 60604

APPENDIX G

ADVISORY SERVICES COVERING INDEX OPTIONS

ADVISORY SERVICES

Institute for Options Research Inc.
The Trester Compleat Option Report
P.O. Box 12340
Reno, NV 89510

The Leveraged Investor
Stock Options, Inc.
P.O. Box 27977
Richmond, VA 23261

Option Analytics, Inc.
Scientific Stock Option Analysis
Box 529
Bowie, MD 20715

The Option Trader
CMI Business Services, Inc.
1602 F. Executive Plaza
555 Sparkman Drive
Huntsville, AL 35805

Value Line Options & Convertibles
711 Third Avenue
New York, NY 10017

APPENDIX H
EXCHANGE ADDRESSES

EXCHANGE ADDRESSES

American Stock Exchange
Options Division
86 Trinity Place
New York, NY 10006

Chicago Board Options Exchange
141 West Jackson Boulevard
Chicago, IL 60604

New York Stock Exchange
Index Options Division
11 Wall Street
New York, NY 10005

Pacific Stock Exchange
Options Division
301 Pine Street
San Francisco, CA 94104

Philadelphia Stock Exchange
Options Division
1900 Market Street
Philadelphia, PA 19103

APPENDIX I
OPTION SYMBOL GUIDE

Options At A Glance — NYA

Index And Options Calendar

- Expiring option classes cease trading today
- Exchange holiday (no options trading)
- No interest rate options trading*
- Expiration date

*There may be additional holidays for interest rate options trading in 1984 but this information is not available at this time.

Trading Hours: 10:00 AM - 4:10 PM EST

[Calendar grids for September 1983 through February 1985]

Symbols—Market Indices

- NYA = NYSE Index
- SPX = Standard + Poors 500 Index
- XAM = ASE Composite Index
- OEX = Standard + Poors 100 Index
- XMI = Major Market Index

New Options Symbols:

_____

_____

_____

Expiration Month Codes

Month	Calls	Puts
January	A	M
February	B	N
March	C	O
April	D	P
May	E	Q
June	F	R
July	G	S
August	H	T
September	I	U
October	J	V
November	K	W
December	L	X

Striking Price Codes

Key	Striking Prices		
A	5	105	205
B	10	110	210
C	15	115	215
D	20	120	220
E	25	125	225
F	30	130	230
G	35	135	235
H	40	140	240
I	45	145	245
J	50	150	250
K	55	155	255
L	60	160	260
M	65	165	265
N	70	170	270
O	75	175	275
P	80	180	280
Q	85	185	285
R	90	190	290
S	95	195	295
T	100	200	300

Access Instructions

- Bunker Ramo: Symbol, Month, Striking Price, Recap1
  To obtain the quote on the NYSE Index February 95 call, key in:

  [N] [Y] [A] [B] [S] [Recap1]

- Quotron: Symbol, Month, Striking Price, Exchange Code, Send
  To obtain the quote on the NYSE Index February 95 call, key in:

  [N] [Y] [A] [B] [S] [.] [N] [O] [SEND]

- GTE: Q, Symbol, Month, Striking Price, Send
  To obtain the quote on the NYSE Index February 95 call, key in:

  [Q] [N] [Y] [A] [B] [S] [SEND]

N.Y. STOCK EXCHANGE

Source: The New York Stock Exchange. Copyright 1983. Reprinted by permission. All rights reserved.

Options At A Glance

Interest Rate Options

Expiration Month Codes

Month	Calls	Puts
March	C	O
June	F	R
September	I	U
December	L	X

Striking Price Codes

Key		Striking Prices	
A	75	100	125
B	76	101	126
C	77	102	127
D	78	103	128
E	79	104	129
F	80	105	130
G	81	106	131
H	82	107	132
I	83	108	133
J	84	109	134
K	85	110	135
L	86	111	136
M	87	112	137
N	88	113	138
O	89	114	139
P	90	115	140
Q	91	116	141
R	92	117	142
S	93	118	143
T	94	119	144
U	95	120	145
V	96	121	146
W	97	122	147
X	98	123	148
Y	99	124	149

Quotation Values

$100,000 T-Bond (Standard) $1/32 = $31.25
$ 20,000 T-Bond (Mini) $1/32 = $6.25
$100,000 T-Note $1/32 = $31.25
$1,000,000 T-Bill   .01 = $25.00

Trading Hours:
9 AM-3 PM E.S.T.

Options on Foreign Currencies

Symbols

XBP	British Pound
XCD	Canadian Dollar
XDM	Deutsche Mark
XJY	Japanese Yen
XSF	Swiss Franc

Expiration Month Codes

Month	Calls	Puts
March	C	O
June	F	R
September	I	U
December	L	X

Quotation Values

12,500 BP · .05¢ = $6.25
50,000 CD · .01¢ = $5.00
62,500 DM · .01¢ = $6.25
6,250,000 JY · .0001¢ = $6.25
62,500 SF · .01¢ = $6.25

Striking Price Codes

Key					Striking Prices						
A	0	25	50	75	100	125	150	175	200	225	250	275
B	1	26	51	76	101	126	151	176	201	226	251	276
C	2	27	52	77	102	127	152	177	202	227	252	277
D	3	28	53	78	103	128	153	178	203	228	253	278
E	4	29	54	79	104	129	154	179	204	229	254	279
F	5	30	55	80	105	130	155	180	205	230	255	280
G	6	31	56	81	106	131	156	181	206	231	256	281
H	7	32	57	82	107	132	157	182	207	232	257	282
I	8	33	58	83	108	133	158	183	208	233	258	283
J	9	34	59	84	109	134	159	184	209	234	259	284
K	10	35	60	85	110	135	160	185	210	235	260	285
L	11	36	61	86	111	136	161	186	211	236	261	286
M	12	37	62	87	112	137	162	187	212	237	262	287
N	13	38	63	88	113	138	163	188	213	238	263	288
O	14	39	64	89	114	139	164	189	214	239	264	289
P	15	40	65	90	115	140	165	190	215	240	265	290
Q	16	41	66	91	116	141	166	191	216	241	266	291
R	17	42	67	92	117	142	167	192	217	242	267	292
S	18	43	68	93	118	143	168	193	218	243	268	293
T	19	44	69	94	119	144	169	194	219	244	269	294
U	20	45	70	95	120	145	170	195	220	245	270	295
V	21	46	71	96	121	146	171	196	221	246	271	296
W	22	47	72	97	122	147	172	197	222	247	272	297
X	23	48	73	98	123	148	173	198	223	248	273	298
Y	24	49	74	99	124	149	174	199	224	249	274	299

Trading Hours:
8:30AM-2:30PM E.S.T.

APPENDIX J

BIBLIOGRAPHY

STOCK INDEXES

1. Balch, W. F. "Market Guides: Indexes of Stock Prices Lately Have Multiplied," *Barron's*, September 26, 1966.
2. Butler, H. L., Jr. and Decker, M. B. "A Security Check on the Dow Jones Industrial Average," *Financial Analysts Journal*, Vol. 9, No. 1, February, 1953, pp. 37–45.
3. Butler, Hartman L., Jr. and Allen, J. Devon "The Dow Jones Industrial Average Re-Reexamined," *Financial Analysts Journal*, November–December, 1979.
4. Carter, E. E. and Cohen, K. J. "Stock Averages, Stock Splits and Bias," *Financial Analysts Journal*, Vol. 23, No. 3, May–June, 1967, pp. 77–81.
5. Carter, E. E. and Cohen, K. J. "Bias in the DJIA Caused by Stock Splits," *Financial Analysts Journal*, Vol. 22, No. 6, December, 1966.
6. Cootner, Paul H. "Stock Market Indexes: Fallacies and Illusions," *Commercial and Financial Chronicle*, September 29, 1966.
7. Dow-Jones & Company, Inc. Educational Service Bureau, *"The Dow-Jones Averages, A Non-Professional's Guide,"* Dow-Jones & Co., Inc. 1983.
8. Fisher, Lawrence "Some New Stock Market Indexes," *Journal of Business, Security Prices: A Supplement*, Vol. 39, No. 1, Part II, January, 1966, pp. 191–225.
9. Gordon, C. E., II and Leuthold, S. C. "Margin for Error: The American Stock Exchange Index Has Exceeded It," *Barron's*, March 1, 1971, pp. 14–15.
10. Kekish, Bohdan J. "Moody's Averages," *Financial Analysts Journal*, May–June, 1967, pp. 65–69.
11. Latané, Henry A., Tuttle, Donald L. and Young, William E.

STOCK INDEX OPTIONS

"Market Indexes and Their Implications for Portfolio Management," *Financial Analysts Journal,* September–October, 1971.

12. Lerner, E. M. *Readings in Financial Analysis and Investment Management,* Richard D. Irwin, Inc., Homewood, Illinois, 1963, pp. 84–110.
13. Leuthold, S. C. and Blaich, K. I. "Warped Yardstick," *Barron's,* September 18, 1972, p. 9.
14. Lorie, James H. and Hamilton, Mary T. *The Stock Market—Theories and Evidence,* Richard D. Irwin, Inc., Homewood, Illinois, 1973, pp. 51–69.
15. Milne, Robert D. "The Dow-Jones Industrial Average Re-Examined," *Financial Analysts Journal,* Vol. 22, No. 6, November–December, 1966, p. 86.
16. Molodovsky, Nicholas "Building a Stock Market Measure—A Case Story," *Financial Analysts Journal,* May–June, 1967, pp. 43–46.
17. Reilly, Frank K. "Price Changes in NYSE, AMEX, and OTC Stocks Compared," *Financial Analysts Journal,* March–April, 1971.
18. Rudd, Andrew T. "The Revised Dow-Jones Industrial Average: New Wine in Old Bottles?" *Financial Analysts Journal,* November–December, 1979.
19. Schellbach, Lewis L. "Yardsticks for the Market," *The Analysts Journal,* November, 1955, pp. 33–34.
20. Schellbach, Lewis, L. "When Did the DJIA Top 1200?" *Financial Analysts Journal,* Vol. 23, No. 3, May–June, 1967, pp. 71–73.
21. Schloss, Walter J. "The Dow-Jones Industrial Average Amended," *The Analysts Journal,* February, 1953, pp. 35–36.
22. Schoomer, B. Alva, Jr. "The American Stock Exchange Index System," *Financial Analysts Journal,* Vol. 23, No. 3, May–June, 1967, pp. 57–61.
23. Shaw, R. B. "The Dow-Jones Industrials vs. The Dow-Jones Industrial Average," *Financial Analysts Journal,* Vol. 11, No. 5, November, 1955, pp. 37–40.
24. West, Stan and Miller, Norman "Why the New NYSE Common Stock Indexes?" *Financial Analysts Journal,* Vol. 23, No. 3, May–June, 1967, pp. 49–54.

STOCK OPTIONS

1. Angell, George *"Sure-Thing Options Trading,"* Doubleday & Company, Inc. Garden City, New York, 1983.

BIBLIOGRAPHY

2. Ansbacher, Max G. *"The New Options Market,"* (Second Edition) Walker and Company, New York, 1979.
3. Ansbacher, Max G. *"The New Stock Index Market,"* Walker and Company, New York, 1983.
4. Bookstaber, Richard M. and Clarke, Roger G. *"Option Strategies for Institutional Investment Management,"* Addison-Wesley Publishing Co., Reading, Massachusetts, 1983.
5. Bookstaber, Richard M. *"Option Pricing and Strategies in Investing,"* Addison-Wesley Publishing Co., Reading, Massachusetts, 1981.
6. Clasing, Henry K., Jr. *"The Dow Jones-Irwin Guide to Put and Call Options"* (Revised Edition), Dow Jones-Irwin, Homewood, Illinois, 1978.
7. Cleeton, Claud E. *"Strategies for the Options Trader,"* John Wiley & Sons, New York, 1979.
8. Fischer, Robert *"Stocks or Options? Programs for Profits,"* John Wiley & Sons, New York, 1980.
9. Gastineau, Gary L. *"The Stock Options Manual,"* (Second Edition) McGraw-Hill Book Company, New York, 1979.
10. Mayer, Terry S. *"Commodity Options: A User's Guide to Speculating and Hedging,"* New York Institute of Finance, New York, 1983.
11. McMillan, Lawrence G. *"Options as a Strategic Investment,"* New York Institute of Finance, New York, 1980.
12. Jarrow, Robert A. and Rudd, Andrew *"Option Pricing"* Dow Jones-Irwin, Homewood, Illinois, 1983.
13. Rodolakis, Antony and Tetrick, Nicholas *"Buying Options—Wall Street on a Shoestring,"* Reston Publishing Company, Reston, Virginia, 1976.
14. Rubinstein, Mark and Cox, John *"Options Markets,"* Prentice-Hall, Inc., Englewood Cliffs, N.J., (forthcoming).
15. Saint-Peter, Norman *"How to Make Money in Stock Options,"* Prentice-Hall, Inc., Englewood Cliffs, N.J., 1984.
16. Trester, Kenneth R. *"The Option Player's Advanced Guidebook,"* InvesTrek Publishing, Costa Mesa, California, 1980.
17. Trester, Kenneth R. *"The Compleat Option Player,"* InvesTrek Publishing, Costa Mesa, California, 1977.
18. Welch, William W. *"Strategies for Put and Call Option Trading,"* Winthrop Publishers, Inc., Cambridge, Massachusetts, 1982.

APPENDIX K

GLOSSARY

Aggregate exercise price: The total dollars required to exercise an option contract. It is the exercise price multiplied by the number of units of the underlying asset covered by the contract.

American option: A put or call option that can be exercised at any time prior to expiration. This is in contrast to a European option which can be exercised only on the expiration date. The distinction is important to theoreticians since the latter are usually easier to analyze. All listed options traded in the United States are American options.

Arbitrage: The simultaneous purchase and sale of identical, substantially identical, or equivalent assets in one or more than one market with the intent of capturing the price differential as a riskless profit.

Asked: The price at which an asset can be acquired from a potential seller. The asked price is usually quoted with the bid price, the price at which an asset can be sold to a potential buyer. The difference between the bid price and the asked price is known as the spread.

Assignment: Notification to a writer by the Options Clearing Corporation that the terms of an option contract must be fulfilled. For a call writer this is an obligation to sell stock at the exercise price. For a put seller this is an obligation to buy stock at the exercise price.

At-the-money: The price relationship where the exercise price of the option is equal to the market price of the underlying instrument.

Automatic exercise: Exchange implemented exercise at expiration of in-the-money options in the absence of specific instructions by the option holder.

Beta: A numerical measure of the sensitivity of movements in the

STOCK INDEX OPTIONS

price of a stock to movements in the overall market as reflected by a broad-based index such as the S&P 500 or the NYSE Composite Index. A beta of 1.10 indicates that the stock will rise or fall 10% more than a corresponding move in the market.

Bid: The price at which an asset can be sold to a potential buyer. The bid price is usually quoted with the asked price, the price at which an asset can be purchased from a potential seller. The difference between the bid price and the asked price is known as the spread.

Black-Scholes formula: A mathematical model derived from option theory used to calculate the price at which an option *should* trade. The model is one means of determining option fair value.

Breakeven point: The stock price (or prices) at which an investment strategy produces zero net gain or loss.

Bullish: A market outlook anticipating rising prices.

Buy-in: An involuntary repurchase of shares previously sold short because of the inability of the brokerage firm to retain the position.

Bearish: A market outlook anticipating declining prices.

Call option: A contract granting the privilege but not the obligation to purchase an asset at a specified price for a specified period of time after which the contract is worthless.

CBOE: The Chicago Board Options Exchange (pronounced seeboh).

Cash settlement: Fulfillment of the terms of exercise for an option contract not by delivery of the underlying instrument but rather by appropriate debits and credits of the amount by which the option is in-the-money.

Class: As a group, all the put option contracts same underlying security or all the call option contracts on the same underlying security.

Closing price: The last price at which transactions are made prior to the closing bell.

Closing purchase transaction: Termination of a short option position by an offsetting purchase.

Closing sale transaction: Termination of a long option position by an offsetting sale.

Closing transaction: The termination of an open position by its corresponding offset. For option buyers this transaction is a closing sale. For option sellers this transaction is a closing purchase.

Collateral: Cash or securities (including T-bills) deposited with a broker to guarantee performance on short positions (stocks and options).

Contingent claim: A term used interchangeably for an option or any

GLOSSARY

security having the features of an option such as a warrant, convertible bond, or convertible preferred stock. Fulfillment of these contracts requires performance by both parties involved. The option writer has the liability to deliver stock in the case of calls or to receive stock in the case of puts. Those obligations are contingent upon conditions which the buyer must meet; namely, paying the exercise price in the case of calls or delivering stock in the case of puts.

Contract size: The specification of the amount of the asset optioned by a put or call contract. For equity options this is usually 100 shares of the underlying stock unless adjusted because of a stock dividend or a stock split. For index options the size or underlying value is determined by the index multiplier and the level of the underlying index.

Conversion: A combination position consisting of three elements—long stock and long puts (that is, long a synthetic call) plus the sale of a call. Conversions are virtually riskless arbitrages permitting traders to capitalize on price discrepancies between securities supplemented by the dividend received from the stock.

Convertible security: Bonds or preferred stock with special provision that they can be exchanged for other securities—usually a common stock issue—at the holder's option.

Cover: To buy back as a closing transaction an option which was previously sold.

Covered writing: An investment strategy in which common stock is purchased and call options are sold on a one-for-one basis.

Credit: A positive account balance resulting from any transaction bringing money into an account such as a deposit or an option opening sale transaction.

Deep-in-the-money: An alternative description for options having substantial intrinsic value. For calls it is the price relationship where the stock price is far above the exercise price. For puts it is the condition where the stock price is well below the exercise price.

Delivery: The transfer of securities when an option is exercised. A call writer who is assigned delivers stock to the call buyer who exercised. A put buyer who exercises delivers stock to the put writer who is assigned.

Delta: The option price change resulting from a one point change in the price of the underlying stock. Also called the hedge ratio.

Discount option: An option selling below its intrinsic value. The premium plus the exercise price is less than the price of the underlying security.

Downside breakeven: The price below which an investment strategy generates losses.

Downside protection: The cushion against falling prices provided by the premium received from the sale of call options.

Downstairs: Trading by members on the exchange floor. As opposed to upstairs which is trading directed from a remote location. Both participants have advantages and disadvantages. Which party has the edge is the subject of continuous debate.

Early exercise: The exercise of an option contract prior to its expiration date.

Escrow receipt: A bank-issued voucher verifying ownership of securities thus permitting the sale of calls in a brokerage account without the need to post additional collateral.

European option: A put or call that can be exercised only on the expiration date. In contrast to an American option which can be exercised at any time prior to expiration.

Exercise: Assignment of an option contract; that is, sale of stock to the writer in the case of puts or purchase of stock from the writer in the case of calls.

Exercise limit: The total number of puts or calls on the same underlying instrument that a single investor or group of investors acting in concert may exercise during any five consecutive business days.

Exercise price: The price at which the underlying instrument changes hands when an option contract is exercised. Also called the strike price.

Expiration date: The day on which the option contract terminates and thereafter becomes null and void. For listed options the expiration date is the Saturday following the third Friday of the month.

Extrinsic value: The value of an option over and above the intrinsic value. Extrinsic value is also called the time value. The price of an out-of-the-money option is entirely extrinsic value.

Fair value: The price at which an option should trade in an efficient market as predicted by option theory. Both buyers and sellers of fairly valued options can, at best, expect to break even.

Floor broker: An exchange member who trades on the exchange floor executing orders for nonmembers.

Floor trader: An exchange member who buys and sells for his own account fulfilling the function of a market maker.

GLOSSARY

Front running: A transaction in options based on advance knowledge of a forthcoming transaction in stocks which will affect the option price favorably.

Fungibility: Complete interchangeability resulting from the standardization of option contracts and the severance of the direct link between a buyer and a seller as made possible by the Options Clearing Corporation. An opening transaction can be offset by a closing transaction in an identical contract.

Futures contract: An exchange traded commitment with standardized terms (including quality, quantity, time, and location) to make or accept delivery of a commodity at a price agreed upon at the time the contract was traded.

Hedge: A position in two related securities, long and short, such that the risk in one position partially or totally offsets the risk in the other.

Hedge ratio: The fractional price change in an option resulting from a one point change in the price of the underlying stock. Also called delta.

Historical volatility: Volatility measured from a sequence of past stock prices.

Holder: The owner of a security.

Implied volatility: That value of volatility which, when inserted into an option model, produces a solution which is the current traded price of the option. It is the volatility which the market currently assigns to the underlying instrument.

Institution: A large organization which commands vast resources and which trades in large volume such as a pension fund, mutual fund, bank, or insurance company.

Initial margin requirement: The minimum margin which must be posted when entering an investment position.

In-the-money: An option having intrinsic value. Call options are in-the-money when the price of the underlying instrument is above the option exercise price. Put options are in-the-money when the price of the underlying instrument is below the option exercise price.

Intrinsic value: The cash value of the option. It is that amount which, when combined with the exercise price, can be applied in acquiring the underlying asset. For calls the intrinsic value is the stock price minus the exercise price. For puts the intrinsic value is the exercise price minus the stock price. In other words, it is the amount by which an option is in-the-money.

STOCK INDEX OPTIONS

Leg-in: Nonsimultaneous execution of transactions in a multiple position strategy. The objective is to establish one portion and to complete others at more favorable prices.

Leverage: The magnification of the potential (both risk and reward) of an investment when a given amount of money controls assets of substantially greater value.

Limit order: An order to buy or sell at a specified price or better.

Liquid market: A market characterized by high volume of trading, narrow spreads, and depth (meaningful size at both bid and asked prices). Buying and selling in quantity can be accomplished without perturbing prices.

Listed option: A put or call with standardized terms traded on a national securities exchange.

Long: A position of ownership resulting from acquisition of an asset. An investor who is long will make money if the asset rises in price. As opposed to short.

Margin: The equity which must be posted by an investor to collateralize an investment position.

Market maker: An exchange member responsible for maintaining liquidity by making bids and offers for his own account in the absence of public orders. Several market makers are usually assigned to a particular security.

Market-maker-system: An approach to implementing trading on the exchange floor where liquidity is provided by many competing market makers. As opposed to the specialist system.

Model: A mathematical formula derived from the theory of options and finance the solution of which gives the price at which an option should trade.

Naked option: An option position either long or short which is unhedged.

Net margin requirement: The collateral required to finance an option sale after deducting the premium received.

Neutral: A market outlook anticipating relatively unchanged prices.

Neutral hedge: A hedge balanced to give highest return when the underlying asset remains unchanged. The upside and downside breakeven points are generally equidistant from the entry price.

Offsetting transaction: A transaction which terminates an option position either long or short. An opening sale transaction is offset by a closing purchase. An opening purchase is offset by a closing sale.

Open interest: The number of option contracts outstanding; that is,

GLOSSARY

those not eliminated by exercise, assignment, or closing transactions.

Opening purchase transaction: A trade establishing a long position in an option, either a put or a call.

Opening sale transaction: A trade establishing a short position in an option, either a put or a call.

Opening transaction: A transaction establishing a new option position. An opening purchase adds a long position. An opening sale adds a short option position.

Option: A contract granting the privilege but not the obligation to buy or sell at a particular price for a specified period of time.

Option period: The lifetime of the option as specified in the contract and within which the buyer must exercise or lose the privilege.

Option price curve: A graph of the expected track or trajectory along which an option price will move in response to a change in the price of the underlying instrument. Because option price is a function of time, the curve is valid only for a short period after which it must be recomputed.

Options Clearing Corporation: An organization owned by the various exchanges which trade listed option contracts. It is an intermediary, acting as issuer of all option contracts and also as the guarantor of each of the contracts.

Options exchange: One of four securities exchanges authorized to trade listed options.

Out-of-the-money: An option for which the intrinsic value is zero. Call options are out-of-the-money when the price of the underlying instrument is below the option exercise price. Put options are out-of-the-money when the price of the underlying instrument is above the option exercise price.

Overvalued: Selling in excess of the expected price as predicted by experience or an option valuation model.

Parity: The market price for an in-the-money option that is equal to its intrinsic value. The time value of the option is zero.

Position limit: The maximum number of options on the same side of the market (calls held plus puts written, or puts held plus calls written) for a single underlying instrument that may be held or written by a single investor or group of investors acting in concert.

Premium: The price of an option. Infrequently the term is used interchangeably with time value.

Profit profile: A graph or table showing projected returns for an investment strategy over a range of prices in the underlying instrument.

Put: An option granting the holder the right but not the obligation

STOCK INDEX OPTIONS

to sell the underlying instrument at a particulr price for a specified period of time.

Ratio writing: An investment strategy involving sale of options in excess of those covered by a long position.

Return: The total change in value of an investment including appreciation and yield (dividends or interest).

Return on investment: The change in value of an asset (including dividends or interest) usually expressed as a percentage of the initial investment.

Reverse conversion: A combination position consisting of three elements—short stock and long calls (that is, long a synthetic put) plus the sale of a put. Reverse conversions are virtually riskless arbitrages permitting traders to capitalize on price discrepancies between securities while earning interest on the credit balance resulting from the short sale. An important adjunct to reverse conversions is the creation of puts which might otherwise be illiquid and therefore unavailable.

Rolling: Repositioning by switching from one option into another having a different exercise price or expiration date. See also rolling up, rolling down, and rolling forward.

Rolling down: The simultaneous closing of an option position at one strike price and opening of a substantially identical position at a lower strike price.

Rolling forward: The simultaneous closing of an option position in one expiration month and opening of a substantially identical position in an expiration month further out.

Rolling up: The simultaneous closing of an option position at one strike price and opening of a substantially identical position at a higher strike price.

Securities and Exchange Commission (SEC): An agency of the federal government which regulates and oversees the securities markets in the United States.

Series: All option contracts of the same class on the same underlying stock having the same exercise price, expiration date, and unit of trading.

Short option position: The position of the writer or seller of a put or call.

Short sale: The sale of a borrowed security in anticipation of falling prices. If the drop materializes the securities are repurchased (covered) at the lower level and the profit is the difference between the original sale price and the subsequent purchase price.

GLOSSARY

Specialist: An exchange member responsible for making markets in specific securities and for keeping the book of public orders. This entails maintaining a liquid and continuous market buying and selling for his own account in the absence of public orders.

Speculator: An investor willing to assume excessive risk in search of disproportionate capital gain.

Spread: An option hedge consisting of a long position in one or more options and an offsetting short position in options on the same security but of a different series, a different strike price, or a different expiration date.

Standard deviation: A statistical calculation which measures the tendency of the data in a distribution to cluster about a mean value.

Stock index futures: A standard futures contract requiring purchase or delivery of the cash value of a stock index at some specified point in the future.

Straddle: An option hedge position consisting of a put and a call on the same underlying instrument at the same exercise price and with the same expiration date. A straddle is purchased if both positions are long. The objective is to profit from a major move in the market in either direction. A straddle is sold if both option positions are short. The objective is to profit from a stagnant market.

Straddle buying: The purchase of a put and a call on the same underlying instrument with the same strike price and the same expiration date executed in anticipation of a major price move (in either direction).

Straddle selling: The sale of a put and a call on the same underlying instrument with the same strike price and the same expiration date executed in anticipation of stagnant market.

Strike price: The price at which the underlying asset will change hands when an option is exercised. Also called the exercise price.

Strike price interval: The distance between striking prices in an option series. For equity options the interval is 5 points for stocks selling up to $100 and 10 points for stocks selling up to $200. For index options the interval is always 5 points.

Synthetic call: A combination position consisting of stock long in conjunction with puts purchased on the same stock. The profit profile is equivalent for outright purchase of a call option.

Synthetic put: A combination position consisting of stock sold short in conjunction with calls purchased on the same stock. The profit profile is equivalent for outright purchase of a put option.

Systematic risk: That part of total risk attributable to the overall influence of the market.

STOCK INDEX OPTIONS

Terms: The provisions of an option contract including the underlying instrument, the exercise price, the expiration date, and the method of settlement.

Theoretical value: The price of an option as computed by an option valuation model.

Time value: That component of option premium which exceeds intrinsic value. It is the amount by which the market price of an option exceeds the amount that could be realized if the option were exercised.

Trading pit: A specific location on the exchange floor designated for trading in a particular option.

Transaction costs: Charges associated with executing a trade including commissions and exchange fees. It also includes a penalty imposed by the existence of the bid-asked spread.

Type: The classification of an option as a put or a call.

Uncovered: Options in an unhedged context. Equivalent to naked options.

Underlying security: The asset which can be purchased or sold in accordance with the terms of the option contract.

Undervalued: Selling at a price below that predicted by an option valuation model.

Unsystematic risk: That part of total risk attributable to a particular firm and its industry group.

Upstairs: Trading directed from locations other than the exchange floor. As opposed to downstairs trading which is trading on the exchange floor.

Volatility: A measure of a stock's propensity to change in price over a period of time, generally computed from historical data. More precisely, it is a statistical calculation; namely, the annualized standard deviation of security price changes.

Warrant: An option to buy stock (generally that of the issuer) at a specified price for a particular period of time. Warrants are similar to call options.

Wasting asset: An investment having a finite life where payoff depends upon time for a workout. Thus, value is proportional to time.

Whipsaw: A rapid sequence of price reversals always out of synchronization with the investor's position.

Writer: The seller or grantor of an option contract.

INDEX

A

Advisory services, 82, 189
Amex Computer Technology Index
  description, 23, 121
  historical chart, 122
  option contract, 159
Amex Major Market Index
  description, 21, 123
  historical chart, 124
  option contract, 161
  versus Amex Market Value Index, 30
  versus S&P 100 Index, 33
Amex Market Value Index
  description, 22, 125
  historical chart, 126
  option contract, 162
  versus S&P 100 Index, 34
Amex Oil & Gas Index
  description, 23, 127
  historical chart, 128
  option contract, 163
Amex Transportation Index
  description, 23, 129
  historical chart, 130
  option contract, 164
Applications
  basic strategies, 64–71
  example transactions, 71–78
  preview, 5
Arbitrage, 89–90
Averages
  calculation, 10–14
  complexity, 8

Averages—*Continued*
  objectives, 9
  versus indexes, 7

B

Broad-based indexes
  correlation coefficient, 40–44
  cyclical percentage changes, 38–39
  description, 21
  graphic juxtaposition, 27–37
  listing, 21
  versus narrow-based indexes, 21

C

Call options, 97–101
  call buyers, 98
  call writers, 98
  option diagram, 100
Cash settlement, 2, 54
CBOE, xvii, 56
Chicago Board Options Exchange; see CBOE
Commissions, 91
Commodity markets, 2
Common stocks having listed options, 181–185
Comparison of broad-based indexes
  correlation, 40–44
  cyclical percentage changes, 38–40
  graphic, 27–37
Comparison of stock options and index options, 4–5, 55
Computer data bases, 82, 187

211

INDEX

Computer software, 82
Contract specifications, 159–172
Contract value, 2, 53
Correlation coefficient
  calculations, 42–43
  definition, 40–41
Covered writing, 75, 91–93, 111
Cyclical percentage changes, 38–39

D

Dow Jones Industrial Average
  attributes, 15
  description, 14, 24, 151
  historical chart, 152
  shortcomings, 15
  strengths, 15
  weaknesses, 16

E

Equity markets versus futures markets, 2
Example transactions, 71–78
  covered writing, 75
  protective puts, 73
  speculative call purchase, 72
  straddle purchases, 77–78
  straddle sales, 75–77
Exercise prices, 53
Expiration cycles, 53, 107
Escrow letters, 93–94
Equity options; *see* Stock options
Exchanges
  for index options, 50
  addresses, 191

F

Fair value, 80
Futures markets, 2

G

Geometric average, 25

H

Hedging strategies, 68–71, 110–117; *see also* Covered writing, Protective puts, Straddles

I

Index concentration, 8
Index options
  basic characteristics, 53
  chronology of delistings, 49
  chronology of listings, 48
  current offerings, 3–4, 159–172
  definition, 47
  grouped broad-based versus narrow-based, 49
  grouped by exchange where traded, 50
  history, 47
  versus stock options, 4–5, 55
Indexes
  calculation, 16–19
  complexity, 8
  concentration, 8
  objectives, 9
  versus averages, 7
  weighted, 17

L

Liquidity, 87–89

M

Manipulation, 94–95
Margin requirements, 54, 55

N

Narrow-based indexes
  description, 22–23
  listing, 23
  versus broad-based indexes, 21
NASDAQ-OTC Composite Index
  description, 24, 153
  historical chart, 154
  versus S&P 100 Index, 35
Nonoptionable indexes, 23–25, 151–158
NYSE Composite Index
  attributes, 20
  calculation, 19–20
  description, 19, 22, 131
  historical chart, 132
  option contract, 165
  shortcomings, 20

INDEX

NYSE Telephone Index
  description, 23, 133
  historical chart, 134
  option contract, 166

O

Open interest, 88
Optionable indexes, 3, 121–150
Optionable stocks, 181–185
Option diagram
  for calls, 100–101
  for puts, 106–107
Option models, 79

P

PHLX Gaming/Hotel Index
  description, 23, 138
  historical chart, 139
  option contract, 168
PHLX Gold/Silver Index
  description, 23, 140
  historical chart, 141
  option contract, 169
  versus gold, 142
  versus silver, 143
Portfolio tracking, 90
Premiums, 53
  determinants, 101–103
Protective puts, 73, 111–114
PSE Technology Index
  description, 22, 135
  historical chart, 137
  option contract, 167
Put options, 104–107
  option diagram, 106–107
  put buyers, 104
  put writers, 106

R

Return concepts, 59–60
Risk concepts
  definition, 59–60, 61
  risk decomposition, 61
  systematic risk, 61
  unbundling, 62, 63
  unsystematic risk, 62

S

Sentiment, 89–90
S&P 100 Index
  description, 22, 56–57, 144
  historical chart, 146
  option contract, 170
  versus S&P 500 Index, 32
S&P 500 Index
  description, 22, 147
  historical chart, 148
  option contract, 171
  versus S&P 100 Index, 32
Speculative/trading strategies, 64–68
Stock averages; *see* Averages
Stock indexes; *see* Indexes
Stock options versus index options, 4–5, 55
Stocks having listed options, 181–185
Straddles
  straddle purchases, 77–78, 114–115
  straddle sales, 75–77, 114–117
Symbols, 109–110, 193–195

T

Time value, 103–104
Timing risk, 90–91
Tracking; *see* Portfolio tracking
Trading strategies; *see* Speculative/trading strategies

V

Value Line Composite Average
  description, 24, 25, 155
  historical chart, 156
  versus S&P 100 Index, 36
Value Line evaluations, 173–180
Value Line Options, 83–85
Volume of trading, xvii, 88

W

Wilshire 5000 Equity Index
  description, 24, 157
  historical chart, 158
  versus S&P 100 Index, 37